The Human Encounter:
Teachers and Children Living Together in Preschools

To the teachers —
Who cared enough about teaching
to allow me to come close,
to see inside their work with children.

The Human Encounter:
Teachers and Children Living Together in Preschools

S. Vianne McLean

The Falmer Press
(A member of the Taylor & Francis Group)
London • New York • Philadelphia

UK The Falmer Press, 4 John St, London WC1N 2ET
USA The Falmer Press, Taylor & Francis Inc., 1990 Frost Road, Suite 101, Bristol, PA 19007

© S.V. McLean 1991

All rights reserved. No part of this publication may be reproduced, stored in a retrieval system, or transmitted in any form or by any means, electronic, mechanical, photocopying, recording or otherwise, without permission in writing from the Publisher.

First published in 1991

British Library Cataloguing in Publication Data
McLean, S. Vianne
  The human encounter: teachers and children living together in preschools.
  1. Schools. Teachers. Interpersonal relationships with students
  I. Title
  371.102

  ISBN 1-85000-724-1
  ISBN 1-85000-725-X pbk

Library of Congress Cataloging-in-Publication Data
McLean, S. Vianne.
  The human encounter: teachers and children living together in preschool/S. Vianne McLean.
    p. cm.
  Includes bibliographical references and index.
  ISBN 1-85000-724-1: — ISBN 1-85000-725-X (pbk.):
  1. Teacher-student relationships — Australia.
  2. Teacher-student relationships — Australia — Case studies.
  3. Preschool teachers — Australia. 4. Education, Preschool — Australia. I. Title.
  LB1033.M35 1991
  372.11'02'0994 — dc20   90-48864
                                                            CIP

Jacket design by Caroline Archer

Typeset in 11/13 pt Garamond
by Graphicraft Typesetters Ltd. Hong Kong.
Printed and bound in Great Britain by
Burgess Science Press
Basingstoke

Contents

Chapter 1: Teachers, Children, Persons	1
Becoming Human	2
Teacher Personality, Belief and Behaviour	3
Early Childhood Teachers	7
Studying Teachers and Children	9
Young Children As Social Beings	10
Social Development and the Early Childhood Curriculum	11
About the Book	14
Chapter 2: Research and Researcher	17
Methodological Overview	17
Overall Plan of the Study:	18
Participants	
Foundations for Trust	
Observations:	22
Timing for Observations	
Role of Observer	
Nature of Observations	
Interviews:	27
Depth Interviews	
Conversations	
Card Sort	
Dependability of Interview Data	
Analysis:	32
Interview Coding Schemes	
Observational Coding Schemes	
Case Study Format	
Summary	36

The Human Encounter

Chapter 3: Rhonda   41

The Setting: 41
    Rhonda's Preschool
    Children, Families, Assistant
    The Teacher
Rhonda's Image-of-Self-as-Teacher: 45
    General Description: Confidence and Organization
    Biographical Aspect
    Rules and Responsibilities
    Being Settled
    The Cognitive Aspects of Teaching
    Respect for Children
    Description of the Program for Children's Social
       Development
Actions in the Preschool: 56
    Smoothness and Order
    Rhonda's Power
    Rules
    Developing a Sense of Community
    Involvement in Children's Dramatic Play
    Resolving Peer Conflict
    Helping Children Gain Access to Peer Play Groups
    Environmental Support of Peer Interaction
Concluding Remarks   68

Chapter 4: Nan   71

The Setting: 71
    Nan's Preschool
    Children, Families, Assistant
    The Teacher
Nan's Image-of-Self-as-Teacher: 75
    General Description: 'They Are as I Am'
    Biographical Aspect
    Authenticity
    Acceptance and Trust in Self
    The Cognitive Aspects of Teaching
    Respect for Children
    Description of the Program for Children's Social
       Development
Actions in the Preschool: 87
    Responsiveness and Questioning

    Directive and Non-directive Strategies
    Helping Children Gain Access to Peer Play Groups
    Resolving Peer Conflict
    Involvement in Children's Dramatic Play
    Rules
    Developing a Sense of Community
    Environmental Support of Peer Interaction
Concluding Remarks   101

Chapter 5: Brenda   **105**

The Setting: 105
    Brenda's Preschool
    Children, Families, Staff
    The Teacher
Brenda's Image-of-Self-as-Teacher: 109
    General Description: Connections and Continuities
    Biographical Aspect
    Staying Calm
    Sense of Time
    The Cognitive Aspects of Teaching
    Respect for Children
    Description of the Program for Children's Social
        Development
Actions in the Preschool: 121
    Contextual Factors
    Calmness and Self-control
    Non-authoritarian Stance
    Resolving Peer Conflict
    Rules
    Developing a Sense of Community
    Helping Children Gain Access to Peer Play Groups
    Environmental Support of Peer Interaction
    Involvement in Children's Dramatic Play
Concluding Remarks   134

Chapter 6: Kathy   **137**

The Setting: 137
    Kathy's Preschool
    Children, Families, Assistant
    The Teacher
Kathy's Image-of-Self-as-Teacher: 140

General Description: Confusion or Ambivalence?
Biographical Aspect
Self-concept
The Cognitive Aspects of Teaching
Respect for Children
Description of the Program for Children's Social
    Development
Actions in the Preschool: 152
    Kathy's Program
    Work vs Play
    Control Strategies
    Developing Independence
    Resolving Peer Conflict
    Rules
    Developing a Sense of Community
    Helping Children Gain Access to Peer Play Groups
    Involvement in Children's Dramatic Play
    Environmental Support of Peer Interaction
Concluding Remarks   168

Chapter 7: Living Together in the Preschool   171

Making Sense of Teacher Actions: 171
    Paradoxes and Ambiguities
    Ideals and Realities
A Tentative Model: 182
    Theoretical Bases
    Image of Self as Teacher
    The Human Encounter
    Situational Factors
    Teacher as Decision Maker
Living and Teaching: The 'Here and Now' and Promotion of
Development: 204
    Managing the Here and Now
    Promoting Social Development
Influence of the Personal Factors of the Children   220

Chapter 8: Looking Forward; Looking Back   223

Teacher Development: 223
    Reflection
Preservice Teacher Education   227

References	233
Appendix: Examples of Coding Systems	253
Index	257

Chapter 1

Teachers, Children, Persons

It is nine o'clock on a clear and still morning. In an otherwise quiet suburban street, there is a hive of activity around the preschool centre. Families are arriving and as parents escort their preschoolers inside, a flurry of infants and toddlers adds to the bustle. Indoors, the activity continues, but sitting on the step between patio and playroom, the teacher is calmly greeting the newcomers, listening to children's stories, and having a few words with parents.

Within fifteen minutes, most of the parents and toddlers will have gone, leaving the teacher, the assistant and a group of twenty-five 4- and 5-year-olds to live together for the next three to five hours. Such a scene is taken very much for granted by families and early childhood educators. But how *do* these persons manage to live together in reasonable harmony? Who is this person called 'teacher', who is charged not only with the survival of this large group of young children, but also with the promotion of their development? How does she see herself as a teacher and how does she interact with others and the environment to create the particular social world that exists within the preschool setting?

Teachers and young children both are members of our human species, with all the joy and wonder, inconsistency and uncertainty that being human entails. If we are to understand something of their complex and often paradoxical relationships, we must go beyond idealized images of early childhood teachers facilitating children's development in fictitiously aseptic environments. By looking closely at the nature of the teacher's interactions with children, and accessing some of the meanings these interactions hold for the teacher, we can come to understand not only the ways this group of people has found to survive the here and now, but also the manner in which they meet in human-with-human encounter.

Becoming Human

Dubos has written: 'Members of the species *Homo sapiens* are not born with the attributes essential for a truly human life but rather with potentialities that enable them to become human' (1981, p. 16). The process of becoming human does not end when 'child' becomes 'adult', but rather our whole life span is likely to prove insufficient for us to maximize our potential for human-ness (Combs, Avila and Purkey, 1978; Rogers, 1967). Becoming human inescapably involves our interaction with others (Fromm, 1968; Greene, 1981; Teilhard de Chardin, 1959). We are social beings and it is through contact with others that we come closer to being all that we might be; to a deeper understanding of ourselves and our relationships with others.

If we accept the notion that adults, like children, are unfinished incomplete human beings, then 'socialization' or 'enculturation' of the younger by the older provides an inadequate description of the process of becoming human. Interactions between adult and child cannot be understood simply as the unidirectional transmission of information from s/he-who-has-arrived to s/he-who-is-still-travelling. All are engaged on the same journey, and the complex web of interaction that binds the person we call 'teacher' with those we call 'learners' may be important to both in their developing human-ness.

The deeply-rooted human dimension has not figured prominently in educational research during the last few decades. Instead, much research has focused on the surface level, examining 'observable teacher behaviours' (Flanders, 1964; Stallings, 1975). Only in the last decade has educational research begun to systematically explore some of the deeper links, with phenomenologists arguing that without consideration of the meanings behaviour holds for the participants, behaviour itself has no meaning (Mischler, 1979; Bussis, Chittenden, Amarel and Klausner, 1982).

Increasingly, research in this tradition is being described as 'interpretive' (Grundy, 1987, p. 13) and indeed, the study reported in this book is concerned with interpretation at a number of levels. It conceptualizes teachers as persons who are constantly engaged in interpretations of classroom events as they make sense of what is going on around them and make decisions about their own actions. It also views the researcher's role as one of interpretation. The researcher is *not* the teacher and cannot know what the teacher knows in any 'pure' untainted form. Thus the researcher also is engaged in an interpretive activity as she strives to understand the teacher's meanings and actions, and to portray these in ways that others will find meaningful.

In effect, this is a story of four early childhood teachers and one researcher. Unlike some other recent research works (Ayers, 1989) this is not a collection of teachers' own stories. This is a story *about* these preschool teachers and the joys and tribulations of their everyday teaching lives. In keeping with other interpretive inquiries, this project did not set out to yield 'hard' generalizable findings. Rather, it provides a detailed account of early childhood teaching which readers can ponder and question, and resonate against their own first-hand experiences of teaching. It is hoped that through this engagement with the story, readers will be stimulated to reflect upon their own teaching lives and the part they play in children's lives.

Teacher Personality, Belief and Behaviour

Humanist writers of the 1960s, such as Buber (1967), Moustakas (1966), Richardson (1967) and Rogers (1969) emphasize that the *person* who is the teacher is a crucial part of the educative process. As Buber writes: 'It is not instruction that educates, but the instructor' (1967, p. 102). Similarly, Rogers suggests the teacher 'is a person to his students, not a faceless embodiment of a curricular requirement, nor a sterile tube through which knowledge is passed from one generation to the next' (1969, p. 106). This belief in the importance of the teacher as person had little to do with findings from empirical research of the time. In reviewing twenty years of research on teacher personality and behaviour, Getzels and Jackson conclude: 'Despite the critical importance of the problem and a half-century of prodigious research effort, very little is known for certain about the nature and measurement of teacher personality or about the relation between teacher personality and teaching effectiveness' (1963, p. 574).

In the following decade, in an attempt to develop a 'blueprint' of effective teaching (Brophy and Evertson, 1974; Flanders, 1964; Soar and Soar, 1972; Stallings, 1975), research attention shifted from teacher personality to teacher behaviour and its relationship to student achievement. Reviewers such as Dunkin and Biddle (1974) and Rosenshine (1971) differ in their views of the usefulness of the accumulated findings of this vast area of research, but according to Doyle the 'general perception of low productivity' (1977a, p. 164) seemed to prevail. In the latter part of the 1970s the focus broadened once more, to include such factors as pupil characteristics, grade level and time on task (Berliner and Rosenshine, 1978). As Doyle wrote: 'The teacher effectiveness question ... is now being asked more often in terms of who is learning, who is teaching and what is being taught' (1977a, p. 170).

A lesser stream of research activity in the years following the Getzels and Jackson (1963) review focused on the connection between teacher belief and behaviour. Underlying this research was an assumption that pervades much of our thinking about people — that behaviour is guided by mental dimensions such as values, attitudes and beliefs. Some support was found for this notion, in studies that combined interviews of teachers with observations of classroom behaviour (Halperin, 1976; Harvey, White, Prather and Alter, 1966). One of the most noteworthy of these was the Bussis, Chittenden and Amarel study, *Beyond Surface Curriculum*, which suggested that 'teachers' characteristic beliefs about children and learning have pervasive effects on their behaviour, influencing the learning environment they create for their children and themselves' (1976, p. 16).

When studies found that the values and beliefs espoused by teachers were not strongly correlated with classroom structure or behaviour, these discontinuities often were interpreted as flaws in the teacher or the program (Berk, 1976; Prawat and Nickerson, 1985; Verma and Peters, 1975). In Toulmin's words: 'Since coherent intentions and a settled plan of life are normally regarded as merits, inconsistencies, vascillation and other forms of indecisiveness are seen as shortcomings' (1977, p. 306).

The assumption that behaviour is driven by belief or attitude has been labelled an overly-simplistic myth by Morton (1980), and Kelman, in reviewing research on measures of attitude as predictors of behaviour, posits a much more complex model:

> Attitude ... is not an index of action, but a determinant, component, and consequent of it. Furthermore, it is not an entity that can be separated — functionally or temporally — from the flow of action, but is an integral part of action. Attitude and action are linked in a continuing reciprocal process, each generating the other in an endless chain. (1974, p. 316)

More recently, Schon (1983) has described a similar reciprocal and indivisible relationship between the reflections of professional practitioners and their actions, a concept he labels 'knowledge-in-action'.

In the 1980s, an increasing body of research following in the tradition of Jackson's (1968) classic study, *Life in Classrooms*, has begun to document the real life experiences of teachers as they interact with students in educational settings. This research is portraying teaching as a difficult and complex process; one that often is fraught with inconsistency, disequilibrium, uncertainty and ambiguity (Bolster, 1983; Calderhead, 1987; Clandinin, 1986; Clark and Yinger, 1987; Good and Weinstein, 1986; Margolin, 1982). With a heritage including work of the Chicago School, the interactionist theory of Kurt Lewin, and the social psychology of George Herbert Mead, these researchers are developing new conceptualizations and methodologies as they try to understand the many complex ways that personality, belief and social context are manifested in the teacher's actions in the classroom.

Fenstermacher (1978) identifies this research approach as the 'Intentionalist Account of Teacher Effectiveness' because of the underlying belief that teacher behaviour is basically goal-directed and has meaning only in terms of the teacher's intentions. Contextual factors also are considered in terms of their meanings for teachers. Rather than measure teacher behaviour against some blueprint, it asks why teachers engage in the practices they do. Researchers such as Clandinin (1986), Calderhead (1987), Elbaz (1983), Lampert (1985), Marland (1977) and Shulman and Lanier (1977) have helped redirect educational research to bring into focus the mental lives of teachers. For example, Shulman and Lanier ask 'How do the ways teachers think — about themselves, their work, their students, their subject matter and materials, the settings in which they appear, and the alternatives they consider — affect the nature and quality of their teaching and student learning? (1977, p. 44).

Because of the researchers' willingness to explore the detailed complexities of individual teacher's thinking, this research approach frequently involves a small number of teachers in more collaborative roles, rather than a large number of 'subjects' who remain ignorant of the research purposes. In so doing, it weakens the traditional distinction between researcher and practitioner, research findings and practice (Torbet, 1981), though it does not eradicate the differences entirely. As Shulman and Lanier state, 'Focus on the wisdom of the practitioner increases the probability that findings will be compatible with how teachers actually think and feel in classroom settings' (1977, p. 49).

The image of persons that both guides, and emerges from, this area of research suggests the teacher is not a passive responder to environmental stimuli, nor a belief-directed actor. Rather, s/he is an 'agent' (Mischel, 1977) who actively mediates between environment and action, who discriminates environmental features in making decisions about personal actions.

Within this highly interactive perspective, contexts are no longer 'out there', able to be dissected cleanly from the individuals operating within them. Rather, the context and the person are interconnected. The influence of Lewin is evident. He writes, 'To understand or predict behavior, the person and his environment have to be considered as one constellation of interdependent factors' (1951, pp. 239–40). Similarly, Levinson, in his study of the lives of men, defines 'life structure' as 'the pattern or design of a person's life, a meshing of self-in-world', and suggests that 'In countless ways, we put ourselves into the world and take the world into ourselves' (1980, p. 278). Within this research perspective, Polanyi's (1967) view that all knowledge includes a personal component is central, and reciprocal, even reflexive connections are considered to bind the context and the person (Mehan and Wood, 1975). As Greene suggests:

> Mind is involved with experience and lived situations. It has to do with the finding of meanings, or the sedimentation of meanings, all sorts of meanings. These become part of and indeed constitute the self; they compose the background against which new encounters and experiences are projected. (1984, p. 287)

In creating meanings for behaviour in educational contexts, teachers are believed to draw not only on their context-specific knowledge about teaching and learning, but also on their understandings of the broader personal, social and cultural context in which they are embedded as persons. If we are to understand anything of the individual's framework for making sense of the environment, we also must know something of that person's life, his/her biography. As Greene suggests: 'Each individual enters into a particular province, no matter how demanding, with some consciousness of his or her own biography and life project, some awareness of his or her location in the intersubjective world' (1984, p. 291). Ball and Goodson propose an even broader focus and make three investigative assumptions:

> First, that the teachers' previous career and life experiences shape their view of teaching and the way he or she sets about

it. Secondly, that teachers' lives outside school, their latent identities and cultures have an important impact on their work as teachers. And thirdly, that we must ... seek to locate the life history of the individual within the history of his time. (1985, p. 13)

It would seem, then, that to better understand teachers and teaching, one must assume that the connections between the internal aspects of the person who is the teacher (such as self-concept, beliefs about learning and teaching, awareness of own biography), the contextual features of the environment (both physical and interpersonal), and teacher behaviour, will be complex, reflexive and multi-directional.

It must also be assumed that, paradoxically, both change and stability will characterize those connections. Many researchers and writers have suggested that teacher beliefs and actions change slowly as teachers move through a process of development (Fuller, 1969; Fuller and Brown, 1975; Katz, 1972; Languis and Wilcox, 1981; Moyer and Kunz, 1985). But as Kelman (1974) suggests, short term situational pressures also may induce the person to act beyond the range of behaviour normally required by his/her attitude.

Thus, teacher belief and action are bound together in many complex ways. Perhaps we should not be surprised that discontinuities sometimes exist between belief and action, but instead be surprised that in the complexity of educational settings, so many continuities exist. Just as teachers and children seem to find a coherence to life in the classroom, it remains for the researcher to find a similar coherence.

Early Childhood Teachers

Traditionally, early childhood education has placed great emphasis on the quality of relationship that exists between teacher and child. The classic early childhood educator Maria Montessori (1870–1952) wrote: 'When the teacher shall have touched, in this way, soul for soul, each one of her pupils, awakening and inspiring the life within them as if she were an invisible spirit ... each one will feel her in a living and vital way' (1974, p. 116).

More recent writers in the field (Gordon and Browne, 1985; Hildebrand, 1985; Read and Patterson, 1980; Yardley, 1971) have continued to emphasize that the teacher as a person is the most important aspect of the child's preschool experience. For example, Lindberg and Swedlow, in addressing beginning teachers, say, 'You are a unique individual and the way you teach will reflect your own personality, attitudes and values. The most important contribution you have to make is your own uniqueness' (1985, p. 7).

Writers in early childhood education long have emphasized the importance of certain personal qualities in teachers. Many of these virtues have never been subject to empirical examination, but are rooted in the philosophy of child-centered education and distilled from the experiential knowledge base of several generations of early childhood educators. A review of recent early childhood texts[1] suggests that teachers of young children should be: warm and affectionate, patient, friendly, flexible, self-confident, compassionate and empathetic, sensitive and responsive, nurturant, optimistic about children's potential, in good physical and mental health, and highly aware of self (i.e., introspective). Some other mentioned qualities are being happy and having a sense of humour, being alert, resourceful and imaginative, being dedicated, genuinely liking children, having a sense of order and an appreciation for beauty and being interested in children, families and the world at large.

One of the cornerstones of traditional early childhood education has been the teacher's respect for young children (Gordon and Browne, 1985; Margolin, 1982; Read and Patterson, 1980; Robison, 1983; Yardley, 1971), a quality that can be traced to Friedrich Froebel (1782–1852), the 'father of the kindergarten'. He wrote, 'We now trust too little to the energetic and uniting power in the child and boy — we respect it too little as a spiritually quickening power' (1901, p. 133). Maria Montessori also held the child in high regard and thus saw virtue in the teacher who could allow the child to take the primary role in his/her own development. She wrote, 'The adult must recognize that he must take second place, endeavour all he can to understand the child, and to support and help him in the development of his life' (1963, p. 79). In a similar fashion, Susan Isaacs (1885–1948), an influential figure in early childhood development and education in the United Kingdom, saw the teacher as a 'collaborator' with children, rather than a director of their learning (Roberts, 1985, p. 54).

Because the child must have room to grow, the teacher must not be overpowering. To quote Froebel once again:

> We grant space and time to young plants and animals because we know that, in accordance with the laws that live within them, they will develop properly and well: young animals and plants are given rest and arbitrary interference with their growth is avoided, because it is known that the opposite prac-

tice would disturb their pure unfolding and sound development ... Thus, O parents, could your children, on whom you force in tender years forms and aims against their nature, and who therefore, walk with you in morbid and unnatural deformity — thus could your children too, unfold in beauty and develop in all-sided harmony! (1901, pp. 8–9)

In more recent times, providing 'room to grow' often is expressed as the need to allow children to experience some uncertainties and frustrations, rather than be overprotected by the teacher (Hildebrand, 1981; Hymes, 1981; Lindberg and Swedlow, 1985; Read and Patterson, 1980).

Despite this long standing interest in the personal qualities of early childhood educators, little research has systematically examined them (Seefeldt, 1973), and two reviews of teacher effectiveness research at the early childhood level have been unable to provide a profile of the 'ideal' teacher (Feeney and Chun, 1985; Phyfe-Perkins, 1982). Feeney and Chun conclude, 'The research reviewed here points to the interaction of many factors that influence effectiveness, including teacher and child characteristics and the physical and social environment of the program. Teaching young children is incredibly complex and multifaceted' (1985, p. 52).

Studying Teachers and Children

The network linking a group of persons within a preschool contains many connections at differing levels of visibility. Even at the most observable behavioural level, there are many types of interaction occurring — among children, parents, teachers and other staff. Underlying these observable connections are other, less visible connections that take into account the teacher's practical knowledge and undertandings about these children and this social world. To understand these connections, the researcher must find ways to help teachers bring this often tacit knowledge (Polanyi, 1967; Williams, Neff, and Finkelstein, 1981) to the surface, making it explicit so that it can be verbalized.

Psycholinguists have developed a technique in which the researcher begins with a very narrow instance of observable behaviour — often a single classroom event (for example, a 'circle time' as in Wallat and Green's 1979 study) then asks the participants a version of the question: 'What's going on here?' Although the approach often utilizes molecular behavioural analysis, the event is interpreted with regard for the participants' own meanings. A related technique is stimulated recall (Clark and Peterson, 1986) in which a record of observable behaviour is used to assist the participant to recall and verbalize what was in mind at the time.

These techniques are now widely used in studies of teacher thinking and decision making, but when the researcher's intention is to take a broader focus on the teacher as person, it would seem some modifications are necessary. The initial scope of observations needs to be sufficiently narrow to allow detailed recording of the surface interaction, yet sufficiently broad to encourage teachers to reflect upon the meanings of their connections with children in these and other situations. The area of interest could be likened to an iceberg: the observable behaviour, like the tip of the iceberg, is visible above the surface, but what is of greater interest is the breadth and depth of meaning that lies beneath. In the study reported here, it seemed a suitable scope for detailed observations might be the teacher's involvement in children's peer interactions.

Young Children as Social Beings

The importance of young children's social development has been supported over the last fifteen years, by research claiming 'long term effects' for early social experience (George and Main, 1979; Moore, 1975; Rubin, 1983; Sroufe, Fox and Pancake, 1983). Some links have been found between early social competence and adult functioning, leading Hartup (1983) in a major review of research, to conclude that childhood competence with peers is critical for later social and personality development.

Over recent years, much research devoted to young children's social interactions has suggested that in many ways, the child is a more sophisticated social being than previously thought (Corsaro, 1985; Hartup, 1983). Researchers such as Arnold (1979), Bronson (1981), Mueller and Brenner (1977), Vandell, Wilson and Buchanan (1980) have shown that children even younger than preschoolers have surprising competence in the social arena. Studies of young children's social language (Chafel, 1987; Garvey and Hogan, 1973; Hamilton and Stewart, 1977; Shatz and Gelman, 1973; Spilton and Lee, 1977) and prosocial behaviour (Bar-Tel, Raviv and Goldberg, 1982; Marantz, 1988; Rodd, 1989; Yarrow and Waxler, 1977) have challenged the image of the young child as a totally egocentric being. It seems at least under some circumstances, young children are capable of recognizing another's plight and spontaneously offering help.

Although considerable research effort has been devoted to such areas as peer popularity (Asher, 1983; Hartup, Glazer and Charlesworth, 1967; Grusec and Abramovitch, 1982; Roopnarine and Honig, 1985), social problem solving (Krasnor and Rubin, 1983; Spivak and Shure, 1974), and effects of physical environment (Charlesworth and Hartup, 1967; Howes and Rubenstein, 1979; Smith and Connelly, 1977; Rubin, 1977; Vandell and Meuller, 1977), little is known about the effects of adults on children's peer interactions (Marantz, 1988). But the small number of studies that have examined the relationship between mothering style and children's peer interactions (or popularity) have suggested that significant adults play an influential part in young children's social development; a difference that is evident in children's interactions with each other (Abraham and Christopherson, 1982; Baumrind, 1977; Corter, Abramovitch and Pepler, 1983; Peery, Jensen and Adams, 1984; Roopnarine and Adams, 1985).

Social Development and the Early Childhood Curriculum

Traditionally, early childhood education programs have claimed to address every aspect of the child's development. Unlike later educational settings, the child's feelings of self-worth, self-control, attitudes to learning and relationships with others have not been relegated to the 'hidden' curriculum (Combs *et al.*, 1978; Evans, 1981; Hosford, 1980; Jackson, 1968; Overly, 1970), but have been within the scope of the planned curriculum.

Children's peer relations also have been acknowledged as a legitimate area of the teacher's concern. As Moore (1981) says, 'learning to get along with others' has been viewed both by parents and teachers as a major developmental hurdle for young children, and entering a group situation for the first time represents a major change in the 3- or 4-year-old's social existence. As Pendleton describes:

> He must join in, play with other children, share, take turns and take some responsibilities for his actions. In this setting, he also is expected to recognize and verbalize his feelings, to substitute verbalizations for behaviours, to physically control his feelings and emotions, to find alternatives for certain behaviour, to enter new situations, to obtain as well as accept help and

support and to recognize the rights and feelings of others. (1980, p. 6)

Despite the lack of solid research evidence on the effects of adult interventions on the development of children's social skills with peers, writers of practical early childhood education textbooks have described a wide range of strategies for intervention, drawn from many theoretical bases.

One major strand allied to Social Learning Theory (Bandura and Walters, 1963), has focused on socializing the child to fit into an adult society (Margolin, 1982). These strategies emphasize the importance of the teacher as a model (Hildebrand, 1981; Hymes, 1981; Read and Patterson, 1980; Yardley, 1971) and are concerned with children acquiring good manners, acceptable behaviour and conformity to rules. As Hymes states: 'Nothing is more basic than teaching children to behave so they are a joy now for others to have around, and so they grow up to become good citizens' (1981, p. 131). In addition to being a model, however, the teacher also is an authority figure; someone who sets the rules and consistently intervenes to enforce them, should the children's self-control be found lacking (Hildebrand, 1981; 1985; Hymes, 1981).

Many of the advocated strategies for the development of children's social skills have originated in behaviourist psychology. The teacher is seen as shaping children's social learning through positive reinforcement when desirable social behaviours are emitted (Hildebrand, 1981; Holmberg, 1972). As an instructor of social skills, the teacher models and rewards children for using communication skills such as verbal phrases for requesting access or turns, using names when addressing others and responding when spoken to.

In the 'ecological' approach, the teacher is seen as a provisioner of the environment; someone who works 'behind the scenes' making environmental adjustments (fine-tuning) to promote certain desirable social behaviours and inhibit less desirable ones (Day, 1983; Montessori, 1964; Hildebrand, 1981). Similarly, the 'maturationist' view (Gesell, Ilg, and Ames, 1949) has been represented, in strategies where the teacher provides opportunity and encouragement, but does not intervene directly (Lindberg and Swedlow, 1985).

Yet another area of teacher strategies represented in early childhood texts has arisen from the humanist psychology movement (Combs, Avila and Purkey, 1978; Robison, 1983; Rogers, 1969). In these strategies the teacher plays an almost therapeutic role, facilitating the interaction through the use of reflective or focusing questions, interpreting the social situation, focusing on feelings and helping children to generate possible solutions for peer problems (Hazden, Black, and Fleming-Johnson, 1984). A related approach identifies children's peer interactions as opportunities for problem solving. In this case, the teacher again is a facilitator who helps children clarify and identify the problem, generate alternatives and find possible solutions (Lindberg and Swedlow, 1985; Shure and Spivak, 1979; Smith, 1982).

In early childhood, moral and social development often have been perceived as being intertwined (Damon and Killen, 1982; Kohlberg, 1970; Krogh and Lamme, 1985; Lindberg and Swedlow, 1985). Some developmental psychologists such as Enright and Sutterfield (1979), Krasnor (1982), and Krasnor and Rubin (1983) have evaluated children's interactions with peers in a value-neutral manner, in terms of the success of one child's strategy in achieving his/her goal, but clearly, teachers have a more demanding task. Their interventions need to be guided by a sense of the 'ideal' moral person; someone who is concerned not only with the success of a strategy in achieving personal goals, but is also aware of the effects of one's own actions on others and who ultimately, develops a sense of social justice (Furlong and Carroll, 1990). If indeed the preschool does reflect the democratic ideals of the larger society, as is claimed (Evans, 1981; Lindberg and Swedlow, 1985; Krogh, 1984; Seefeldt and Barbour, 1986), the teacher, in promoting children's social development, must also be guided by an 'ideal of citizenship'.

Writings on early childhood curriculum strategies for social development also reflect wider societal issues. For example, the interest in peace education has been reflected in an emphasis on teaching young children non-violent strategies for conflict resolution (Ward, 1985). Similarly, in a social context of increasing multiculturalism, early childhood educators have become concerned with the children's development of tolerance and a valuing of racial and cultural differences (McLean, 1990). As other groups within society have shown a heightened concern with fundamental moral and social values, there has been renewed interest in 'books with a moral' to promote desirable social attitudes in children. Group games and exercises also have been devised specifically to promote certain desirable social attitudes (Krogh and Lamme, 1985; Sapon-Shevin, 1980; Smith, 1982).

Thus it can be seen that practical early childhood education texts reflect many of society's changing emphases and represent a range of theoretical positions on social development. As changes have occurred, it seems that many early childhood writers have not foregone earlier approaches but have simply added to them. Sometimes, these diverse strategies do not fit well together. They often originate in quite different world views and represent differing perspectives on the processes of human development and desired outcomes from early education programs.

Although the promotion of social development has received considerable attention in early childhood texts, the suggested strategies often provide conflicting advice and little is known about how early childhood teachers, in practice, deal with this area of development. The teacher's involvement in preschooler's peer interactions is a complex phenomenon; one shrouded with overlapping concerns of moral development, social competence, group control and person-with-person relationships. Because this is an area of the curriculum that has no simple answers, it was hoped that a record of teacher actions in these situations would provide a means of accessing that teacher's interpretations of particular child-child situations and decision making. Further, it was hoped that this focus would provide a window on the ways internal, personal factors interact with situational factors to produce unique patterns of teacher-child interaction.

Helping children to live together in harmony, to find satisfaction, even joy in their contacts with each other, would seem to be particularly important in terms of the process of becoming human and thus is appropriate in a study where teaching is seen to be an essentially human endeavour; an intersection, a point of contact between people (Hughes, 1958; Rogers, 1969).

About the Book

In interpretive research, it is acknowledged that there can be no such thing as a strictly objective account. The act of research is itself an interpretation and thus every outcome, every word picture that is created, includes something of the researcher. In this sense, then, what follows is not only a story about teaching, but also a story about researching.

The story of the research project already begun continues in Chapter 2, with a brief methodological overview and a reflective account of the conduct of the study. In order to maintain the idiosyncratic quality of the data, it was decided to compile it as a series of discrete case studies. These are contained in Chapters 3 through 6, beginning with 'Rhonda', then moving to 'Nan', 'Brenda' and lastly, 'Kathy'. (Note these names are pseudonyms.) In trying to convey a detailed yet concise picture of each teacher and her work with a particular group of children, the case studies make use of some of the teacher's own words and include thickly-detailed instances of teacher-child interactions.

Although the case studies must inevitable reflect something of the researcher's own changing perspectives, discussion of what was learned from these teachers is confined to Chapter 7 where these understandings are considered in relation to other research and writings in education. In the final chapter (Chapter 8), the professional development of early childhood teachers is considered and questions are raised about the ways in which enhanced understandings of the practices of real life teaching may usefully inform preservice and inservice teacher education programs.

Note

1   These personal qualities have been catalogued from the following texts: Bacmeister, 1980; Gordon and Browne, 1985; Hildebrand, 1981; 1985; Hymes, 1981; Margolin, 1982; Read and Patterson, 1980; Robison, 1983; Seefeldt and Barbour, 1986; Yardley, 1971.

Chapter 2

Research and Researcher

Methodological Overview

The methodological techniques used in this investigation were based on a phenomenological perspective on knowledge and the pursuit of understanding. The approach[1] places heavy emphasis on observing phenomena in their natural context, without the imposition of *a priori* categorization schemes, and attempts to maintain the 'wholeness' and complexity of the phenomenon. 'Context stripping' (Henry, 1971; Mischler, 1979) or 'decontextualization' (Bronfenbrenner, 1979; Taylor, 1973; Yamamoto, 1984) is seen as a major obstacle in the search for understanding of human phenomena. As Owens writes:

> If one seeks to understand the realities of human organizations and the behavior of people in them, the naturalistic view would hold that those organizations must be examined in all the rich confusion of their daily existence. Human behavior must be examined *in situ* if it is to be understood. (1982, p. 6)

In a similar vein, Yamamoto writes: 'A cardinal possibility for understanding may be lost if humans are either prematurely removed from their natural habitat to simplified and isolated settings for investigation, or presorted into certain convenient categories of characteristics and behaviors' (1984, p. 69).

Underlying this research perspective is the assumption that people are 'knowing beings' (Bogdan and Biklen, 1982; Fenstermacher, 1978; Magoon, 1977) and that no knowledge can be free from the influence of personal interpretation (Polanyi, 1967). Grundy, in writing of Habermas' theory of human interests writes: 'A view that knowledge exists somehow apart from people and is "discovered" by them is not what is being accepted here. Rather, knowledge is recognized as being something which people together construct (1987, p. 8). Further, knowledge is seen as an essential component of behaviour. To construct understandings of human actions, one must seek the meanings situations hold for the actors. To understand human phenomena, the inquirer must attempt to see through the eyes of the participants, as well as his/her own.

In such interpretive investigation (Grundy, 1987), 'thick description' (Geertz, 1973) is used in an attempt to 'make sense' (Rowan and Reason, 1981; Taylor, 1973) of the meanings of action held by people embedded in particular contexts. Rowan and Reason describe this as one of the canons of the hermaneutic approach and state: '... the interpretation should make the phenomenon maximally reasonable in human terms' (1981, p. 134).

Such research is inherently incomplete: 'truth' is not waiting to be discovered once, and for all time (Gendlin, 1973). Within the 'hermaneutic circle', knowledge is not a possession, but an ongoing search. As Rowan and Reason state: 'we should not seek knowledge as a thing we have, but rather be involved in a personal, circular, contradictory process of knowing, of inquiry' (1981, p. 136).

Many of the assumptions underlying this approach are similar to those of ethnographic anthropological investigation. Although the present study is not strictly a cultural inquiry, ethnographers have provided a framework through which to examine the ways in which the participants reflexively both construct and respond to the meanings they hold about life within their classroom. To quote Geertz:

> Man is an animal suspended in webs of significance he himself has spun. I take culture to be those webs, and the analysis of it to be not an experimental science in search of law, but an interpretive one in search of meaning. (1973, p. 5).

This study also was a search for meanings. It explored the person who was teacher, and her many complex, multi-faceted connections with children and the physical environment, that together comprised life in these preschool settings.

Overall Plan of the Study

Although it was acknowledged that the features of life in classrooms are a construction of both adult and child participants, preliminary studies (McLean, 1986) had shown that there were profound methodological difficulties in accessing a 4- or 5-year-old's meanings of everyday social interactions. Thus, this became a study of teachers in the interactive contexts of preschool settings, rather than a study of both teachers' and children's understandings.

In a sense, the study was a search for patterns or 'configurations', a term Henry attributes to Dilthey and describes as 'a complex interweaving of values, institutions, emotions and actions' (1971, p. xxi). In seeking Bolster's 'coherent explanations of how [the] classroom works' (1983, p. 303), the study sought to identify patterns in the teacher's observable behaviour, patterns between teacher and child in interaction, patterns within the teacher's beliefs and reciprocal connections between beliefs and actions.

Because of the complexities of classroom life, it is not possible to observe and analyze everything. Careful decisions have to be made, so that although an aspect of classroom life is considered in fine detail, the holistic perspective on classroom life is maintained (Bolster, 1983; Erikson, 1977). For the reasons described in the previous chapter, in this study observations were focused on the teacher's involvement in children's peer interactions, and these written records were then used as a way of assisting each teacher to talk about the meanings of the events. Through other interviewing techniques, some of the more personal dimensions, such as her beliefs about children, learning and teaching, and perceptions of her own development were explored.

Participants

The four early childhood teachers who participated in the final phase of the study were drawn from a pre-existing study group within a community preschool network in Australia. Members had been invited to join this group because of their extensive experience and excellent professional reputation. The group set out to reflect on their own teaching, to broaden and deepen their own insights through interaction with colleagues and to write a statement about the philosophical approach that characterizes early childhood education in this network. (The group has no longer meeting at the time of this study.)

It could not be claimed that this was a representative sample, but as writers such as Bogdan and Biklen (1982) and Lincoln and Guba (1985) have emphasized, because probabilistic inference is not used to draw conclusions, representativeness is not crucial in interpretive investigations. The focus is idiographic (Allport, 1981; Cronbach, 1975;

Magoon, 1977; Yamamoto, 1984) and aims to 'provide an in-depth understanding of the complexity of a particular classroom, rather than an experimental derivation of a selected number of elements whose relationships can be replicated elsewhere' (Bolster, 1983, p. 305).

The decision to select teachers of recognized ability reflected a number of factors. Several recent major educational initiatives had focused on excellence (Frymier, Cornbleth and Donmayer, 1984; National Commission on Excellence in Education, 1983) and it seemed that if the research effort was to be limited to a very small number of settings then it was important that these settings should provide a worthy example for others (Leinhardt, 1986).

Further, it was acknowledged that in asking participants to closely examine their own teaching practices and beliefs, the study would be personally demanding. It seemed likely that teachers who recently had received affirmation of their teaching ability might be willing to undertake the risks involved in this type of self-questioning and to open themselves to the close scrutiny the study required (Laing, 1969).

Of the eight teachers in the study group, four were selected to participate in the final research project. All were women. (Although an increasing number of men are graduating from early childhood teacher education courses, to date male teachers form a very small minority of Australian early childhood teachers.) The participants ranged from approximately 30 to 50 years of age and each held a three year diploma from a Kindergarten Teachers College. In this final selection of four teachers, 'maximum variation sampling' (Lincoln and Guba, 1985; Yamamoto, 1984) sought to maximize the diversity in the social contexts in which the teachers worked. 'Rhonda' taught in a small rural and dormitory community on the outskirts of the city. 'Nan's' preschool was located in a suburb with mainly affluent families. 'Brenda' taught in an Aboriginal preschool in a depressed urban area and 'Kathy's' centre was located in a suburb with mostly middle-income families.

The decision to include Kathy in the study has created many ongoing ethical and personal dilemmas for me as a researcher. At the initial meeting, Kathy expressed her pleasure at being invited to participate, but after the first two days of observation, it became clear that Kathy's teaching was under considerable stress. I suggested she might like to withdraw at this point, but Kathy indicated she wished to continue, even though she was feeling 'burned out' with teaching. The decision to proceed reflected my desire to utilize this rare opportunity to explore the connections between a teacher's perception of self as 'burned-out' and what was happening in her classroom. Bolster writes of the value of such opportunities: 'Unanticipated contingencies potentially illuminate rather than confound understanding, since reaction to the unexpected often highlights the salient meanings assigned to what is normal' (1983, pp. 305–6). What I did not anticipate was the anxiety I would later experience as I made decisions about how to use these data, how to portray Kathy and her work honestly and with compassion.

Foundations for Trust

Qualitative researchers have differed on the extent of foreknowledge of the situation that is needed by the researcher (Erikson, 1977; Glaser and Strauss, 1967; Rowan and Reason, 1981; Yamamoto, 1984), but it would seem that one must be oriented to the culture as a whole (Lincoln and Guba, 1985) and have some 'shared reality' with the participants (Dawson, 1979; Elden, 1981) before any narrowly-focused work can begin. In this study, I had considerable foreknowledge, being a graduate from a Kindergarten Teachers College, and having been a preschool teacher for several years. This common background was a great advantage in building rapport with the teachers, but it also brought some difficulties. As the study proceeded, the extent of my taken-for-granted knowledge of early childhood education only gradually was revealed. Despite periods of cognitive dissonance as these beliefs were exposed and challenged, it is quite likely that some tacit areas of my knowledge base still remain unacknowledged.

At an initial meeting, each teacher was given the fullest possible picture of the study, bearing in mind its emergent nature. My interests and philosophical orientation were openly disclosed (Kelman, 1968) because in Patton's (1980) terms, this was to be 'overt' observation. By answering the teachers' questions honestly, and giving as much information as I could, it seemed a positive foundation would be laid for the development of trust — an essential component of rigor in qualitative research (Coles, 1967; Dawson, 1979; Elden, 1981; Haas and Shaffir, 1980; Lincoln and Guba, 1985).

In this study, a generally high level of trust appeared to prevail, but there were some differences in the level of trust both within each relationship and among teachers. Trust seemed lowest in the few days between the first observation and the teacher's sighting of the first full observation transcript. Once the teachers read the first transcript, the level of trust rose and remained high throughout the study. The relationship with Kathy was an exception. Perhaps because of her stressed state, the level of trust never seemed to reach the level that characterized relationships with other teachers.

During the data-gathering phase, I felt quite at ease with the information I was being offered by these teachers and the understandings we developed together. Only when I came to make the first public presentation on this study, did I find myself appalled at the prospect of disclosing such personal information. Although in an intellectual sense, I understood the need for close trusting relationships, only through personal experience did I come to fully appreciate the inherent paradox in this research approach, whereby the understandings gleaned through these trusting relationships are then disclosed to a wide audience. Even after minor changes were made to protect the anonymity of these teachers, my sense of betraying a trust has endured. I have learned that the gathering of data is relatively straightforward. It is in the compilation and dissemination of findings that many dilemmas must be faced by the qualitative researcher.

Observations

In keeping with Geertz who emphasizes the need to 'attend to behavior with some exactness' (1973, p. 17), this study set out to create an accurate and detailed stable data record (Erikson, 1977) of the teachers' involvement in children's peer interactions. The production of such detailed records, however, makes many demands of the observer, as Yarrow and Waxler state:

> Though exceedingly practiced, the human observer, by many criteria, is a poor scientific instrument: nonstandard, not readily calibrated, and often inconsistent or unreliable. Counterbalancing these failings are the human capabilities of extraordinary sensitivity, flexibility, and precision. The challenge is to discover how to conduct disciplined observing while making full use of the discriminations of which the human observer is capable. (1979, p. 37)

Timing for Observations

In studies such as this, prolonged immersion in the setting is an important component of rigor (Bolster, 1983; Coles, 1967; Dawson, 1979; Lincoln and Guba, 1985; Owens, 1982), but it is impossible to specify any concrete period as being an adequate duration for all contexts and purposes (Patton, 1980). Bearing in mind the teleological nature of the pursuit of understanding, it seems likely that any period could be considered insufficient.

In this study, observations were carried out in every session of the 4- to 5-year-old group over a period of a little less than three weeks. (The overall period differed marginally between sites because of different patterns of attendance.) Further insights may have arisen had observations continued, but this time span was sufficient to observe a wide range of interactions between teachers and children and to see patterns repeated on many occasions. It seemed a level of saturation (Glaser and Strauss, 1967) had been reached.

Although it was expected that teachers initially would feel uncomfortable in the presence of an observer, it was hoped that through the almost continuous observation over a period of weeks, the strangeness of the situation would be overcome. To help deal with the discomfort, teachers were encouraged to talk about their experience of being observed and, although they were rarely oblivious of the observer, this did not seem to be a problem. As Brenda said:

> It's made me a bit more conscious of what I say. But you get really involved in something and you don't worry. You know you're there, but you just sort of get too concerned with what's happening with the group of children, to be worried.

Several of the teachers reported that although they remained aware of the observer's presence, after the first few days it was no longer threatening. In commenting on an observation from the first day, Nan said:

> [That situation] was very stilted. That I felt at the time. It was Monday morning, it was my first experience of you being close. I felt it was stilted and not flowing and it was a bit forced.

Later, Nan added:

> It didn't take me long to feel comfortable — I did just feel comfortable, so that it became — I was able to look beyond the selfconscious feelings and the worry about whether I was doing the right thing and get on with the job.

Occasional spontaneous comments, such as a teacher softly commenting: 'Did you see that?!', as she hurried from a scene suggested that at least at times, these teachers enjoyed having the observer share some special moments of the day.

A consecutive observation schedule also was selected because of a desire to capture the continuity of life in classrooms and this made it possible to consider today's events, in the context of what happened yesterday. Even over a period as short as three weeks, distinct changes in a teacher's perceptions of children were noticeable and this continuity added much to the breadth of understanding that was possible in the study.

Role of Observer

Because of the desire to create detailed observational records that would have a high level of accuracy, participant observation (Patton, 1980) was rejected in favour of a more distanced observational role, though as Le Compte and Goetz (1984) point out, *any* observation within the classroom inevitably involves a degree of participation.

From my experience in preschools, I knew that a responsive stranger quickly could become the centre of attention for friendly children and this engagement could hinder accurate recording. There also seemed a danger that my presence would act as a constraint on children's behaviour, if I became involved in their interactions. So, I became a 'passive, compliant and restrained person' (Henry, 1971, p. 459) who remained uninvolved, even in stressful situations. Like Brearley (1970), I found this a difficult role at times, as I had to repress my usual responsiveness to children. Despite my unease, it seemed to work well. After the first two days, the children very rarely approached me or even made eye contact, often leaning to one side to stare around me, as if I were a piece of furniture. It seemed I had been judged totally uninteresting. After observations ended, three of the teachers reported that children did not comment on my absence. The children in Brenda's centre were an exception. They often greeted me with warm smiles and when I returned to the centre after being ill and missing a day, one boy called cheerily, 'G'day Vi! Where ya been?'

Throughout, I tried not to display my interest in children's behaviour and carefully kept my expression blank as peer interactions occurred close to me. On many occasions, the children seemed completely oblivious of my presence and their peer behaviour when I was very close by was quite different to that seen around other adults. For example, they would act aggressively to each other, often without even glancing towards me, to monitor my reactions.

Although it would appear that my impact on the children was minimal, Valerie, an Aboriginal child in Brenda's group, reminded me that I was still visible. On one occasion, she walked through the playroom, carrying a child-sized chair behind her. In the other hand, she carried a piece of paper, folded to notebook size, and a pencil. Periodically, Valerie lowered the chair, quickly sat on it and crossed her legs, then balanced the paper on her knee. After looking around at the children near her, Valerie scribbled madly for a few seconds, then stood up, picked up the chair behind her and moved on. The observer had been closely observed.

Nature of Observations

Two major types of observational strategies were used. Event sampling (Cohen and Stern, 1970) focused on the teacher's involvement in children's peer interactions, and in order to understand the temporal context (Bolster, 1983; Henry, 1971) in which these events were embedded, a general running record, or 'stream-of-behavior chronicle' (Le Compte and Goetz, 1984, p. 49) was kept throughout each session. In this chronicle, particular note was taken of any salient happening, and the teacher's movements, general atmosphere of the group, and dispersion of children across areas, was noted periodically.

Event sampling requires the observer to watch for occurrences of a specific type of event, then to record what happens in a detailed narrative form. As mentioned above, the events targetted in this study were those occasions when the teacher became involved in children's interactions with each other. This included occasions when the teacher spoke to a single child about his/her interactions with other children and occasions when the teacher made adjustments to the immediate physical environment where children were located (for example, adding materials, extra chairs or props for ongoing dramatic play).

Even with the help of a small audiotape recorder with a powerful directional microphone, the observer needed to 'shadow' the teacher closely, as she moved through the environment. The tape was activated as an event began and details such as time, location, identity of children and non-verbal behaviours were recorded in written site notes. A written 'skeleton' of dialogue facilitated later matching of the audiotape with site notes.

Observations were recorded throughout free play times, as these large segments of the program provide many opportunities for children's interactions with peers. Free play times typically occupy more than two thirds of the 'active' program time (i.e., excluding the lunch and rest routines in full-day programs) and may extend for ninety minutes or more without interruption. They are characterized by low structure, with children usually free to select their own activity from both indoor and outdoor areas concurrently, or from indoors and, at another time, outdoors.

Early in the study, it was decided to extend event sampling to include the tidy-up routine that followed free play time. At tidy-up time, the nature of the teachers' involvement with children often underwent a major change, as they organized children to work together to put materials away, under time pressure. These differences seemed particularly salient to the study.

At the conclusion of a target event, whenever possible I remained on the scene after the teacher left, to capture something of the children's interactions as they reverted to purely peer contacts. These data were of particular interest to the teachers. However, to remain behind for even a few seconds meant risking the loss of the beginning of the next event. If the teacher left the scene with a purposeful stride, I followed quickly. If she slowly drifted away, I stayed for a minute or two, whilst monitoring her movements.

Although the audiotapes were sometimes difficult to transcribe, the combination of written notes and audiotaped dialogue enabled very detailed descriptive narratives to be constructed. Owens writes:

> Thick description is more than mere information or descriptive data; it conveys a literal description that figuratively transports the readers into the situation with a sense of insight, understanding and illumination not only of the facts or the events in the case, but also of the texture, the quality and the power of the context as the participants experienced it. (1982, p. 8)

By combining the detailed event descriptions with the chronicle, it was possible to create a single session narrative that often was forty or fifty pages in length. In this way, the occasions in which the teacher became involved in children's peer interactions remained contextualized and the continuity of the live events was maintained, at least to some degree, in the written account.

In addition to observations of interaction, note also was taken of the ways in which the teacher provisioned the physical environment. Ecological studies (Day and Sheehan, 1974; Mincey, 1982) and others

(Krogh, 1984; Minuchin and Shapiro, 1983) have suggested that the physical environment is a powerful force in social interactions. The ways in which teachers made use of the environment to enhance children's peer interactions provided another perspective on the ways they were involved in helping children live together in harmony.

Interviews

Approximately seven hours of audiotaped interviews were completed with each teacher, usually commencing late in the first week of observations and continuing for several weeks after the observations ended. (The tapes were made available to the participants.) All interview tapes were fully transcribed, a situation Patton (1980) has described as ideal, but the transcripts contained an immense amount of detail-far more than could be fully utilized in this study.

Throughout the interviews, an accepting, friendly atmosphere was maintained and rapport was generally high. For the most part, participants were encouraged to make their own connections, explore tangents and pursue items that most interested them. Although there was some repetition, in accordance with Spradley (1979), it was believed redundancy would add strength to the patterns that were discerned. The open-endedness of the interviews enabled the participants to raise and return to issues and the recurrent nature of these issues then alerted the interviewer to their importance.

Overall, fewer interviews were conducted with Kathy and these were of doubtful dependability. Although Kathy was keen to discuss some aspects of her teaching, she was reluctant to examine other areas and as Torbet (1981) has described, had a repertoire of strategies to avoid doing so.

Two types of interviews were conducted — 'depth' interviews and a form of stimulated recall (Clark and Peterson, 1986) identified as 'conversations'.

Depth Interviews

Massarik describes the 'depth' interview as being characterized by: 'an intensive process on the part of the interviewer to explore thoroughly ... the views and dynamics of the interviewee' (1981, p. 203). One aspect explored in the depth interviews was the teacher's biography. The hermaneutic approach emphasizes the importance of the 'ontological dimension' (Kisiel, 1973, p. 278) on an individual's interpretations or understandings. As Rowan and Reason state: 'The first lesson of hermaneutics is that we are historical beings; and that our understanding is an historical process' (1981, p. 132). The phenomenologist Dallmayr credits Shutz with recognizing the importance of the person's recollections of his/her own personal history and writes: 'he found the source of meaning in the stream of lived experience or internal time-sense or more specifically, in the reflective glance upon such experience' (1973, p. 154).

In this study, it was assumed that recollections of past experience could influence the ways in which the participants conceptualized themselves as teachers and thus have some bearing on the ways in which they interpreted and became involved in classroom events (Ball and Goodson, 1985). For this reason, considerable attention was given to the participants' reflections on their accumulated experience as teachers. They were asked why they had stayed in teaching for so many years and what plans they had for the future.

Participants were asked to reflect on their development as person and as teacher and to comment on the changes they perceived in themselves and their teaching actions. They were invited to explore some of the connections they saw between their personal development or life outside the preschool, and their teaching.[2] As another strategy to access this area of interest, participants were asked if they felt comfortable with the notion of teaching as performance. (If the participant suggested that she performed on occasion, this was pursued with 'structural' questions [Spradley, 1979, p. 116] about the types and circumstances of performances.) One of the most useful questions in exploring the person-teacher connection was: 'How do you change when that door opens at 9:00 a.m.?' This question generated a great deal of interest among the participants and introduced a whole new area of interest to the study — the ways the teachers mentally prepared themselves to face each day.

Although the two types of interviews could be distinguished as being general and specific in focus, in actuality there was a good deal of crossing over of topics beween the two.

Conversations

The highly-interactive 'conversations', based on Erikson and Shultz's (1981) second-generation interviewing technique, usually began with an invitation to the teachers to comment generally on the written observations. Because it took a great deal of time just to read a long observational transcript, teachers were asked to read the transcript in advance. With the exception of Kathy, it seemed the narratives were a powerful tool for helping the teachers recall events. They readily verbalized recollections of their feelings and thoughts, and gave details about individual children, that had guided their decisions. On occasion, they pointed out aspects of their personal experience of events, that were not adequately covered by the observational narrative. The reliving of an unpleasant experience was clear in Brenda's halting words as she commented on the narrative of a particularly rough day:

> That day, the Thursday, when I was outside on my own and there was all that ... going on. [I] just want to comment that — the chaos that I was feeling inside when I was reading through — There was one point, when you said my voice showed frustration ... I remembered that day particularly, feeling — just feeling so many things were going on and I was — sort of having a lot of trouble coping with all those situations. Just from reading the observations, that didn't come through very much at all.

Invariably, during these conversations, the teachers talked at length about the nature of children in general, specific children in the group, their goals for children and the strategies they used to try to achieve these. The conversations also provided for several levels of 'member checking' (Dawson, 1979, p. 9; Lincoln and Guba, 1985, p. 236; Owens, 1982, p. 14). They enabled a checking of the initial observation with the teacher's recollections, some access to the teacher's meanings associated with specific events, checking of the emerging patterns of interaction, and some cross-checking of positions between teachers. For example, early in the study, Rhonda's statement that *any* teacher intervention in peer interactions would lead to greater adult-dependency in children caused me to reconsider my assumptions and to raise her position for comment with other teachers.

These conversations were always stimulating and sometimes were punctuated by exciting moments, as both the teacher and myself found nourishment in the other's ideas and suddenly saw connections where none had been noticed before.

Card Sort

At the conclusion of the interviews, an informal card sort was used to prompt teachers to discuss their philosophical positions on early childhood education. Half of the cards contained generalized statements about children and teaching, distilled from a teacher's statements in the preliminary study, and the remainder contained concocted opposing position statements. Participants were asked to sort the cards on a five-point agreement/disagreement scale, while 'thinking aloud' about their choices. Because the statements had not been systematically tested, the actual sort data were not utilized, but the teachers' comments as they completed the tasks were recorded.

With the exception of Kathy, the teachers disliked this task immensely. Throughout, they complained about the impossibility of dealing with generalizations and clearly indicated their greater comfort with the particularistic dimension of their knowledge. At the end of the task, these three teachers left a large number of cards in the 'too-hard basket' and would sort them only after placing on record a list of conditions or qualifications. For example, Nan finally dealt with the troublesome statement 'It is my professional responsibility to actively direct the way these children learn' by saying:

> I don't feel confident in specifying the direction a child should go. I don't think I should play God and say that I know the very best. But — by trial and error, with individual children, I find out which is the best way for that child to go, in my opinion.

Kathy approached the task quite differently, sorting the cards without complaint and saying this was 'more fun than answering questions' (see Chapter 6).

Dependability of Interview Data

As Lincoln and Guba (1985, p. 299) have suggested, there can be no foolproof measure of dependability in data of this kind, but throughout the sessions, all possible care was taken not to impose my views on the participants. When I raised patterns I had perceived, for checking by participants, this was done in a tentative manner. Although it is not possible to say to what extent this was successful, participants sometimes unhesitatingly refuted my ideas, saying, 'No, that's not how I see it', and went on to propose an alternative explanation.

In the interviews, the participant's words were being noted as data (Fenstermacher, 1978) but beyond this, the interviews also were a form of observation. As Combs et al., (1978) have suggested, verbal behaviour in interviews provides *clues* to underlying meanings, rather than providing a pure measure of those meanings. Similarly, Taylor points to the paradox that even in a hermaneutic inquiry that strives for congruence, verbalized interpretations and lived interpretations must retain a degree of incongruity. He writes:

> [The question is] whether the interpretation can ever express the same meaning as the interpreted. And in this case, there is clearly a way in which the two will not be congruent. For if the interpretation is really clearer than the lived interpretation then it will be such that it would alter in some way the behavior if it came to be internalized by the agent as his self-interpretation. (1973, p. 62)

Because so many areas of the teacher's practical knowledge are tacit or implicit (Popkowitz and Wehlage, 1977), it cannot be assumed that what teachers are able to verbalize is necessarily a mirror-like reflection of what they mean (Porter and Portenza, 1983). Therefore, an element of 'clinical judgment' (Porter and Potenza, 1983, p. 163), of 'listening with the third ear' (Reik, 1948), of 'high-quality awareness' (Reason and Rowan, 1981, p. 245) is called for on the part of the inquirer. As Yamamoto writes: 'To study anything of human significance, one must sooner or later go to where people are, and explore their actions, reactions, and interactions, both inside-out and outside-in' (1984, p. 69).

In this study, both the inside-out perspectives of the participants and the outside-in perspective of the observer were explored and considered. Although a determined effort was made to understand the participants' perspectives, my own perspective was not totally subjugated (Laing, 1969). In keeping with the acceptance and exploration of multiple realities typical in phenomenological inquiry (Emig, 1983), whenever possible, differences in perspective were brought to the surface and discussed with the participants.

Because teaching was conceptualized as a complex and paradoxical phenomenon, with some inherent ambiguity and inconsistency, it was not possible to utilize the degree of consistency as evidence of dependability of these data. Rather, apparent inconsistencies in teacher statements, and between statements and actions were carefully considered as interesting areas worthy of closer examination. There was constant recycling between the interview and observation data, so that one was not used as a 'predictor' of the other (Popkewitz and Wehlage, 1977). When apparently inconsistent statements were discussed with teachers, what often emerged was a paradoxical or particularistic element; both statements were true under different circumstances. For example, Nan explained her apparently inconsistent policy about parents lingering at the beginning of the session:

> It was important for [Dennis's Dad] to say something to me about Dennis. And if I brushed him off and said: 'Not now, off you go', it wouldn't have been said. It's messy sometimes. It's messy because the parents stay around for a while. And I don't encourage them in some ways ... Sometimes the kids don't get involved if everyone's hanging about. So I think it's legitimate for the parents [to] draw the line. They know when they really need me, or when I'm too involved, they go away.

In raising apparent discrepancies for the teacher's comment, extreme care had to be taken to communicate a non-judgmental position. Because of the powerful place our culture ascribes to 'consistency' as a virtue (Toulmin, 1977), there was a danger that participants might immediately alter their statements in order to appear consistent, and in this way, conceal the actuality. In Kathy's interviews, her apparent fragility and defensiveness meant that many apparent inconsistencies had to remain unexplored.

Analysis

Because it was assumed that teachers' behaviour would hold particular personal meanings, for each participant the interview data were analyzed first. In this way, the information that emerged from the interview data was able to inform the analysis of observational data.

Interview Coding Schemes

The initial coding system, developed in a preliminary study, consisted of three global areas; *The Child*; *The Interface*; *The Teacher*. Subsumed under *The Child* were a small number of categories including 'competence' and 'individual differences'. The major category, *The Interface*, contained a large number of subcategories related to the ways in which teacher and children come together in the preschool setting. *The Teacher* was the largest category, with four subcategories: Personal Factors; History; Teaching Activities Not Directly Involving Children; and Professional Networks.

Though this global coding system was retained throughout the study, repeated reworking of the data (Bogdan and Biklen, 1982) identified recurrent themes for each teacher, which were reflected in the subcategories established (see Appendix). Thus, whilst a core of categories remained for all teachers, there were also some idiosyncratic categories applying to each teacher. For example, in Brenda's case, the recurrent themes that ran through her talk about her own development and her teaching were identified as: Interrelatedness; Talking things over; It all takes time; Being positive. Each of these was assigned a code under the Personal sub-category of *The Teacher*.

Codes were marked on the transcript and data were sorted by noting a page reference and a brief precis of items on index cards for each subcategory. Much cross-referencing and multi-listing occurred so that a single item was often categorized in a number of different ways. In addition, from the 'conversations', the teacher's comments on particular classroom events were collated and later entered on observation summaries, as a cross-referencing between interview and observation data. When the major analysis of the interview data from one teacher was complete, a detailed 'case record' (Patton, 1980, p. 305) was compiled and with a similar case record from the observation data, made up each teacher's case study.

Observational Coding Schemes

The observational coding system that had worked so well in the preliminary study quickly showed it was a poor fit with these teachers' involvement in children's peer interactions. The system had two main categories: Process Behaviours (in which the teacher assisted with communication, but did not take control of the situation from the children); and Product Behaviours (in which the teacher entered with directive inputs that did take control from the children). Very early in the data analysis process, this distinction became a murky one, making it impossible to categorize some teacher inputs as one or the other.

After a series of trials with other categorization schemes, and well into the study, a new typology emerged that was able to account for all teacher interventions observed. The six categories were: Developing a Sense of Community; Helping Children Gain Access to Peer

Groups; Involvement in Children's Dramatic Play; Use of Social Conduct Rules; Resolving Peer Conflict Situations; Arrangement of the Physical Environment to Support Peer Interactions.

In addition to these mid-level categories, more micro-level coding also continued, so that smaller chunks of teacher behaviour could now be cross-referenced across types of intervention. For example, an item of 'Questions children in a peer situation' might also be listed under 'Resolving peer conflict situations', or 'Involvement in children's dramatic play', depending on the context in which it had occurred.

As with the interview data, although major categories were maintained across all settings, for each teacher some categories were unique. For example, Brenda's emphasis on 'Talking things over' in the interview data also emerged in the observation data, so a category by the same name was established.

This system captured something of each teacher's uniqueness, as well as providing a core of common areas that would enable some 'soft' comparisons to be made between teachers. But this reduction of data also decontextualized information and fragmented the flow of interaction. To help overcome these problems, a brief summary of all of the target events in each session was kept in temporal order. Erikson and Shultz (1981) have used the metaphor of a bead necklace, to explain that it is not just what goes on within each 'bead' of interaction, but also how the beads are strung together, that constitutes the pattern. These summaries enabled me to see some of the patterns across target interactional events.

As the data analysis proceeded, it became clear that a crucial dimension of the teacher's decisions about involvement concerned the identity of the children. To help these patterns stand out in the data, the children's names were colour coded, and this helped me realize to what extent a few children in each centre dominated these interactions. For example, in Nan's centre, Julie was coded green and the colour green appears to run continuously across the pages of the summaries.

As Geertz (1973), Henry (1971) and Coles (1969) have written, categorizing the human phenomenon often comes at the cost of spontaneity, richness and complexity. In devising these systems for analysis, I tried to ensure that each stage of analysis remained linked to the raw data through careful referencing. Return trips to the interview transcripts and observation narratives occurred with great frequency during the analysis and writing, and enabled the recontextualizing even of small fragments of teacher-child interaction. This referencing also provided an 'audit trail' (Owens, 1982, p. 12; Lincoln and Guba, 1985, p. 210) that allowed a rapid return to the stable data record, to check the dependability of precis or conclusions. This desire to stay as close as possible to the stable data record also was a major consideration in the format of the case studies.

Case Study Format

The case study approach (Stake, 1978) was thought to be particularly appropriate for this study because of its ability to build on the reader's tacit knowledge, communicate the interplay between inquirer and respondents and to provide 'thick description' and extensive contextual information (Lincoln and Guba, 1985). Further, case studies were able to portray these teachers as discrete individuals and not lose their particularistic qualities in an impersonal aggregate of pooled data. Each case study produced in this investigation closely conformed to Emig's description as 'an intense, naturalistic examination of a given individual' (1983, p. 163).

The case studies begin by describing the teacher and the setting, to help the reader 'make sense' of later examples; to 'receive a measure of vicarious experience' (Lincoln and Guba, 1985, p. 359). A major section describes the understandings that have emerged from the interview data, including the teacher's beliefs, attitudes about children and teaching, and the connections that have been discerned between the person and the teacher. After searching for a conceptual frame that would be sufficiently broad to encompass all of these dimensions, the term 'image-of-self-as-teacher' was selected.

Several recent researchers and writers in education have used the concept of image to provide a holistic framework for organizing notions about the teacher's personal practical knowledge, but there is little consensus on what constitutes an image (Calderhead and Robson, 1988). Elbaz (1983) conceptualizes image in terms of the teacher's linguistic statements about practical knowledge and introduces metaphor as a clue to underlying meanings. Clandinin (1986), in a manner congruent with Schon's (1983) concept of 'knowledge-in-action', conceptualizes image as including not only the teacher's linguistic expression of practical knowledge, but also the enactment of that knowledge in practical teaching situations. In this study, although the use of the term 'image-of-self-as-teacher' is used primarily with interview data, the understandings drawn are not limited to the surface meanings of the teacher's words, but go beyond to include links to teacher actions (through the 'conversations' about classroom events) and the researcher's interpretations of the teacher's knowledge.

The final subsection of the Image-of-Self-as-Teacher describes the teacher's comments about her program for children's social development. This information was distilled from many interviews and conversations, as the teachers spoke of the importance they accorded social development; what they wanted for these particular children; and the strategies they used to try to attain these goals.

As the name suggests, the fourth section, Actions in the Classroom, provides thick description of the teacher's actions in the preschool context. Very wide differences were observed in the relative importance placed upon the six areas of teacher involvement in children's peer interaction and the ordering of subsections reflects this diversity.

In the summary section, connections between the image-of-self-as-teacher and actions in the classroom are explored and a brief description of the inquirer's and participant's perspectives on participating in the data gathering phase of the study is given.

Summary

Because the philosophical assumptions include the inherently subjective nature of all knowledge, the existence of multiple realities and the impossibility of observing a phenomenon without becoming part of it, the traditional approaches to ensuring rigor are quite inappropriate in interpretive research. Inquirers following this approach have no set of standard procedures to ensure rigor, no rule book to follow (Smith and Heshusius, 1986). However, a number of writers in this area (Dawson, 1979; Halpern, 1983; Lincoln and Guba, 1985; Owens, 1982) have begun to collate techniques to increase the likelihood that research procedures will produce credible, dependable, transferable findings.

In keeping with the 'inquirer as instrument' notion, many of the techniques are related to the inquirer her/himself and the relationship that is formed with the participants. As Owens states:

> In order to avoid unreliable, biased, or opinionated data, the naturalistic inquirer seeks not some 'objectivity', brought about through methodology but, rather, strives for validity through personalized, intimate understandings of phenomena stressing 'close in' observations to achieve factual, reliable, and confirmable data. (1982, p. 10)

Lincoln and Guba (1985) suggest that claims for credibility can be based on a prolonged period of engagement, evidence of persistent observation and the use of multiple methods (or observers) to triangulate findings. Dawson (1979) adds the importance of the interpersonal conditions under which the data were gathered.

In this study, although the time in each setting was not extensive by ethnographic standards, the persistence of the observation schedule was intensive and a large amount of data (almost 1000 pages of narratives and transcripts per teacher) was generated. Several different observational and interviewing techniques were used to permit a degree of triangulation and to overcome the weaknesses that exist in any single method of data gathering (Dawson, 1979; Patton, 1980).

Adequacy of the interview data was increased through a 'testing-out' strategy (Douglas, 1976) in which the inside-out perspective of the participant was compared with the outside-in perspective of the inquirer and participant's statements were compared across many interview sessions, held over a period of time.

In keeping with the strategies suggested by Dean and Whyte (1969), to minimize the danger of participants giving inaccurate information on highly subjective areas, assurances were given that the participants would remain anonymous. Emphasis was placed on developing a high level of rapport and trust and in the one case where the level of trust was questionable, this was fully acknowledged.

Dawson (1979) emphasizes the importance of the observer's examining his/her own commitments and biases and, in the hermaneutical tradition (Smith and Heshusius, 1986), this occurred throughout the study and is continuing. As a solo researcher, 'peer de-briefings' (Lincoln and Guba, 1985) were particularly important and my 'knowledgeable peer', a recently graduated Doctor of Philosophy in Early Childhood Development and Education, was able to challenge my assumptions and help me to reflect further about the compilation of data and the conclusions I was drawing.

Writers such as Coles (1967), Heron (1981), and Magoon (1977) emphasize the importance of seeking corroboration for observations, from the participants. In this study, copies of narratives were discussed at length with the teachers and minor corrections noted. For the vast majority of events however, teachers corroborated the accuracy to a high level. For example, Brenda said:

> I was amazed at how much you'd taken in; I couldn't get over it. And also the accuracy. I thought a lot of what happened —

how you'd written it — was the same as ... The perceptions were what I'd had as well.

Nan said: 'It must be awfully demanding. I can't believe how much detail is in it. I've never seen it before.'

As observations were recorded as uncoded narratives in this study, observation and coding were quite distinct processes, but to provide a measure of inter-observer reliability, a second observer was used on several occasions. In an approach similar to that used by Holmberg (1980), the second observer used her own notes and the audiotape to compile a separate narrative account. Both completed narratives of the same events were then compared by a third person and an estimate of their agreement made. Twenty six events from two settings were compared using six broad categories, including location, participants, initiation of the event and dialogue. Overall agreement across all six categories was .97 and a finer-grained comparison of utterances alone, yielded a .80 level of agreement.

To ensure a degree of 'referential adequacy' (Lincoln and Guba, 1985, p. 313; Owens, 1979, p. 14) careful records were maintained, beginning with site notes, observation narratives and interview transcripts, and continuing though coding cards and memos. All of these materials were archived and an 'audit trail' (Halpern, 1983; Lincoln and Guba, 1985; Owens, 1979) created.

Although every effort was made to ensure rigor, in the end, it must be left to the reader to establish the worth of these findings for him/herself. As Lincoln and Guba state:

> There is no possibility that the naturalist can present a design (even ignoring its emergent character) that will absolutely persuade the skeptic that the results of the study will be worth attending to. Naturalistic studies simply cannot be warranted in the same way as are conventional studies. (1985, p. 329)

Notes

1 Some difficulties exist in terminology, as many overlapping labels have been used to describe this group of research approaches. For example: Naturalistic (Lincoln and Guba, 1985; Owens, 1982); Symbolic-Interactionist Ethnographic (Bolster, 1983); Hermaneutic (Kisiel, 1973; Rowan and Reason, 1981); Constructivist (Magoon, 1977); Qualitative (Smith and Heshusius, 1986).

2 This information later led to the production of a short video entitled 'Changing Perspectives: Teachers Becoming Mothers', in which five pre-school teachers discuss the ways in which their approaches to teaching have changed through the experience of having children of their own.

Chapter 3

Rhonda

The Setting

Rhonda's Preschool

The preschool was located in a rural community where some small farming continued but an increasing number of residents commuted daily to the city. Despite the rapid growth of the area, the community retained its small town atmosphere in what was still a delightfully unspoiled environment.

After twenty years of service, the preschool centre had a very well-established and well-used appearance, but was in good condition. The broad patio provided an unusually rich environment where much of the children's activity occurred. The playroom was spacious and very neat, with children's work carefully displayed. Each day, fresh flowers were placed around the room, and a vast range of materials was displayed at all times. Suspended from the ceiling, a large sign stated with some authority that every cooperative society has rules to protect its members and listed ten of the rules that applied in this setting.

Outdoors, the playground was of moderate size, with mature trees and shrubs. There was a great deal of fixed equipment, placed in a rather haphazard way, but providing many opportunities for play. Fowls lived in a coop at the rear, and foraged in the playground each day. Overall, the preschool had the appearance of a 'doing' sort of place. It provided an immense range of things to do and it is hard to imagine a child could ever become bored in this very rich and diverse environment.

Two groups of children attended, each for four half-day sessions a week. The sessions included two blocks of free play time, in which for the most part children had free access to both indoor and outdoor areas. However, on occasion, Rhonda made the choice for them, refusing access to certain activities and emphasizing others. These limitations often came in the latter part of the session, after children had had some free choice time and after some inappropriate activity had occurred.

Clock time had some importance in this program. Tidy-up routines consistently occurred at 11:00 a.m. and 2:40 p.m., but other segments of the program were more flexible. For example, the timing of snack ('morning tea' or 'afternoon tea') varied considerably from day to day. The basic morning timetable was as follows:

8:30	Arrivals.
8:35 — 9:10	Language group. (Sometimes up to forty-five minutes.)
9:10 — 10:00	First Block of Freeplay. (One day each week, Rhonda was involved in a library routine for the first thirty minutes of freeplay.)
10:00 — 10:20	Morning Tea. (Rhonda usually stayed until the last child finished — sometimes another fifteen minutes into the second freeplay block.)
10:20 — 11:00	Second Block of Freeplay time.
11:00 — 11:18	Tidy-up Time.
11:18 — 11:27	Music Group.
11:30	Departures.

Children, Families, Assistant

The group comprised twenty children, aged from 4.6 to 6.0 years. Five of the oldest children had been eligible to attend school this year, but their parents opted to keep them in preschool. Three of the 'younger fours' probably would have another year of preschool after this, before commencing school.

Rhonda described the families as 'caring' and indicated that they were 'pretty typical' for this preschool. Although the fathers worked in a wide range of occupations, including the professions, clerical work, business, primary industry research and farming, they 'were not scraping, financially'. None of the mothers were in full-time paid employment, though several did some part-time work.

For this group, Rhonda was assisted by A., a mother with two children of her own. A. had completed a certificate course as a teacher's aide and had worked with Rhonda for four years.

The Teacher

Rhonda was a slightly built woman of approximately 40 years of age. After being in poor health for several years, she was now maintaining a reasonable level of fitness. Rhonda dressed in a neat, but practical way; usually in jeans and several sweaters. Whenever she ventured into the playground, Rhonda wore a large straw hat, in keeping with her very strong concern for sun cancer prevention.

Although Rhonda was quite capable of moving very quickly when necessary, her movements generally were unhurried. Rhonda often spent prolonged periods of time working with just a few children. Many occasions were noted where she stayed in one location for twenty or thirty minutes, and once she spent fifty minutes working on a new construction toy with a small group of children. In this time, she made only one very brief foray — to the storeroom, to get paper that a child had requested. During this time, children came to Rhonda if they needed her, and she occasionally called to children elsewhere. But for the most part, Rhonda and the children around her worked in a relatively undisturbed way.

At these times, Rhonda made use of what she called 'economical' teaching strategies. For example, she used non-verbals very effectively; often holding out her hand to an interrupting child, in a gesture that was both an acknowledgement and a command to wait, or a pointing gesture that said: 'Sit here!'

When children sought consolation after a minor injury or disappointment, Rhonda typically hugged or patted them. Occasionally, she used physical contact as a control, for example, leading a child by the hand, and made some affectionate contacts, such as putting her arm around a child's shoulder, but these were relatively rare behaviours.

Rhonda's verbal behaviour was varied. She was usually softly spoken, but her words were very carefully articulated and her voice contained a ring of authority. She (almost) never sounded hesitant or doubtful. In common with her non-verbals, Rhonda's verbal behaviour also was 'economical' at times. When she noticed children behaving inappropriately, Rhonda called to them in a stern way that brought immediate compliance. For example:

- John! No! You know the rule.
- Tom! No! That's a dangerous thing to do.
- Sally! Come down.

Rhonda did not feel obliged to fill silent space with words and as she worked beside children, there often was a companionable silence as all concentrated on their work.

One distinctive aspect of Rhonda's verbal behaviour was her use of difficult words casually interspersed in the conversation. For example:

- As Carmel pokes her loose tooth out between her lips, 'Oh Carmel! That's *grotesque*.'
- As the children debate the issue of a second 'motor' in their 'boat', Rhonda says, 'The second one must be an *auxiliary* engine.'
- When they are exploring the new construction set, Rhonda identifies a piece, 'Look. This is a *pivoting* piece.'

A feature of Rhonda's interaction with children was her sense of humour. Although Rhonda did not use any terms of endearment, she often addressed children in an affectionate, but teasing manner. For example:

- When another child draws Rhonda's attention to Emily's poor handling of the apple pulp, Rhonda smiles at Emily and says, 'Oh! What a messy kid she is.'
- When Amy begins the board game with a run of bad luck, Rhonda comments, 'Oh Amy! Back to your old tricks again — landing on sad cards.'

Rhonda also enjoyed sharing a joke with children. Once, she dispersed the children from a grouptime by prompting: 'Knock knock.' The children replied on cue: 'Who's there?' Rhonda replied: 'Howard'. 'Howard who?' asked the children. 'Howard-ya-like-to-go-back-to-work?' said Rhonda. The children went back to work, amidst roars of laughter.

Overall, Rhonda was very responsive to children. She listened carefully to their stories, laughed with them and showed interest in their actions. Very often, she paraphrased the children's remarks, in a way that was very supportive of the child's communication. However, only very rarely did Rhonda comment on a child's emotional state.

In many ways, Rhonda defied our neat categorization schemes. Although generally warm and responsive, there were times when Rhonda was quite inflexible, as the following sections will show.

Rhonda's Image-of-Self-as-Teacher

General Description: Confidence and Organization

Rhonda described herself as 'an organizer' and in her forthright manner, said she sometimes 'organized [others] to within an inch of their lives'. This predilection for organization was perhaps the most notable feature of Rhonda's descriptions of her teaching.

She also described herself as 'never playing it safe', 'always wading in, boots and all', and this was in keeping with the image she presented as teacher. Rhonda expressed her opinions with great conviction. Her confidence was evident in statements such as 'I do the job well' and her description of herself as 'a natural teacher'. Interestingly, after reading the observation narratives, Rhonda described herself as 'bossy'.

Rhonda seemed to be troubled by few areas of uncertainty. Often, she spoke of issues in stark terms, usually expressing only a single side. For example, lack of parent punctuality was a continuing problem for Rhonda. Parents often brought their children a few minutes late and she found this very frustrating. Rhonda said she had 'counted it up' and fifteen minutes each session added up to two hours each week, that she lost. (In this context, she did not mention what might be happening in the parents' lives, that made it difficult for them to be punctual, though in another context, Rhonda spoke of trying to remember that parenting was more difficult than a non-mother such as she could understand.)

In an attempt to enforce punctuality, Rhonda began the session with a grouptime. She was aware that in some ways, this was problematic. For example, parents who were just a few minutes late could not speak to her. The assistant was fully occupied receiving children, and thus could not take half of the group for a separate story, as Rhonda preferred. In her determination to enforce punctuality, Rhonda also was prepared to pay a cost in terms of her positive relationships with the children. She acknowledged this in her description: 'I'll say to the children; you've missed story. You were too late today. You'll have to see if you can get ready earlier next day. And try to force them that way.' As Rhonda discussed the problem of punctuality, it was clear that her reflection on this matter did not lead her to reframe or reevaluate the importance of the problem, but rather was a search for new strategies to resolve it.

It seemed the calendar also was a powerful organizing force for Rhonda. She held very definite ideas about children's capabilities at 3, 4 and 5 years of age. In keeping with this age-definition, certain teaching behaviours, such as participation in dramatic play, interpreting social situations and mediating peer disputes, were seen as appropriate (even desirable) in the 3-year-old group, but were considered inappropriate when dealing with the 4- to 5-year-old group. When a child did not behave in accordance with his/her age-definition, problems arose. For example, Rhonda spoke about Duncan:

> Duncan and I had a lot of clashes last year. 'Cause he's quite strong willed and he's quite capable, and he was capable of doing lots of things which I wouldn't let him do. Simply because in a group you've got children who are less capable and less responsible and when they're very young like that I find that if you let somebody do something that he's capable of, they'll try it and it might be extremely dangerous for them but they're too immature to understand that. So you've got to sort of stop (!) some activities with children and Duncan and I had a lot of hassles about that last year.

The classic teaching dilemma described here, between conflicting individual and group needs, seemed to be interpreted by Rhonda mainly in terms of Duncan's personal characteristics. Soon after, Rhonda commented on the current year: 'Duncan's matured out of that very difficult stage. He's a different boy'.

Strong beliefs constrained Rhonda's behaviour. She spoke of sometimes being highly amused by a child's 'outrageous actions', but feeling she had to conceal her amusement, because the child was behaving inappropriately and she felt obliged to discipline him/her. Rhonda described 'putting on a really angry voice and doling out whatever discipline is necessary' and then seeking a few moment's privacy to express her amusement. As might be expected, Rhonda was very comfortable with the notion of teaching as a performance. She readily agreed that there was a lot of performing in her teaching, yet she also spoke of valuing authenticity, as when she said: 'Most of the time ... I just try to be me.'

During discussions, only two issues emerged in which Rhonda

evidenced some ambivalence. One of these involved the concepts of mothering and teaching, and the other dealt with her role in motivating children. Whilst acknowledging that teaching and mothering shared many common tasks, such as 'blowing noses, cleaning up messes, and wiping bottoms', Rhonda suggested that the two were really 'poles apart' and that she was 'definitely not the mothering type.'

In discussing her role in motivating children, Rhonda made some very strong statements, then retracted them a few minutes later, in favour of opposing statements. For example, Rhonda read a (given) statement about the need to motivate children and responded: 'No. No. Definitely not. There have been very few children I've ever had to motivate ... These children are absolutely not passive, no.' Very soon after, Rhonda reflected: 'You really *do* have to motivate them, don't you?' When the change of opinion was surfaced for comment, Rhonda gave a detailed rationale for the new position, with a conviction equally as strong as the original. Once again, Rhonda had 'waded in boots and all'.

Biographical Aspect

Rhonda was the oldest of three children and had extensive contact with younger children throughout her childhood. In her final year at high school, Rhonda was uncertain about career choices, but took the advice of a guidance counsellor, who suggested she become either a kindergarten teacher or a social worker. Rhonda said she 'couldn't face the thought of going to university with all those radicals', so that left kindergarten teaching. Once at the Kindergarten Teachers College, Rhonda found her course 'spellbinding'. Although she had trouble memorizing theory for exams, Rhonda felt she was a 'pretty good student'. It was in practice teaching, however, that Rhonda really found fulfilment. She said:

> I lived from teaching practice to teaching practice. I really thought that teaching was just — Oh, it was just lovely, wonderful. And I was a different person when I was teaching. You know, it just seemed to fulfil something in me ... I just sat down and children just naturally came to me. And I just naturally sort of knew what to say.

Following graduation in the mid-1960s, Rhonda moved interstate, where she taught in a preschool attached to a primary school. This proved to be a very difficult placement for a beginning teacher, as the teacher in charge of the centre was ill and frequently Rhonda was left as the only teacher, with a group of fifty children. Sheer survival was Rhonda's pressing need during this time.

After a year in that position, Rhonda moved to another city, where she married and worked for six years in a church nursery school, with 3-year-olds. She returned to her home state in the mid-1970s and after being unemployed for ten weeks (Rhonda's only break from teaching in twenty years) found work as a preschool teacher. Rhonda had been in her present position in this community early childhood centre for eight years.

From college days to the present, Rhonda found support for her belief that she was a 'practical sort of person'. As each teaching position was discussed, she made some mention of her strength in this area. For example, in one position, Rhonda team-taught with a young American teacher, who had 'wonderful theory' but 'no grasp of the practicalities' of teaching. Rhonda and this person 'learnt from each other'. Speaking of the present, Rhonda described how she evaluated new information on teaching approaches. The crucial test for her was: 'Does it work?'. This pragmatism was very much in keeping with her emphasis on practical efficiency.

In discussing her development as a teacher, Rhonda saw more continuities than changes. She spoke of a firm core of essential beliefs that continued from year to year. Skills became more polished, some adjustments were made as children and their contexts changed, but Rhonda believed, 'You're still basically you'.

There was an interesting difference between the perceptions of self that Rhonda espoused and the outside-in perceptions of the researcher. From the outside, Rhonda appeared to hold very strong beliefs that sometimes prevented her from seeing other points of view, yet Rhonda spoke of herself as being generally more tolerant, more accepting, seeing 'more grey, less black and white' in her world, than previously. On one occasion she mentioned a danger of becoming 'too wrapped up in doing something the right way, [when] sometimes, the right way in theory isn't the right way for that particular family'. Other self-references were more in keeping with the outside-in perspective. For example, Rhonda said her own development had made her more confident, more mature, more settled and more certain about what she wanted from life, than she used to be.

Prior to this study, Rhonda had not had cause to reflect on the course of her own development and she explained why this self-reflection was difficult for her. She said, 'It's really hard to tell [how you've changed] because you've grown along with yourself all the time. It doesn't sort of seem as if you've changed.'

Rules and Responsibilities

Rules and responsibilities were concepts that featured prominently in Rhonda's descriptions of teaching. For example, Rhonda felt a strong sense of responsibility to the profession. A lot of time and money had been invested in developing her skills as a teacher. Therefore, Rhonda felt a responsibility to stay in the profession as long as she could and to pass on her skills to a new generation of teachers. Rhonda also felt keenly the responsibilities of work with young children:

> [You] realize that once [the children] are over the threshold, they're your responsibility. And you're in charge of them and do the best you can with them. I think you realize that responsibility as you open the door. And as you close it ... When they're all gone, you can finally relax and stop keeping an eye on every single corner of the room and playground. Because you do tend to. You must.

Rhonda also mentioned the responsibility to form a good relationship with children and parents, even though they might make that difficult at times, and taking responsibility for making decisions, when the children were judged incapable. Rhonda emphasized the need for children to accept responsibility for their actions and believed this was particularly important in relation to the rules of conduct. She believed it was her responsibility to set the rules in place and the children's responsibility to obey them. When rules were broken by the children, it was her responsibility to discipline them. She said:

> They know the rules. There's no two ways about it. They are already doing, or are going to do, something which is against the code of behaviour and therefore it's my responsibility to stop them and they're aware of that. They know that, they don't resent it.

Rhonda wanted to create a highly predictable social environment for the children, where they understood the consequences of their actions. She accepted that a measure of uncertainty was unavoidable, but tried to minimize this through careful control. Yet Rhonda did not value passive children. She repeatedly emphasized the importance of independence and described the whole preschool experience as a process through which children were 'weaned from dependence to ultimate independence'.

Rhonda believed the way to accomplish children's independence was through the establishment of a classroom culture governed by a set of absolutely consistent ground rules. She described the first six weeks of the 3-year-old group as a 'hard battle', in which she 'nearly went demented', as the rules were learned by the children. Once the children knew the rules and were obeying them, Rhonda believed they felt secure and were able to approach problems with confidence. Carmel (a 5-year-old) who was having difficulty obeying the rules, was seen to be in this predicament, because she did not attend this centre as a 3-year-old. She had missed the grounding.

With the older group, Rhonda said she was not as quick to 'jump on' children who disobeyed, because she wanted the children to assume some of the responsibility for rule enforcement. Rhonda reported she was very pleased to see peers reminding each other of the rules, because 'after all, this is their group'. She did not see the rule structure as engendering conformity and placed great importance on individuality.

Being Settled

In addition to the common constraints of rules and responsibilities, another aspect of life that Rhonda valued both for self and children was 'being settled'. When she was subject to transfer in a government education system, Rhonda could not 'feel settled' and it was this uncertainty that finally led her to resign. One of the positive changes Rhonda saw in her own development, was an increased feeling of 'being settled'.

In relation to the children and the program, Rhonda also placed high value on 'being settled'. She described this group as a very good one, because they were 'very settled'. (She defined this as 'having good work habits'.) In encouraging these work habits, Rhonda saw her own behaviour as an important influence. For example, she explained one of the benefits of staying out of children's peer conflicts:

> [You're] not all the time jumping up and down. That's very disruptive for the children who are having problems with concentration. If you're all the time jumping up and down having

to go to some sort of conflict situation, they're ratty by the end of the day if you're doing that.

Rhonda believed that children could be 'conditioned into a pattern of doing useless things like running wildly and not settling and just being involved in highly boisterous, physical activity'. (Rhonda did go on to say this type of activity had some value, but it caused children to miss out on lots of things.) It was clear that a calm group, working diligently, was the ideal towards which Rhonda was striving. 'Being settled' was a high priority within her program.

The Cognitive Aspects of Teaching

As she discussed teaching, Rhonda mentioned several types of mental activity. Although she did not describe specific mental preparations to face each day, as Rhonda showed me around her magnificent home garden she said, 'Now you should understand how I come to work feeling so tranquil each day.' So it seemed Rhonda also may have valued a calm mental state to face the challenges of teaching.

A more important type of mental activity 'in-advance' was the care with which Rhonda planned her program. Her emphasis on setting the ground rules in the first weeks showed that she left little to chance. Yet Rhonda did accept quite a high degree of uncertainty in the open-ended activities she provided. She explained:

> I've learnt from experience what's going to happen. And I tend to stand back and watch the children and how they are going to tackle the situation rather than trying to predict what they might do. When I was a younger teacher, I always had everything planned right down to the last detail and then was terribly upset when it all fell apart because somebody didn't tackle it the right way. And I've learnt that there's no right way and there's no wrong way now. That there's only each person's individual way.

Rhonda made some references to rapid on-the-spot decision making, though she felt her judgments were tightly constrained by the same set of rules as governed the children's behaviour. When a rule was disobeyed, the only degree of freedom mentioned by Rhonda was the amount of time she waited before 'jumping on' the child. With some children, Rhonda felt she needed to move very fast, to forestall an escalation of the misbehaviour. For example:

> With Tom and John, I don't allow any transgression whatsoever. Because they don't yet have a sense of when it might hurt somebody else. And Tom would start off like that — he would end up jumping on somebody's back or poking them in the eye ... And I tend to stamp on them a lot earlier than I would on somebody else.

Decisions about timing also were important in other interactions. Rhonda believed the ability to laugh at yourself was an invaluable aid in dealing with life and she said she tried to instil this in children by gently making fun of them and trying to coax them into 'taking life a little less seriously'. But timing was crucial. Rhonda explained that after almost three years of such attempts with Cameron, he still was likely to burst into tears, if she did not judge the moment well. Timing also was important in allowing children to reach their own decisions. If Rhonda judged children had been given adequate 'self-decision' time, but had failed to make a decision, she would then make it for them.

It seemed that on-the-spot decision making might be a little less complex in Rhonda's highly regulated program than in other, more spontaneous ones. Rhonda claimed her mental activity placed more emphasis on the past than on the present. As she explained:

> I'm an if-only person. I know I shouldn't be ... if only I'd done such-and-such, I'm sure it would have been better. You shouldn't be like that. I try very hard to be a foward-thinking person but my mind is back there.

Yet Rhonda made many statements that referred to a future orientation in rationales for her actions with children. At times, she referred to the distant future. Some examples:

> Life's tough — they've got to learn to work it out. And if they learn how to work out simple situations now, it's going to be so much better for them later on, I think. ... how are they going to get on in the world? I mean, I sort of look at my job as a life job. A life education for them. It's not just getting them to the stage where they're ready to go on to the next stage. You've got to set some patterns now, before it's too late.

> If you don't instil in the children good values and ... making them see that learning is right, how are they ever going to get on in society and ever going to become the great people? I mean one of these days I might be able to say, look at him. I taught him when he was at preschool and now he's Prime Minister of Australia or whatever.

At other times, Rhonda's concern was more for the short term future, particularly the future that awaited the children on the primary school playground:

> In the school across the road, there's five, six hundred children there and there's two teachers on playground duty. Now it's just impossible ... There could be nobody [to help children with their problems] ... I think the more practice they get in this sort of a situation, the better off they'll be.

Respect for Children

Rhonda's comments on children were a sometimes puzzling mixture. At times, children were spoken of with the greatest respect. For example:

> Children can cope with far more than anybody gives them credit for.
>
> They are inherently competent learners.
>
> They are very good at accepting different expectations for different environments.
>
> These are intelligent, bright, experienced children, who have a sixth sense about who respects them and who does not.

Yet other statements seemed to suggest that Rhonda's respect for children might be at least in part, contingent on their compliance within her organizational framework. For example:

> I don't see the point in allowing them to come to preschool, spending good money to send them here, and then having them wander around sucking their thumb or running wildly in the

> playground the whole day and not having achieved anything ... And so they work.
>
> I enjoy seeing a child come in at 3 years of age — uncivilized — and going away from me at 5 and a half, a partially civilized being.

Rhonda clearly was comfortable with her dominant position in the social world within the preschool. She seemed confident that she was the person who knew best and willingly accepted the responsibilities associated with the job. This also was reflected in her comments about interactions with other adults. For example, as she spoke of staff needing to hold high expectations for children, Rhonda said:

> That's probably the most difficult area that I have training assistants. I always pick people who are mothers because I'm not a mother and they bring different experience to the job. But mothers tend to have low expectations generally, or unrealistic expectations. And I have to teach them piece by piece what to expect from each individual situation and each individual child. And that's rather difficult. But once we all — have learnt that skill, it operates very well.

Description of the Program for Children's Social Development

Rhonda considered her highly regulated program promoted children's social interaction in much the same way as a preventative medicine approach promotes good health: by establishing the rules of conduct in advance, many potential conflicts and interpersonal problems were thought to be avoided. Emphasis also was placed on developing the kindergarten group as a community. For example:

> [A sense of community] is important. If they don't have a sense of community, then they won't take care of the equipment, for a start. They won't take care of each other. I suppose I should have put that first ... And they don't have respect. Being part of the community means helping, caring for other people. Sharing your skills is also a very good way of developing their self-concepts. I mean, it gives them such a lift if they can do something for somebody else.
>
> And that's part of the secret too, that they've got to be needed in this little community. They've got to have their

own jobs and responsibilities, as well as their rights. That's important.

Rhonda discussed several strategies she used to foster this sense of community. She said she drew children's attention to the achievements of others, reminded children of absent members of the group, and modelled social conversation.

Another aspect of the social development program that Rhonda emphasized heavily was the acquisition of manners. She explained this was a personal conviction:

> I think [manners] are very important ... Manners are an outward sign that you care about other people. They might be just a sign, but it does symbolize that people care about other people ... Nobody says please and thank you any more. We do. And it's valuable to me. Although I must say it's not valuable to many of the families, though. Quite a lot of the families have — not criticized but queried whether I should be insisting ... but I just think it's important enough to persist with it.

Rhonda made many statements about the importance of staying out of children's peer interactions as much as possible. She said she had been much more involved in children's dramatic play when they were in the younger group, but now tried to limit her involvement to 'fringe' roles. From this position, Rhonda believed she could 'dart in and grab someone who is being troublesome', 'make suggestions to enhance the game', or 'whizz off and get something like scissors and felt pens', without disturbing the peer interaction.

Rhonda reported that at one time, she routinely became involved in mediation of peer conflicts, but stopped this intervention because she feared it caused a form of dependency in the children. Now, she said, she tried to avoid these situations whenever possible. In terms of the children's acceptance of her refusal to help, Rhonda said:

> This group are fairly used to it now. At the beginning of the year they tried to drag us in, a lot. But they're used to the fact that I'll be there if they really need me, and A. too. But unless they *really* need me, then they know I'll keep sending them back. And so quite often they don't come. They keep on trying themselves.

The Human Encounter

(Rhonda pointed out that one problem in 'sending them back' was that they sometimes took a modified version of her message that served their own interest.) When Rhonda was forced to become actively involved, she said her response sometimes was to remove the child causing the problem, or to redirect the children to the quieter handiwork activities, where they could 'settle down'. Rhonda also entered children's peer interactions if she felt a failure was inevitable:

> You know sometimes they get tired. Sometimes something else has happened that's upset them and you know they're just going to keep persevering with whatever the play is they've started, simply because they are so tenacious ... But it's not going to be successful or there's very little chance that it's going to be successful. And I tend to jump in and, I suppose, prevent a failure if I can. Because social failures ... do upset the children, much more than failure in any other area. They see it more keenly and feel it more keenly. So I do tend to jump in. Bossy again.

In summary, from the outside-in perspective of the researcher, Rhonda's image-of-self-as-teacher contained several interesting areas of discontinuity. However, it was clear that after a twenty-year teaching career, Rhonda had a core of strong beliefs and saw little need to reexamine them. She was aware of many connections between herself as person and as teacher and seemed very comfortable with the place her own values played in her teaching.

Actions in the Preschool

Smoothness and Order

On first impressions, Rhonda's preschool appeared to be a particularly smooth operation in which the children were almost invisible, as they worked diligently at their largely self-selected tasks. This perception seemed to be shared by the children: Gary (aged 5 years) comments, 'There's not many people here.' Rhonda replies, 'No, there's only a few away today. I think everyone is so busy, it just looks as if they are away'.

Another early impression was the high level of independence shown by these children. They did not clamour for Rhonda's attention

Rhonda

and left her undisturbed for long periods. This impression of orderliness and purpose carried over to transition times, where the children gathered and dispersed without any of the disorder that is so often seen in preschool programs.

As the period of observation lengthened, it became clear that not all days were quite as tranquil as those first few. But more importantly, out of this smooth, harmonious culture, gradually there emerged an extensive and consistent rule structure.

Rhonda's Power

At all times, Rhonda was in control of this group. Her control often was unobtrusive as she raised her voice only occasionally and in many ways accorded the children great freedom. But when Rhonda made a decision for a child, there was very rarely any dispute. A frequently-seen example was when Rhonda decided children (usually boys) should stop noisy interactive play with peers and move to more sedentary activities. Sometimes, these children briefly would advocate a continuance of their play, but Rhonda was unyielding. Similarly, when Rhonda directed a child to a particular chore at tidy-up time, there was no room for debate.

Rhonda displayed great certainty in her actions with children. She never wavered or appeared to be considering options. As mentioned above, on occasion, Rhonda used strong, concisely worded directives that sometimes were negative in tone, but never ambiguous. For example:

- 'Come down this minute!';
- 'Melinda! Sit down!';
- 'Tom! No!'.

A less blatant use of power was Rhonda's frequent phrasing of directives as her personal preference and her wishes seemed to exert a powerful influence on the children. Some examples:

- 'I need you to put your shoes on,'
- 'Tom, I need you to get a block and take it down,'
- 'You're doing nothing and that's upsetting me.'

Praise and punishment also played a large role in Rhonda's class room. For example, 'being helpful to others' was very highly valued. When children were helpful to others, Rhonda praised the action:

- Larina voluntarily gives some of her blocks to Martin, then brings this action to Rhonda's attention. Rhonda praises her: 'Oh that was kind of you'. When children failed to be helpful, sanctions followed. For example:

Darren is playing on the tumbling mat instead of helping to put it away, as directed. Rhonda says sternly: 'Darren! If you're going to be unhelpful, you can do another job. Get the broom and sweep the edges of the sandpit.'

(It seemed that sweeping the sandpit edges was a form of punishment, as Rhonda allocated this chore on other occasions, when she was displeased with a child's behaviour.)

Verbal chastisement probably was the most common form of punishment observed, but as shown in the examples already given, Rhonda did not berate the children at length. She acted quickly and decisively, with a concise statement indicating her displeasure and a direction indicating what the child was to do about it.

Rules

As indicated, rules played a very important part in the social world of this preschool setting. The rules went beyond those listed on the notice, into every facet of preschool life. There were rules about clothing: hats had to be worn outdoors, shoes had to be removed for climbing and at music time. There were rules about safety: ladders were not allowed on the climbing decks, neither were skipping ropes. Sawing was allowed only at certain points around the carpentry bench. Running indoors was not allowed. The only way to get on or off the old tractor was at the rear. There were rules about equipment: carts were not allowed inside the shed during free-play time, hands were to be washed before looking at books. There were rules about routines: no library bag meant no library book this week. Morning tea time was not for playing with friends. Waiting for a grouptime to begin, children should be quiet and patient. Children must help with the chores at tidy-up time.

Infringements of the rules sometimes were sternly dealt with, but at other times, the enforcement was softer. An interesting feature was the frequency with which children brought to Rhonda's attention, rule infringements by others. Some examples:

- Larina tells Rhonda that indoors, Tom just ran. Rhonda says, 'Not again! He finds it hard to remember, doesn't he? Maybe you could remind him.'
- Martin draws Rhonda's attention to Gary, who is outdoors without a hat. Rhonda says, 'On no! Did someone remind him?' Martin says, 'Yes.' Rhonda responds, 'Oh good.'

The children displayed a remarkable grasp of the many rules governing life in this setting. For the most part, they operated within the rules and Rhonda's interactions with them were warm, positive and encouraging. Only when children disobeyed the rules, did Rhonda become disapproving and these occasions were both rare and short lived.

Developing a Sense of Community

In keeping with the importance she placed on a sense of community, Rhonda used a number of strategies to help children become more aware of others, and to appreciate their rights. But some of these strategies were difficult to categorize. For example, Rhonda would simply chat with children, modelling good listening skills, asking clarifying questions and demonstrating interest in others. A more clearly defined strategy was the drawing of children's attention to the achievements of others. For example, she suggested objects made with construction toys should be displayed for others to see.

Rhonda actively encouraged children's helping behaviour, by prompting one child to seek help from another, or directing a child to help others. As indicated above, when children did help each other, she commonly praised them with the words: 'That was kind of you.' On one occasion, Rhonda took an even more active part in a sequence of peer helping:

Tom has arrived at preschool with one foot bandaged. It is library time and Rhonda is checking out the books children have selected. Tom is having difficulty hopping and carrying his books at the same time. Rhonda says to Tom, 'Cameron can hold your books for you.' Turning to Cameron, Rhonda says, 'Cameron, can you hold his books please?' Cameron does as he is asked and carries Tom's books. As they arrive at the table, Rhonda says, 'Thanks, Cameron. That's fine'.

More frequently, Rhonda was present only at one end of a helping sequence, for example, directing one child to help another, but not being present to praise after the event, or alternatively, not being present to prompt a helping event, but praising it afterwards.

Other strategies to promote child-child contacts, such as encouraging children to express their wishes or grievances to others, were not observed. Only a few examples were recorded where Rhonda tried to facilitate children's communication with each other:

- Joanne is telling a story during morning tea, but others keep interrupting her. Rhonda says to the small group: 'Listen to her.' A few moments later, when Carmel tries to interrupt again, Rhonda says:

- 'Carmel, wait a minute.' Joanne's story continues.

Carmel is trying to show the boys a seed pod she has found, but they ignore her. Rhonda says to them: 'Look what Carmel has.' Then, to Carmel, Rhonda says: 'Bend down and show Martin. He has some in his garden too.' The boys glance very briefly at Carmel's seed pod before carrying on with their constructions. A few moments later, as Gavin 'flies his aeroplane' around the room, Carmel follows, trying to get his attention. Rhonda watches. As Gavin arrives beside Rhonda, she says: 'Carmel was trying to show you something.' Once again, Gavin glances very briefly at the object in Carmel's hand, before 'flying off'.

The scarcity of this type of involvement was in keeping with Rhonda's statement that she tried to stay out of children's peer interactions whenever possible.

As part of developing a sense of community, Rhonda helped children be aware of others' welfare. As well as directing children to share materials, Rhonda asked children to modify their behaviour in other ways, out of consideration for others. For example:

Rhonda is working with two boys at a board game, when Carmel passes nearby. She is carrying two sets of bells and jingles them as she walks. Rhonda says: 'It would help if you would put those away. These boys are trying to concentrate.' Carmel does not speak, but walks to the music corner and puts the bells away.

Rhonda emphasized the social aspects of life by drawing children's attention to their working as a team. She also reminded the group of absent members and the return of a child after an absence was marked with a warm welcome. When a child was withdrawn from the preschool, Rhonda carefully explained this to the children. Rituals also were important in this centre. The marking of the daily roll, Rhonda's standing at the door to farewell each child and the weekly rituals of library and 'show and tell' — all were unvarying.

Observations of Rhonda's actions supported her emphasis on politeness and manners. She provided a good model, habitually using 'please', and thanking the children when they complied with her wishes. The children typically displayed good manners towards each other and rarely did Rhonda have to remind someone to be polite. Another social skill emphasized by Rhonda, was the use of names. If children neglected to use her name as they answered the roll, Rhonda would stop and stare fixedly at the child until s/he added 'Mrs. X'.

Interruptions whilst Rhonda was speaking or listening to another child, were dealt with in a variety of ways. On occasion, Rhonda would say 'Please wait', or use a 'stop' gesture without even making eye contact with the interruptor. At other times, she directed, 'Just a moment please', and on a few occasions, ignored the interruptor completely. Very rarely, was the interruption accepted.

In Rhonda's diverse responses to Larina's frequent interruptions, it was clear that Rhonda's choice of strategy was not determined solely by the identity of the interruptor. One day, Larina repeatedly interrupted Rhonda at the cooking table. Rhonda responded with a range of behaviours including ignoring Larina, helping her as requested and redirecting her to other adults. Two days later, Rhonda responded very warmly to Larina's interruption:

Rhonda and Tom are working with a construction toy, when Larina approaches. She says to Rhonda, 'Would you like to come in our boat? We've got whiting in it.' Rhonda responds, 'Oh that'd be lovely, delicious! But just at the moment, I'm busy here. Is it nice and warm in the sunshine?' Larina mumbles noncommitally and Rhonda goes on, 'We might have morning tea out there. Is it warm near your boat?' Larina says that it is and soon after, Rhonda leaves to organize morning tea.

In this instance, Larina's bid for attention was a skilled one: she had a definite plan and used a clever tactic in the mention of whiting. Rhonda's liking for this fish was well known. The acceptance of Larina's interruption also may have been related to fortuitous timing, as morning tea was imminent.

Involvement in Children's Dramatic Play

Sometimes Rhonda paused as she passed, or looked up from where she was working to observe children in dramatic play, but usually she did not become involved. On one occasion, Rhonda was organizing a skipping activity with a small group, when nearby other children's dramatic play noisily disintegrated. Rhonda observed, but her only involvement was to caution the children as equipment fell.

Occasionally, Rhonda acted as a worker, helping children build with outdoor blocks, but she looked to them for directions. When Rhonda visited children's play sites, she acknowledged the children's roles, but only rarely did she take on a fringe role herself. Some examples:

- Rhonda asks the girls if she can come to their concert, then sits in the 'audience'.
- Rhonda suggests to the boys who are about to set out in their block fishing boat, 'I'd like some fish for tea, thank you. Bring me home some whiting.'

When Rhonda visited children in dramatic play situations, she commonly opened with a general question such as, 'What's going on here?' Sometimes, her inputs were pleasant 'small talk', reinforcing because of her approval and interest, but not attempting to offer new ideas or otherwise facilitate the play. On a few occasions however, Rhonda did offer extending ideas. For example:

Rhonda is visiting the 'cargo boat' being built by Cameron, Milton and Martin using the outdoor blocks. She asks a series of questions that invite the boys to extend their thinking. Rhonda asks: 'What sort of cargo will you put in it?' Cameron pauses, then replies: 'Australian cargo.' Rhonda responds: 'Mmmm, Australian cargo. Things that are made in Australia, will you? Will you carry toys in it?' (There is an interruption as Rhonda calls to a child entering the shed.) Then Rhonda asks: 'How will you load the cargo? Will you have a crane to load it?' Cameron offers: 'Through the door.' Rhonda repeats: 'Through the door. Will you have a truck?' But Cameron is on another tack and announces: 'I'm the boss of it.' Rhonda switches to a different form of questioning: 'You're the boss of it. And what does the boss of it have to do?' Cameron responds: 'Steer.' Rhonda asks: 'sort of like the captain?' Cameron agrees: 'Yeah'.

Although Rhonda did not often get involved in dramatic play situations, on a few occasions, she acted as an organizer, who directed children's actions until the play got underway. Sometimes this involved only a brief comment such as, 'Will this show get off the ground before afternoon tea?' but at other times, it involved a long series of directives and focusing questions. Apart from the 'fishing trip' mentioned above, two other events of this type were of particular interest. Both involved a measure of peer conflict and will be dealt with in the following section.

Resolving Peer Conflict

Conflicts between children were not as frequent or as physical in this setting as in some other centres, but conflict situations did arise from time to time. It sometimes was difficult to tell if Rhonda was aware of them, as her behaviour gave no clue. Other peer conflicts clearly were observed by Rhonda, but she did not intervene. Some examples:

- Rhonda sits at the cooking table, surrounded by children. Suddenly, loud angry voices can be heard nearby. Rhonda rises in her chair, and looks over children's heads to the home corner, where Gavin and Joanne are arguing heatedly. After just a few seconds' observation, Rhonda sinks back into her chair and continues with the cooking. Gradually, the voices fade.

- Gary and Tom are playing with a construction toy. Rhonda sits at the same table, working with Larina. Tom holds up a piece, saying to Gary: 'Here's a space helmet.' Gary responds angrily: 'No, that's mine!' Tom goes on: 'I'm going to make a spaceship.' Gary says loudly: 'No, I'm going to make a spaceship!!' Rhonda manipulates her own construction and doesn't become involved. Within a few seconds, the disagreement has faded and the sporadic conversation resumes.

When Rhonda did become involved, typically it was after prolonged observation, or in response to a child's report of misdeeds by others. Once Rhonda decided to enter however, her interventions were decisive. In this event, Rhonda played an organizing role:

In the block corner there is a cardboard house that the 3-year-old group has made from a large carton. At the beginning of freeplay time, there is great interest and many children try to cram into the house. Several children are inside and a child calls urgently: 'One at a time! One at a time!' Others raise their voices anxiously, as the box teeters from their struggles. Gary calls to Rhonda, who is watching from nearby: 'There's too many people in there.' Rhonda walks slowly to the box, without comment. She watches silently as the children make accusations about each other. Finally, Rhonda speaks: 'Let's think. How could we use blocks with this building? How could we use blocks around this building? Perhaps we could build something around the outside.' Within seconds, Rhonda is allocating jobs. She asks one child: 'Could you build a letterbox?' She asks another: 'Could you build a fence and flowers? Could you build a sandpit?' Rhonda tells the children to come out from inside the house and rules: 'We'll take turns at going in here.' More tasks are allocated, then as the children begin to bring blocks from the shelves, Rhonda asks questions to clarify their tasks, such as: 'Martin, which part are you building?' and 'Who's going to build the sandpit for the children to play in?' Rhonda stays at the scene or nearby, for much of the first freeplay time.

Rhonda's organizational strategies were successful in getting this group of children on-task, *if* the task was to build constructively. However, the play that eventuated was largely parallel, with little interaction between children building different items.

The second prolonged involvement occurred with a group of girls planning a 'dance concert'. They had taken a long time to dress for the occasion, in dancing skirts and veils. However, they could not agree on the form the concert should take:

> Rhonda is ready to start the dancing music, but the girls are involved in a heated argument that already has raged for several minutes. Finally, Rhonda enters, saying: 'Joanne has a good idea. Listen to her.' Rhonda says to Joanne: 'Tell us your idea first.' As Joanne speaks, Carmel is visibly agitated and tries to interrupt. Rhonda says: 'Carmel, wait a minute', as Joanne gives a rambling description of her choreography. When Joanne finishes, Rhonda says: 'Alright, I see. Right. Now that's Joanne's idea, so let's hear Carmel's.' Carmel explains her idea, rather more concisely than Joanne. Rhonda responds: 'And what about Melinda's idea? She has another idea.' Melinda defers to Joanne's idea. Rhonda makes an arbitrary remark (in Joanne's favour): 'Well, look. Why don't you use Joanne's idea first, because it was a good idea, and then your idea can be next, Carmel.' Carmel is unhappy with this and continues to try to voice a problem she sees, as the others go off to adjust their costumes yet again. Finally, she succeeds in explaining her concern to Rhonda: 'There's not enough people [for Joanne's idea]. There's two and two and one! What would we do with the one?' (Joanne's plan calls for pairs and they have five girls.) Rhonda relays this observation to the others: 'Carmel is saying that there's two (she touches two girls) and two (touches two more) and then one left by herself. So how are we going to work out that problem?' Joanne suggests that she will dance twice, once in the first pair, then again with the left-over child at the end. Rhonda is enthusiastic: 'That's a good idea.' Rhonda goes on to recommend Joanne's solution to the others, then starts the music. As Carmel continues to advocate her own plan, Rhonda directs her from the dancing area, saying: 'You can sit this one out with me.' Carmel sits out the dance, on Rhonda's knee.

In Rhonda's use of positive interpretive remarks, it was clear she supported Joanne's position. In speaking about Carmel's plan, Rhonda's remarks were phrased in a strictly neutral fashion, suggesting this point of view did not enjoy the same degree of support.

In these 'organizing' interactions, two interesting comments could be made about Rhonda's task orientation. Firstly, it seemed she perceived the children's preparations as being secondary to the following play event and this suggested that the focus of the play might be defined differently by children and teacher. For example, in the 'fishing trip' play, the boys may have been content with the building of their boat, but Rhonda wanted them to go fishing. Similarly, in the dancing concert. The girls had spent much time preparing their dancing costumes and arguing about the choreography. The actual performance did not seem as important to them, as it did to Rhonda.

Secondly, Rhonda's strong task orientation seemed to lead her to respond to peer conflict by trying to get children back on-task as soon as possible. In the dance concert interaction, Rhonda's attempts to facilitate the children's expression of their own points of view seemed to be aimed at moving them to the performance phase, rather than specifically focused on working through their conflict.

In other peer conflict situations observed, Rhonda's inputs were often a single strategy. For example, she sometimes made a statement that identified or directed a solution: When Tom tries to place a chair under the table, John is in the way and refuses to move. Rhonda directs Tom to put the chair under the other side of the table. When Joanne complains that Ann won't give her the veil she wants, Rhonda suggests they swap veils. When Joanne complains that other children are raiding her cubby house, Rhonda says, 'Well, there's one solution. You could move your house.'

When differences arose between children, or their actions seemed inappropriate, Rhonda sometimes made a ruling or pronouncement. For example:

- After a near miss with blocks falling from the deck, Rhonda announces: 'We've decided that the blocks are too dangerous here, so we're going to hand them over the side and bring them down. Right?' (Actually, it was Rhonda who had decided. There had been no discussion.)
- When Tom anxiously says he needs *that* piece of the construction toy, Rhonda responds: 'You can have a turn after Larina.'

Only one instance was observed where Rhonda responded to a child's report of strife with a peer, by sending the child back to try to resolve it:

Rhonda

Joanne comes to Rhonda with a story about Ann's bad language. Rhonda says: 'Yes, Ann sounded as if she was very angry with someone. What's the problem down there?' Joanne tries to explain: 'She, she, wanted to be quiet and I was being quiet but the big kids weren't.' Rhonda responds: 'Well, tell Ann a different way of saying people be quiet. Could you?' Joanne leaves Rhonda and returns to the home corner, from whence she can be heard, saying forcefully: 'Don't say shut up!'

Helping Children Gain Access to Peer Play Groups

Rhonda rarely became involved in children's access issues. Only three examples were noted, when Rhonda tried to recruit playmates for a child and they all involved Cameron, a shy child who often worked alone. When Emily is looking for someone to play a board game with her, Rhonda asks Cameron, on Emily's behalf. Cameron declines and Rhonda plays with Emily herself. Cameron is sitting in his block 'cargo boat' alone. (The peers who helped with its construction have left to do other things.) Rhonda sits in the boat with Cameron for some time, then asks Tom as he passes by: 'Would you like to come over for a ride on the boat? We're taking a load of horses to Storm Island.' Tom declines, saying he is busy elsewhere. Soon after, Carmel arrives to ask Rhonda's help. Rhonda says: 'I think Carmel might be coming.' But Carmel also declines, leaving Rhonda and Cameron in the boat. Joanne has been talking about using the outdoor blocks to make a train, but she hasn't made a start. Rhonda acts as organizer, encouraging Joanne and Ann. As they carry the blocks, Rhonda directs Cameron to join them, saying: 'Come on Cameron. Help us.' He does. As soon as the train is completed, the helpers leave. Joanne is left alone. Plaintively, she approaches others, inviting them to join her. For example, saying to Leigh: 'Leigh, would you like a ride on my train? It's very beautiful.' No one accepts and soon after, Joanne abandons it.

Rhonda's only additional involvement in an access-related incident came when Sally approached a group of girls but was rebuffed. (Rhonda successfully distracted her with a suggestion of sand 'cooking'.) Although access issues were a part of the children's lives in this setting, as they were in other settings, with the exception of Cameron, Rhonda stayed uninvolved.

Particularly late in the session, Rhonda's interventions sometimes did split up peer play groups. When Rhonda stopped groups of boys outdoors and suggested they move to 'handiwork' activities, they frequently ended up at different tables, but this seemed as much related

The Human Encounter

to available space and their personal preferences, as to Rhonda's purposeful splitting of the group.

Environmental Support of Peer Interaction

This rich environment provided an abundance of materials that children could use in interactive play. The open-endedness of almost all activities also provided opportunities for cooperative action and children frequently worked together on projects.

Rhonda sometimes made adjustments to the environment during the session, in support of children's interaction. For example, adding old curtains for dramatic play, bringing more utensils for sand 'cooking' from the shed, telling a child where to find a tray for the 'restaurant' and helping Darren weave 'bait' into his fishing net.

Minor alterations to the physical environment frequently were used by Rhonda as a way to avoid peer conflict. For example:

- In the block corner, when a wall of blocks is knocked accidentally, Rhonda suggests rebuilding it in an out-of-the-way corner.

- When Melinda is about to take some of the drawing paper that Leigh is using, Rhonda stops her and says: 'You can't have this piece of paper. Leigh's copying something. There are lots of pieces of paper on the shelf.'

- On the climbing structure, Gary is about to take a block that Tom has placed, but Rhonda intervenes: 'No, not those ones. Tom put them there for steps. If you want some different ones, climb down and get some'.

In a number of ways, Rhonda reminded children that this was a shared environment and emphasized the need to act with consideration for others. For example, the rule prohibiting carts in the shed was to make access easier for other children and Rhonda explained why she was reluctant to 'mind' materials for a child, because others might wish to use them.

Concluding Remarks

The patterns of life in this centre were not easily observed or captured. Rhonda found reflection rather tiresome. She considered this 'probing' a peculiarly American trait, one that 'we Australians' did not believe in. Although Rhonda was cooperative in interviews, there were times when she made it clear that she did not consider this to be a particularly enjoyable way to spend her time. When describing her experience of participation in the study, Rhonda said, 'It's been difficult, frustrating, more time consuming than I thought it would be — but interesting'.

Observations of the surface interactions at first gave little indication of the extremely complex underlying structure and only over time did the structure become even partly visible. Even then, Rhonda continued to be an enigmatic figure, who sometimes used unlikely combinations of behaviour. Rhonda's descriptions of herself as an organizer, a 'bossy' teacher, a person of strong convictions, who sometimes 'waded in boots and all', fitted well with observations of her actions in the classroom, but there remained some discrepancies between the outsider's perspective and Rhonda's insider's view.

It is messy to try to conceive of a teacher being both warm *and* cool, responsive *and* rigid, without recourse to the comforting label: 'inconsistent'. Yet Rhonda was all of these things, and in ways that were quite consistent. Rhonda-the-organizer operated a program that was highly organized, in which ambiguity and uncertainty were minimized through her own carefully controlled actions. Although to the observer, the extensive rule base and limited flexibility seemed incompatible with a valuing of children's spontaneity and a concern for authenticity, for Rhonda, they fitted together perfectly.

We cannot know whether the presence of this rule system did aid children's growth of independence, or whether the teacher's limited involvement in peer interactions did facilitate children's abilities to solve their own problems. All that can be said is that Rhonda made her own coherent whole of these apparently disparate pieces.

Although not particularly reflective about her teaching, Rhonda was a keen observer of children, and had come to understand how to operate her program smoothly. She had created a formula that met her needs, and at the same time, provided many learning opportunities for children. Is it surprising then that she had found little cause to seriously reexamine the formula over recent years?

Rhonda forces us to reexamine our neat categorization schemes of teachers. From the outsider's perspective, Rhonda's image-of-self-as-teacher and her actions in the classroom were paradoxical, yet Rhonda herself perceived no such paradox. For Rhonda, her beliefs and actions were highly consistent.

Chapter 4

Nan

The Setting

Nan's Preschool

Nan's preschool was built in the early 1970s, in a relatively affluent suburb. An early concern with aesthetics had been maintained through later developments and the preschool provided a model environment for young children. The large playground was shaded by tall trees and dotted with ferns and gardens. Many birds were attracted to this suburban oasis of natural bush and, particularly in the early morning, the environment exuded a rare quality of peace and tranquility.

In common with many Australian preschool buildings, there was no firm distinction between indoors and out. Sliding doors created an easy flow from playroom to patio to playground. The playroom was spacious with excellent natural lighting. There were two areas of particular note: one corner resembled an artist's studio, with tables and easels as workspaces and display shelving containing a vast range of materials. These materials always looked as if the artist had just rummaged through them, making this work area look like 'the real thing'; not a place where children 'played' at being artists.

The other area of note was the science table placed in the wide doorway onto the verandah. Each day, it contained a fascinating mixture of things, from fresh azalea blooms, to leaves and gum nuts, large picture books on pottery or embroidery, or newspaper cuttings on the health problems of eucalypt trees.

A notable feature of Nan's program was the flexible provisioning of the physical environment. Throughout the session, Nan 'fine-tuned' the environment, adding or removing materials, depending on the immediate needs and interests of the children. She seemed to have almost unlimited resources. There was a great deal of flexibility evident also in the location of activities. Books and cushions might be taken up to a 'tent' the children had made, in the far corner of the playground. Crayons and paper for leaf rubbings might appear on the deck of the treehouse. An easel might be carried out under a shady tree. Convention clearly was not a major consideration in the organization of this environment.

Nan's program also was a flexible one. Some parents came early, some arrived late, and all were accepted without question. If parents were late collecting children at the end of the session, this was not seen as a problem. Within the session, timetabling also was flexible. Music grouptime could range from ten to twenty-five minutes and it was hard to say when tidy-up time began, because there was no announcement. Messy areas were unobtrusively cleaned up, while other children continued with their activities undisturbed. However, the approximate timetable for a morning session was as follows:

9:00	Arrivals.
9:00 — 10:25	First block of free play time. (Free choice of indoor or outdoor activities.)
10:25 — 10:30	Milk time. (A very brief and casual routine, with children pouring their own milk from pitchers.)
10:30 — 10:45	Music time. (Whole group.)
10:45 — 10:55	Fruit time. (Usually outdoors. Children shared fruit as they sat on log benches.)
10:55 — 11:30	Second block of free play time.
11:30 — 11:50	Tidy-up time.
11:50 — 12:00	Language Group. (Sometimes two half-groups, sometimes the whole group.)
12:00	Departures.

This group attended four half-days, in a mix of morning and afternoon sessions.

Children, Families, Assistant

Twenty-one children, aged 4.4 to 5.11 years were enrolled in this group. These relatively well-to-do families were mostly two-parent, with fathers employed as professionals or businessmen (though one was a council bus driver). No mothers were in full-time paid employment, though several had part-time jobs and their children received some short-term supplementary care.

An important staff member was A., a trained nurse who had been part of this centre for many years. Nan and A. worked as a team, with Nan sometimes deferring to A. during group sessions, allowing her to select materials for her half-group segments and involving her fully in the daily and weekly planning and evaluation meetings.

The Teacher

Nan was a person of great vitality and energy. She was approximately 48 years old, but in appearance and behaviour was ageless. Nan dressed for comfort and convenience, in well-worn jeans, sweatshirt or tee-shirt, and sneakers. Often, Nan sat on the patio step to greet children, but would frequently bounce to her feet, to talk to a parent. Throughout the day, this energetic pattern continued, with Nan sitting comfortably on the floor, crawling inside a tent, or scrambling under a low shrub to visit a 'cubby house' within. Yet Nan also displayed great stillness. She would sit by the easels and with what appeared to be total concentration, watch a child paint. Nan would sometimes hover near a group of children for a considerable time, observing silently.

Typically, Nan engaged in quite long interactions with small groups of children, but sometimes she 'patrolled', making quick observations and having only minimal contact with children. After the patrol, Nan would re-engage with children and settle at one location. Even so, Nan seldom stayed with one group more than a few minutes and often interacted with three or four small groups almost concurrently; spending a few minutes with each, in a cyclical pattern.

There were many affectionate physical contacts between Nan and the children. Children would come to her for a hug, lean against her, or sometimes sit on her knee. Occasionally, Nan used physical contact in a controlling manner, drawing a child down to sit beside her at an activity or reaching out to stop a child running past. On occasion, Nan used physical contact almost in a consoling manner, as she exercised control over a child. For example:

- As Nan tells Julie it is time she moved onto other activities, she gently pulls Julie to her and hugs her.

- Dave is moving around the other boys in the group, as Nan tries to focus their attention on the problem with the block construction. She reaches out and draws Dave to her, then loops her arm lightly around his shoulders as she speaks in a louder, more clearly articulated tone: 'How can we — *How can we* make this the same level all along?'

Nan's speech patterns showed great diversity. There was a quality of informality and authenticity that seemed to suggest Nan was not playing an obvious 'teacher' role. Nan's interest in children's communications was clearly expressed. She frequently paraphrased children's comments, or made a comment that indicated the child's message had been received. With some of the less confident children, such as Karen, Richard and Harry, Nan spoke very softly and carefully, as if she was trying not to overwhelm them. With more robust children, such as Julie, Emma and Dennis, Nan sometimes used a brusque tone that was a mixture of a serious direction and a sort of teasing gruffness. For example:

- Dennis has brought a leaf to show Nan and she suggests he do a leaf rubbing. After Dennis begins, he remembers that he was not planning to stay and says: 'I was in the middle of a game, you know'. Nan says gruffly, but following with a smile: 'Well go!'
- In the large crate, Nan has set up a delightful cubby house for Julie. After Julie arrives, Nan takes her to see it. Sitting inside, they have a long conversation, but then Nan says brusquely, 'Well, I'm not staying here all day. Do you want somebody else to share your house?'.

In her interactions, Nan used many non-directive remarks, often placing the onus back on the child to problem-solve by saying: 'What can we do about that?' When Nan was directive, however, her tone sometimes was stern, particularly with Julie or Dave. For example:

When Julie surreptitiously brings out her toy microphone and amplifier (a working amplifier!) and causes an uproar, Nan says sternly: 'I'll have that, thank you. No, Julie, you know it's too disruptive to bring all these things. We don't bring special toys from home.' The toy is placed back in Julie's locker. A few moments later, as Julie once again brings out the toy, Nan says angrily: 'Office. In the office until later. NOW!'. Julie puts the toy in the office.

There were times when Nan sounded appreciative, angry, amused, disbelieving, teasing, interested, even pleading. But most of all, she sounded alive and real. Her speech was as varied and vital as her actions.

Nan's Image-of-Self-as-Teacher

General Description: 'They Are as I Am'

One of the most striking features in Nan's words about herself as teacher, was the strong sense of connection she saw between herself and the children. Nan considered herself an unfinished being, travelling a developmental path, just as were the children. In terms of her program, Nan valued very similar things for herself and the children, for example; 'usefulness'. In speaking of the teacher's role, Nan said:

> In that creek play situation, I wasn't being a blatant leader, but — being there and being useful. You know, I think it's wrong for the teacher to sit on the bank and keep her feet dry and her stockings clean ... If you sit there and say, Stephen, be helpful, and you're not being helpful yourself — I can't do that.

For children, Nan also placed great importance on being useful to self and others. For example, Zita was described as a 'good group member', because she 'is there, is responsive and accepting'. Tony was hailed as a child who was doing well, because, 'He is contributing some good ideas now'. However, Dennis and Duncan were causing Nan some concern, because it seemed their friendship simply was 'not useful' to either boy.

Another valued aspect of the program for Nan and the children was being able to 'relax and enjoy' being together. To feel comfortable with others was very important. Nan saw her ability to relax with children and parents as one of the major ways in which her teaching had changed for the better with her own development. Nan looked closely at how comfortably children interacted with their peers, and helping a child such as Richard to 'feel comfortable with people' was a 'big priority' in Nan's program.

Nan readily referred to her own feelings or experiences, to make sense of children's actions, as well as her own. She spoke of her recollections of experiences as a child and her desire to protect children (such as Richard and Alan) from social rejection:

> I think that's probably at the bottom of my thinking. I actually know that feeling. I didn't make friends easily as a child, and I think that's important to me. There are things I'll never forget. About having my lunch pinched and sitting by myself and feeling very miserable about things like that. I just know how children would feel, if they didn't feel comfortable with people.

This sense of a very personal connection recurred many times, as Nan talked about all manner of things: 'I think this is at the bottom of [my involvement]: it's just a very personal thing with me.' 'I know how good I feel, when someone says it to me.'

Nan's sense of connection also extended to parents. As the mother of three, Nan was very conscious of her own motherhood and frequently shared her recollections with parents:

> Being a parent has changed me a lot as a teacher. It's given me confidence. That's the sort of person I am. I don't say that people who aren't parents can't be good teachers. But for me, it was a real advantage. Because as a single person, I didn't have the confidence to project this side — They were the ones with the experience in child rearing. You know I don't hesitate to use personal situations ... It's warm and the parents relate to it. So I talk about when my kids were little, problems I had and how ignorant I was.

In a similar way, Nan emphasized the many continuities she saw between home and preschool, between her life within her family and as a teacher. For example: '[A good day] starts with how I feel. And if I feel happy and optimistic, then, well, it's like being at home. When everybody's feeling good and happy, everything ticks along without any hitches.' When Nan had a not-so-good day at the preschool, she took it home with her. She explained:

> I went home and blew up ... And [husband] and I had a beer ... and I sounded off. It was [daughter] who copped it. They always ask, What sort of day did you have, Mum? Was it a good day? I said (*with great feeling*) It was a bloody awful day!

Nan quite deliberately brought her family into her professional life. Her husband regularly visited the preschool, as did her children. She brought photos of her own parents and made many mentions of her personal life to the children. Nan felt this made her 'more real' in the children's eyes, it 'projected (her) more as a person'.

Biographical Aspect

Nan was the second of four children. Her older sister was recognized as the 'brilliant one' in the family and Nan was the 'mediocre student who did not complete high school'. For eighteen months, she worked in an office, before realizing, 'there had to be more to life than office work'. Nan didn't know much about kindergarten teaching at the time and couldn't remember who suggested kindergarten teaching to her, but after studying at night to complete high school, Nan entered the Kindergarten Teachers College.

In the mid fifties, this was a very small college with only ten students in Nan's year. Nan did not excel academically, but worked hard. She said: 'This is really part of finding yourself: finally you realize that life's what you make it, and if you don't make an effort, nobody else is going to do it for you.' In retrospect, Nan was highly critical of the college program. She felt it had contained far too much unsupervised practical experience and not nearly enough theory. In addition, the teachers with whom Nan worked were not good models:

> You did the very structured thing. Structured in the sense of having a very strict timetable and being a 'Teacher' teacher. That's how I see it now. Whereas ... we've talked about the teacher being a facilitator or a leader, or other things, but not necessarily being an evident person who's in the dominant position ... And I was never relaxed in the early part. I was very selfconscious and I was such a tight person myself, I couldn't relax. I was always worrying what people thought of me.

After graduating, Nan began her teaching career working with preschoolers with disabilities. She then worked for eighteen months at a suburban preschool before moving to the outback, where she helped establish a new preschool in a small town. Nan saw many good things coming from this experience. Then, after a few years working as an advisory teacher, Nan married and moved to the country to become a farmer's wife. Eight years later, a severe rural depression caused Nan, her husband and three young children to return to the city. As the most employable parent, Nan rejoined the paid workforce while her husband assumed the role of homemaker. This was a major milestone in Nan's life and she was 'very frightened' by it. At that time, many preschool groups were wary of employing a mother with young children, but after struggling with several part-time jobs, Nan was appointed to her current position in the mid 1970s.

The ten years spent in this centre Nan described as 'enriching and stimulating ones'. She saw this period as a time of great personal development, not so much 'up', but 'out'. Paradoxically, Nan saw her development during this period as being prompted by a negative situation — her fear of the new position. She said:

> I felt inadequate when I came into this job and wasn't quite sure about how I'd cope with these people, these very clever people. And I started, in a panicked way, to do some reading ... And I was challenged a few times in this job, by people who were intelligent and on the ball and wanted to know what I was doing with their kids. And fair enough. And I had to know what I was doing and why I was doing it. And that made me go away and read up and think and talk to people.

Through these processes of accepting questions, pondering them, reading, and talking to people, Nan gradually developed 'her philosophy'. She spoke of this philosophy in very real terms. It was the acknowledged, central core of her image-of-self-as-teacher. Nan was able to trace specific elements of her philosophy to various mentors, books, or her own reasoning. Clearly, Nan was a highly introspective teacher, who frequently reexamined her beliefs and actions, and sometimes made changes to them.

Nan's use of other people in this process was noteworthy, considering that she was the only qualified teacher in the centre. Questioning by parents was an impetus to begin, but other teachers, preschool advisors and tertiary lecturers also played a part. One of the most important figures in Nan's deliberations was the assistant in the preschool:

> Questioning the reasons for doing things, I found really helped me to form the philosophy. Why do I do this? Why do I do that? And it all just fell into place, it all just had a meaning ...
> I didn't do it all by myself. A. has been my sounding board through all these years. And we'd talk and talk and complain

and come to conclusions and test. And when parents tested us, we would talk about it between ourselves.

Whenever Nan spoke of her development as a teacher, she suggested threads of her personal development were intertwined. She saw the two as being inseparable. Nan believed that a major change in her development as a person also occurred in conjunction with the emergence of her philosophy of teaching. She said she had undergone a 'big life change', an 'identity crisis', that had brought a 'vivid change in [her] attitude to life'. Nan said:

It seemed to happen in a day: this is me. I'm myself. I'm not going to try and be anyone else. If people don't like me the way I am, there's no point in worrying about it. I just make myself sick and upset because of that. So from that day on really, I've just become my own person and I think that has helped me to develop in a lot of other ways.

This change in attitude also helped Nan have the confidence to enrol in a BEd program at a university. After five years of part-time study, she still was some distance from completing the program, but the courses were providing 'stimulation, intellectual vitality ... feeding!' Nan accepted that her own development was going to be a process without end. When asked if she thought she was still developing, she said: 'I hope so!'

Authenticity

Nan placed high store on being genuine, on behaving naturally as a person. When the concept of teaching as a performance was raised, Nan was horrified. She said: 'No. No, I don't [play a role with the children]. I hope it doesn't seem like that. No, I don't think so.'

In keeping with this desire for genuineness, Nan also valued spontaneity, in herself, parents and children. In speaking of the need for spontaneity in counselling parents, Nan said, 'That's something you need; a spontaneity. I'm right now. They're right now. Do it now. You just ... judge by feeling'. Nan did not wish to threaten spontaneity by constraining children tightly, or making them conform to rules. She said:

> I think this program is right, because children can relax and can get to work and can have — the lack of pressure. They can feel relaxed and just become involved and not be hindered by feelings of whether they're doing the right thing. Occasionally we find a child who's a bit worried about rules or whether they're going to please. But you can usually help that child.

Nan's valuing of authenticity in her own actions did not mean she thought her behaviour should simplistically reflect some inner state. She was not bothered by the marked adjustment of her responses, according to the identity of the other person. Nan saw no contradiction here. She said:

> They're people. And our interactions with every person we know are different ... I'm very careful with Richard. I think he's sensitive and falls apart so easily. And if I were to rouse at Richard, he wouldn't come back. (*laughter*) I wouldn't hesitate to rouse on Tony or Dennis. I mean, I do it regularly ... They'll answer me back probably. I bounce them. I just — think that's my way of interacting with them.

Nan was visibly uncomfortable, when she became aware of her own statements about children, that suggested an element of manipulation. She said: 'But here I am, making all these judgments about people, all the time. Feeling like a king, aren't I?' When invited to pursue this further, Nan laughed it off and moved on. Much later, she commented again, on her omnipotence: 'I don't feel confident in specifying the direction (a child) should go. I don't think I should play God and say that I know the very best ...'

Acceptance and Trust in Self

Nan displayed a high level of trust in her personal feelings and preferences. She based her judgments about her own actions on what 'felt right' and had a clear sense of what was right for her and what was not. For example, she spoke of visiting a teacher who had been getting a lot of attention for her innovative program: 'It was interesting and yet I came away saying, it's not me. There's no way I could operate a program like that.'

In terms of knowing what was right for children, Nan also relied on a very personal, almost intuitive measure:

> Julie was one of the youngest in the preschool group last year
> ... and there's a certain amount you can do but you can't push
> them on. They just have to mature at their own rate, so you
> don't sit over them and hover and see if they can do this level
> of puzzle or that level. I just felt it was right for her to puddle
> along at her own pace last year, with a reasonable amount of
> input and attention from us.

Nan accepted that some of her personal commitments (such as environmental conservation) and interests would impact upon her program and she was comfortable with this knowledge. Two examples:

> Our own ideas of conservation and our own philosophy of life
> have grown and dovetailed into that [*Teacher's Manual*] as
> well, so that 'Attitude to the Environment' doesn't just mean
> planting a garden. It means leaving nature where you find it
> out there and looking after the lizards and not chopping down
> trees and giving warm fuzzies to the plants. (*laughter*) Quite
> crazy sometimes.
>
> [When visiting music educators asked Nan what she would say
> to an early childhood teacher who didn't like music] I like
> singing and I like music and feeling and dancing. And so I
> would say to the person who doesn't like music: don't do it
> ... If I do something I really don't enjoy doing, the children
> aren't going to get any benefit from it at all.

Nan's acceptance of self meant she was able to acknowledge some shortcomings without attempting to rationalize, or berate herself. She simply stated them and moved on. One of Nan's most frequent self-criticisms was her 'wordiness'. As she read the observational records, Nan felt she had said far too much, on occasions. In terms of her involvement in dramatic play, Nan admitted to difficulties in knowing when to '... hop off or when to shut up, or where to draw the line'.

Another selfcriticism was voiced during the last few days of the observations, when Nan and her assistant were working through a tense period in their relationship. The cause was never identified but Nan was particularly upset by the unusually strained atmosphere and discussed it at length in a conversation session:

> (*With a whine of frustration*) Ohhhh, it just makes me cross
> that I get so affected by things like this. I do, and I think it's

> part of being an animated warm person most of the time. So that when it's not all going my way, I collapse a bit ... It is very much tied up with emotional feelings in me ... In one sense, I can switch off to those [unhappy feelings], if it's not here [in the preschool] ... But when it's here, then — you know — It doesn't happen very often.

Nan's statements suggested that she was living an examined life, both within the preschool and outside of it. Nan did not see herself or her teaching in an idealized way, yet the image she presented was one of calm confidence and acceptance of self. Nan appeared to be a person and a teacher who had 'got it together'.

The Cognitive Aspects of Teaching

In addition to this introspective examination of her beliefs and actions, Nan described teaching as involving wide-ranging mental activities. For example, Nan described the process by which she prepared herself mentally, to face the day:

> I really like to have time here by myself before anyone comes ... At home, there's a fair bit to do ... so that time [alone here] is really important to me. Just to put on a record or walk around, mooch around and get ready. And have my own little think. Just enjoy the morning here, because it's so beautiful, really peaceful. That just gives me a nice calm introduction and then I'm right. My head's in order. If I come in a rush and — once or twice I've been late and ... it was a disaster ... And so I'm relaxed when they come.

Nan admitted there were days, when she was feeling troubled, that she had to make a particular effort to attain a positive, relaxed state in preparation for the children's arrival. The way she did this was interesting:

> I only have to tune in to a few individuals in the group and I'm right. I think, now what's happening today? What day is this? What group is this? Oh yes. Well I've got such and such in mind — Then, I'm right ... That's the way in for me, and it works.

Nan also spoke of many on-the-spot types of mental activity. She spoke of the need to make quick decisions about her own input and evaluate the situation before making further decisions. In one example, Nan described Julie's response when she was asked to come and do some work alone:

> The shutters just came down. *(Nan gestures a blind falling down over her face and a blank expression.)* I can see this blank expression on her face and the resentment really building up. So, right, that wasn't the way to do it. I followed though [on] what I was doing that particular instant, but I didn't pursue it or pressure too much.

Another example occurred as Nan recalled her efforts in trying to foster the play in 'Richard's Shop':

> Maybe I could have given him more leads there or got a few more props. We're strong on the imaginary telephones and what-not. I was tempted to go and get some, but I thought, no, he might — If I go, what's going to happen then? You know, there were a few factors involved.

Nan recognized that not all of her inputs were carefully reasoned. Some actions were spontaneous, others had acquired an almost 'automatic' quality. For example, Nan spoke of the mental effort she once had made to acquire the skill of open-ended questioning. Now, she no longer needed to consciously examine and re-phrase every statement before uttering it. Open-ended questions had 'become part' of her. Similarly, Nan accepted that not all of her actions would be ideal ones. She said: 'I know there are times when I'm being absent-minded when I talk to children, or they demand attention in some ways and I just give them a glib answer. But I think mostly, we're with it.'

Post-hoc mental activities also were very much part of teaching, for Nan. She routinely evaluated children's activities on a daily and weekly basis and used this as the basis of ongoing planning. Nan also evaluated her own actions and pondered their usefulness. In one interesting example, Nan reflected on her attempts to try to get Alan accepted by other children. Although unhappy with some of her inputs, Nan thought Alan had had a better week because of her intervention. She said she had 'thought back and forth about that. And things like that, you would reconsider and see if there was another way around.'

The Human Encounter

Respect for Children

In many of Nan's statements there was a suggestion that the best was already in children, the teacher just had to help it emerge. Some examples:

> [The social element] is just part of their everyday life and [the program] is just getting the best out of them.
> Some social [peer] groupings don't seem to be satisfactory. They don't bring out the best in the people, in the individuals.

Nan spoke of children in a positive respectful way, but she did not idealize them. She mentioned many positive qualities and abilities such as their capacity for independence, their competence, their inherent motivation, their ability to teach her some things. But in almost all of these cases, Nan refused to generalize. For example, although Nan believed most young children were self-motivated, she insisted some were not. She said that without adult intervention, Dave, Bill and Eddie would 'just float along and go nowhere'. Some children would 'Superman up among the trees all day, if they had the chance'. In a similar vein, Nan acknowledged that young children could sometimes be hurtful to peers, sneaky, or manipulative.

Nan saw children as being sufficiently robust to accept an honest evaluation from adults and capable of evaluating their own work:

> I really don't accept things that I know are less than their capabilities ... And for them to have their own personal satisfaction, I think it's important that we don't accept (shoddy work) and say, 'oh that's lovely'. 'Are *you* pleased with it?' That's my response to a painting. Sometimes they'll say, 'Yuk!!' and I'll say, 'Well, aren't you pleased with it? Why don't you put it in the bin?' ... I think that's an important part of learning — to evaluate the things you do. They don't want to hear us saying gooey-gooey things about it. They really are accepting about it and it helps them to stop and think.

Nan did not consider children to be powerless. She saw that they were able to shut her out if they wished, refuse to follow her suggestions, or ask her to join in a game, even though she sometimes would prefer to stay out.

In keeping with her individualistic descriptions of children's characteristics, Nan was uncomfortable when asked to generalize on the amount of trust she had in children. Nan accepted that basic trust in children was a central part of her program, but she continued to assert that some children could be trusted, others could not.

Description of the Program for Children's Social Development

Nan saw the social dimension as an integral part of young children's lives and she gave considerable attention to this area of development in her program. One of Nan's major goals was for children to be comfortable with peers: 'What do I want for children in a social sense? To feel comfortable; being able to feel comfortable in people situations. It's part of growing and fostering self confidence and independence.'

Nan spoke on several occasions, of the way in which children's selfconfidence was bound up with their success in social interactions. For example, in speaking of what she wanted for Richard in a particular interaction, Nan said she wanted him to 'feel important and a part of the game.'

From her own childhood, Nan had vivid memories of rejection by peers and it seemed much of her involvement in children's peer interactions was aimed at softening the blow of social rejection. She worried about this with Alan:

> [For me] to leave him [in unsuccessful peer access situations] and not follow it up, I think, would really crush him and would prevent him from coming back another time ... If they're feeling uncomfortable and rejected, why would they bother to go back in another time?

Nan mentioned several distinct strategies she used to try to ensure children's peer success. One was the direct teaching of social skills, which included verbal skills for seeking access and expressing ideas; 'subtle tricks' for gaining access, for example, 'contributing something special'; and listening skills, so the child didn't miss an invitation, should one be offered.

Secondly, Nan spoke of her involvement in the formation and disbandment of peer play groups. Nan actively planned which combinations of children were likely to be most productive. For example:

- Roxanne does get pushed out by Julie, quite often ... I don't encourage her to play with Julie. I don't think it's good for her to be in that situation a great deal.

- I don't remember if it was A. or me who lit on the combination [of Duncan and Harry] some months ago. Harry has been the solitary child in the group for a long time ... Duncan has been a follower ... with Dennis and Emma. But I just felt he wasn't getting anywhere. He'd always be on the edge of things ... But to break him away from the following thing with Dennis, I felt was important. Partly because Dennis doesn't take him anywhere anyhow. So I couldn't see that as a useful partnership ... So we went through the list one day and said, what about Duncan and Harry together? Mmmm, there might be some possibilities there.

It seemed Nan was just becoming fully aware of the extent of her involvement in the creation of peer play groups. For example, in speaking of her 'contrived' peer play groups as being distinct fom 'natural' peer groups, Nan paused, then went on: '... the natural groupings — I [wonder] how natural are they, when we foster and encourage it? [I wonder] if they, in fact, have arisen from our fostering in the first place. That's another question.'

A third related area was Nan's direct intervention in assisting children to gain access to a peer play group. Nan was happier, she said, when children spontaneously invited others to join them, but if that didn't happen, she would take the initiative, and ask a child already in the group to issue an invitation to the outsider. Nan said she also would accompany a child seeking access and if neccessary, speak for that child to request entry.

Observations suggested there were many complex rights and responsibilities attached to peer play group membership in Nan's program, including the issue of 'ownership' of the particular game, yet as the discussions of observations continued, Nan had difficulty dealing with this issue. On one occasion, she seemed surprised to realize: 'Yes, I did make a big thing of it, didn't I?' It appeared that this might have been one of the less examined areas of her program.

In other areas of her program for children's social development, Nan mentioned such things as children developing a sense of responsibility towards others and to the environment. Nan tried to make children more aware of others and their feelings. Although the program emphasized personal freedom, Nan believed children had to learn that this freedom existed only within the boundaries of not harming others.

In terms of peer conflict resolution, Nan mentioned several

strategies she used. They included talking the conflict through, offering alternatives, treating it as a problem-solving situation and occasional role playing (with A.) of non-violent conflict resolution. Nan also mentioned an instructional component when she might say: 'Hitting doesn't help', and said she used positive reinforcement, to praise peer interactions that were going smoothly.

In summary, Nan appeared to enjoy the interviews and willingly seized this opportunity to reexamine her own development and her interactions with children.

Actions in the Preschool

Responsiveness and Questioning

In her relaxed demeanour and great responsiveness, it was evident that Nan enjoyed being with children. She was respectful, listening carefully to children's statements before responding in ways that showed her interest. There was a lighthearted quality to this setting, where laughter was a common sound. Yet Nan's teaching behaviours were diverse.

With her frequent use of non-directive teaching strategies, Nan seemed to maintain an ambience of informality. In many situations, her inputs were phrased as questions that put the conversational 'ball' back in the child's court, but did not pressure the child to respond. For example:

- As Harry is smoothing his clay with water he says: 'Mine's got water on it.' Nan responds: 'Oh, that feels lovely, doesn't it?'

- When Dave shows Nan his Polygon shape, Nan responds: 'That's an interesting shape, isn't it?'

These question-responses often focused the children's attention on some further aspect of the topic:

- When Dennis tells Nan they could use electricity to break open the lock on their 'treasure chest', Nan says: 'Could you? What would that do?'

- When Andrea (a shy child) arrives late after a birthday party, Nan helps her out of her party clothes, while asking many softly-spoken questions about the party: 'What was the baby's name? It was a little girl, wasn't it?' Andrea says very softly: 'Mary.' Nan sounds very pleased: 'Mary. Mary Dean?' Andrea says very softly: 'Yes.' Nan goes on: 'And she's one?' In a rush, Andrea says: 'Mary *Jane* Dean.' Nan responds: 'Mary *Jane*, as well! What did you give her for her birthday? Did she have a cake?' Andrea responds so softly, her voice is almost inaudible: 'Yes.' (The interaction continued, with similar interchanges, until Roxanne entered with a story about her birthday.)

Nan used questions for many other purposes. Some were invitations for children to problem-solve, others focused the children's attention on their interactions with peers. Through the use of these and other non-directive teaching strategies, Nan offered children many opportunities for decision-making.

Directive and Non-directive Strategies

During the long free play segments of the program, Nan rarely made openly directive statements, but these were more frequent during tidy-up times, when chores had to be done. (They also appeared with greater frequency in Nan's interactions with the so-called 'robust' children, such as Julie, Dennis and Dave.) For the most part, Nan used an extensive repertoire of non-directive teaching strategies.

To encourage children to work at some activities (particularly painting) Nan sometimes offered to sit and watch them. This did not seem to imply coercion, but conveyed her interest in their efforts. Almost without exception, children responded enthusiastically and seemed to enjoy Nan's presence. At times, Nan also used the materials herself, both for her own pleasure and as an enticement to children to participate. Nan gave much verbal encouragement and practical support to children's activities, but she did not use lavish praise. Just as Nan described in the interviews, children were encouraged to evaluate their own work.

Yet in practice, not all of Nan's apparently non-directive strategies were totally free from direction. Some of Nan's questions communicated her wishes, in a way that implied a directive. For example:

Nan is trying to prompt three children to include Julie in their play. Nan asks: 'Do you remember the other people who were here with you on Friday? Who else was in this game?' Tom says: 'Julie and — Emma.' Roxanne repeats: 'Julie and Emma.' After a few words on another topic, Nan goes on: 'When you've had a little play with these things, it might be a nice thing to invite Julie and Emma to join you.' No one replies and Nan prompts: 'Is that a good idea?' Roxanne replies, without enthusiasm: 'Yes.' (The prompting was unsuccessful.)

There were many occasions when Nan used questions to lead children to an action she desired. Although Nan only rarely made demands or commanded an action to occur, children often acted upon the implied directives in her statements. In this way, an apparently facilitative strategy could contain an element of manipulation. For example:

It has been a wet morning and children have been confined indoors. The noise level is high. As Don, Martin and Desmond run noisily past Nan, she reaches out and catches Don. She says: 'Come over here with me.' Don squirms, but Nan insists he accompany her. She directs him to hold a bowl of felt pens as she finds a roll of paper. He says: 'I don't want to.' Nan disagrees: Yes, you do.' Don says: 'They won't [want to draw].' Nan leads the way, saying cheerfully: 'Bring it over here. They won't be able to resist it.' As Nan unrolls the paper on the floor, she calls: 'Martin and Desmond, come and see what *Don's* got ready for you.' The boys immediately fall to the floor along the length of paper and reach for felt pens. Don says nothing, but soon joins the others.

Helping Children Gain Access to Peer Play Groups

Nan's behaviour, both with the children and in daily planning meetings, suggested she was very much involved in the initiation, maintenance and disbandment of children's peer play groupings. Through the selection of activities, environmental fine-tuning and interventions, Nan planned to promote some peer groupings and discourage others. Children were not directed to play together, but many subtle (and some not-so-subtle) strategies were used to achieve desired ends. For example: Nan is visiting Karen and Andrea at the Polygon table. She chats to Andrea about her recent absence, then goes on: 'I was thinking while you were away, that you and Karen might like to play together sometimes. And here you are. In fact, I was thinking that we might make some fingerpaint together.' Andrea responds enthusiastically. Later, Nan includes Richard in the invitation, as he is apparently enjoying being with these girls today.

Underlying many of Nan's interventions there seemed an assumption that playing alone was not as valuable as playing with others and Nan had many strategies aimed at increasing a solitary child's interaction with peers. (Julie was an exception. After several days in which Julie dominated her peers, Nan specifically redirected her from social situations to more solitary activities.)

Nan promoted non-specific peer play groups, by asking a solitary child in play if there was someone he/she would like to include. Sometimes, Nan suggested a particular child be included. For example:

> Nan is visiting Harry at his (solitary) dramatic play site, where he has made a pot of 'raspberry soup'. Jason is watering the garden a few feet away. As Jason turns off the hose, Nan says to Harry: 'Jason might be ready for some afternoon tea. Ask him if he wants some.' As Jason passes close by, Nan stops him and asks about the garden. She looks to Harry, but he doesn't speak and soon Jason has moved on.

Nan sometimes used very facilitative strategies in an attempt to establish peer groupings, for example, accompanying Richard as a supportive presence, while he asked other children if they would like to join him at an activity using coloured water. Although Nan prompted many types of direct child to child verbal contact, only rarely did she give an 'outside' child suggestions for verbal strategies to gain access to a peer play group. Nan was more likely to prompt the 'insiders' to issue an invitation. Occasionally, Nan provided a prop for the child seeking access to use as a 'passport'. For example:

> Zita is looking in as Tom and Roxanne are playing in the home corner. Nan watches briefly, then suggests: 'Zita, I've got something you might like to take into that game. Come and see.' Nan provides Zita with several containers of frothy soap mixture. When Zita carries one into the home corner, Tom and Roxanne are excited and with a little further prompting from Nan, all three carry off the containers to use in the outdoor cubby house.

During the first two days of the observational period, Nan sometimes used quite vigorous measures in attempts to establish particular peer play groups. Nan reported feeling anxious at this time and on reading the observational record afterwards, decribed her input as 'forced and stilted'. Although the following example does not do justice to Nan's usual sensitivity, it is of interest because it illustrates the narrow line that separates facilitation and manipulation. In an attempt to provide some social successes for Alan, Nan was trying to help him gain access to the Don-Martin-Desmond group. (Note that this group was Nan's choice, not Alan's):

Nan accompanies Alan to the block corner, where Desmond, Don and Martin are playing. She says: 'Desmond, would you like to tell us what you're up to with these buildings? Alan and I are interested.' Desmond mumbles a brief reply. Nan continues: 'Desmond, Alan was thinking he'd like to be with you. Would it be alright if he came and joined in this game?' Desmond doesn't respond, but Don looks surprised as he says: 'With us? — I don't mind.' Alan stands beside Nan as she negotiates his entry. He says nothing, but Nan continues: 'He's very good at drawing. Very good at making signs. Do you think you might be needing some signs?' Don says: 'Yeah', but the other two boys are silent. Nan turns to Alan and asks: 'What do you think about that, Alan?' Alan doesn't reply and Nan suggests: 'Why don't you go and have a chat with them, and see what they need?' Soon after, Nan leaves the block area. Alan attempts to make contact with the other boys, but it is not successful and soon they leave him to carry on with their play.

Throughout this sequence, the boys displayed little enthusiasm for this play alliance. On this occasion, Nan's attempts to promote Alan's qualities as a group member were unsuccessful, but later in the week Nan helped Alan gain access to other peer play groups, where he enjoyed much more success. (Corsaro, 1985, p. 289 suggests that adult intervention in access situations is useful, even if the immediate outcome is unsuccessful. Although children may resist, the intervention provides children with an encounter of the 'boundary' between the adult and child worlds and this is an important source of social learning.)

In maintaining peer play groups, Nan also used many strategies.

Some of these were facilitative, in that they assisted children to resolve peer problems without surrendering control of events. For example, Nan encouraged children to make direct contact with peers within the game:

- Nan is helping several children make a large house from interlocking timber pieces and asks where they would like the door. Immediately Roxanne says: 'That side.' Nan suggests: 'Ask Alan. Does he agree with you?' Alan does not and convincingly argues his case for the door on the other side.

- Richard (a quiet child) is hovering on the fringe of a group of children, but is not part of the game. Julie is in a commanding position as mistress of the 'brown house' (crate). Nan has been watching and now asks Julie: 'I'd like to know why you have so many [make-believe] fires in this house. Is it because someone leaves the iron on or the stove, or something?' Julie replies: 'It's the telephone in the kitchen, blowing a fuse and going up in sparks.' Nan responds: 'Truly?! I think we'd better get the telephone technician out. Do you think that might be Richard? What about you go and visit him? You can't ring him up unless you go down to the public phone.' Nan stays with the children for some time, facilitating their contacts with each other.

A less facilitative strategy was the (unstated) group membership rule that tried to protect the child who had gained access. Nan often reminded children of the need to include 'other members of your group' when they moved to a new activity. It seemed a child had the right of refusal, if he or she did not wish to go with the group, but the group should issue the invitation.

Nan focused her disbandment efforts on one very stable peer play group that was seen as being a less than desirable combination: the Don-Desmond-Martin group. Martin was the dominant member. Don was a socially competent child, but he was reluctant to take any action without first getting Martin's permission. Desmond rarely initiated contacts with adults, or children other than Don and Martin. Martin's domination of Desmond was, at times, quite cruel.

Nan's actions with this group seemed to be focused primarily on encouraging Don to be more independent. For example, Don usually arrived first, then stood idly by the door until Martin arrived. Despite Don's determination to wait, Nan strongly encouraged him to become involved in activities before Martin arrived. One day, when Martin and Desmond were both absent and Don played with other children, Nan drew his attention to the pleasures of playing with others. But Nan's strategies met with only mixed success. For example:

- Don says wistfully: 'I'd like to go out to play —' but he looks towards Desmond and Martin who are working on a puzzle. Nan says: 'You don't have to wait. Come now.' Nan and Don go out into the playground.

- Don seems to be uninvolved with the block play and Nan asks: 'Are you ready to do your painting? You look like you need something new to do.' Don says: 'I'll ask Martin.' Nan comments: 'You can make your own decisions.' Don replies: 'No, I'll ask him.' He does.

It was a reflection of the complexity of the teacher's decision making that whilst Nan was acting out of concern for Don's welfare in trying to split him from this group, it was not certain that his departure would be a positive outcome for the other two. Don was the spokesman for the trio, and he seemed to provide a buffer for Desmond against Martin's jibes.

Resolving Peer Conflict

Nan used the physical environment as a preventive approach to peer conflict. She provided an abundance of materials, often adding more tape, extra scissors, an additional chair, so that conflicts over materials were minimized. Nan also was vigilant to potential conflicts over use of space. For example:

- When children want to leave their block building standing until the following day, Nan moves screens to protect it from accidental demolition.

- When the boys roll out drawing paper across the room, and it seems that it might be in the way of those building with blocks, Nan realigns the paper, so that it avoids the block area.

The Human Encounter

Conflicts between children were infrequent and in almost every case, Nan's inputs were calm, low-keyed and brief. On many occasions, Nan quickly smoothed over minor conflicts with a few words, refocusing children's attention on the task at hand. In other conflict situations, Nan began by asking a series of information-gathering questions. For example:

> The children in the boat play are in conflict, with much shouting. Nan moves rapidly to the area and asks Tony: 'Mr Pilot, what's this noise all about?' Several children speak at once and the conflict continues. Dave is shouting angrily at Eddie and Don, but there is a suggestion that at least part of the conflict is playacting, as he shouts: 'Get out of it, doggie!' Nan asks: 'Don't you want them to play?' The others say that Eddie and Don have been 'wrecking their things'. Nan says: 'Eddie, would you find Don and you two come with me.' Nan accompanies the boys to the patio and interests them in the clay.

In other conflict situations, Nan asked questions, but then paid little attention to children's answers. It seemed she already had knowledge of these situations, and might have been using this strategy to give herself a little time to decide what action to take. Often, Nan quickly decided which children deserved her support and then redirected others from the peer conflict situation. For example:

> Nan observes some loud action involving five boys. Moving rapidly, she follows the boys to the climber. As she approaches, Dennis and Tony both look upset. Dave runs away and Eddie and Bill hide in a large drum. Nan says to Dennis: 'I think this game's getting a bit too rough. What do you think, Dennis?' Dennis begins to explain: 'Well, you see there's this —' Tony also is speaking. He says: 'It's Dave and Alan. And Dave's in that barrel, no Eddie, and Alan was round there and —' Nan cuts both boys off: 'They're very excited, aren't they?' Tony begins again: 'There's Dave down there and Bill and —' Nan interrupts once more: 'Well, you two (Dennis and Tony) get on with your game and these two might come down with me.' After calling Bill and Eddie from the drum, Nan accompanies them to the patio, saying: 'You can start with a painting, you two.' (Later, Nan located Dave and chastised him for his behaviour.)

Although Nan clearly had decided which side to support in children's peer conflicts, she did not often make 'ruling' statements. One instance observed occured when Zita and Alan were arguing over who would have next turn in the block 'gaol'. Nan ruled that Zita should have the turn, because she had been in the game longer and had been more involved in the construction.

Nan also made only limited use of interpretive statements that subtly conveyed her support for one party in peer conflicts. In the following example, Nan's interpretation also downplayed the conflict:

> Karen and Andrea are working at the collage table. Karen is standing, though there are vacant chairs nearby. As Andrea vacates her chair to bring more materials from a nearby shelf, Karen quickly sits on the chair. A few seconds later, when Andrea returns, she says crossly: 'Karen!!' Nan asks: 'Is that where you were sitting, Andrea?' Andrea nods her head and Nan says: 'I don't think Karen realized that.' Nan pulls up an adjoining chair and says to Karen: 'You sit here.'

A form of interpretive comment as a refutation was used on several occasions when Julie claimed others were scheming to take over her play. The first time Julie voiced this claim, Nan attempted to explain that others *might* want to take over because she was being 'a little mean' in not letting them play. There was little evidence of this actually happening however, and Nan became increasingly frustrated with Julie's persistent complaints. Nan made interpretive statements such as: 'Julie, nobody's interested in this game, except you and Emma. Emma *is* interested and she'd like to make it a good game.' And later: 'Julie, no one's remotely interested in your house.' 'No one even knows you're here!'

In two observed peer conflict situations, Nan made reference to the value of talking over problems, but in neither case did this process actually eventuate:

- Dennis and Tony are in conflict over the direction of the boat play. Nan says: 'What a conflict of opinions. What shall we do? Have a talk about it?' Don interrupts with a request to get off the boat and Nan raises this problem with the boys in conflict. Their difference of opinion is forgotten.

The Human Encounter

- It is almost the end of a rather hectic session. Because of the rain, the children have been confined indoors. Dave and Bill are arguing heatedly over the future of their block building. Eddie also is present. Nan arrives and asks what is going on. Only Eddie answers her questions. Nan tries to compliment the boys on their achievements, but the argument continues. Eddie is visibly agitated and tries to make the peace by saying: 'It doesn't matter.' Nan moves in and holds Dave's arm as she says firmly: 'Well, it doesn't matter a *lot*, but it helps if you talk things over when you're working.' Nan goes on to say it will be tidy up time in two minutes and she expects the boys to tidy the blocks. Then, she suggests a quick walk outside as the rain has stopped at last.

Across many situations, Nan used a distraction or redirection to swiftly conclude peer conflicts. She was not observed to engage in prolonged interactional sequences as children tried to resolve their conflicts with peers.

Involvement in Children's Dramatic Play

Nan's involvement in children's dramatic play followed a relatively stable pattern. She often observed the play from nearby, sometimes without becoming involved. When she entered the play, often it was in response to a child's invitation. (Julie was particularly aware of Nan's observation and often invited her to join in.) When Nan entered dramatic play sites, she asked many focusing questions, that aimed to help children clarify their ideas, rather than simply to provide her with information. To some extent, the questions also offered extending ideas, although these questions sometimes occured later in the sequence. For example:

Dennis invites Nan to join several others on a boat trip. As Nan arrives at the boat, she asks: 'Pilot, where are you going?' Tony says: 'We're going to Storm Island and ah — Fiji, and — ah — Norfolk Island.' Nan responds: 'Oh, I see. And how much does it cost?' Another child says: 'Twenty dollars.' Nan says: 'Well, that's reasonable. Are you ready to go now?' (Nan's involvement in this play lasted for ten minutes and other excerpts will follow.)

In these situations, Nan typically did not enter fully into a role, but played what might be termed, 'the curious visitor'. Nan accepted the children's roles and addressed them accordingly (for example, calling Tony 'Mr Pilot'). She did not take over the play, but offered extending details to the children's ideas. In the boat play event, Nan became more involved than usual, acting out the rescue of shipwrecked sailors with vigour and urgency:

> Nan is sitting in the boat with the children. Tony says they've passed a shipwreck and Nan says: 'How exciting! I wonder if there are any survivors. (Pointing to a fern in the garden) Oh look! There's one! Have you got a rope?' In an urgent tone, Nan tries to involve the others: 'Quick! Get a rope! Don't just sit there!' Tony and Stephen are participating fully in the drama, but other 'passengers' sit passively. Nan urges them to care for the 'survivors'. Gradually, Don and Dennis are drawn in to the fantasy and the play continues.

More commonly, Nan's fringe role allowed her to move in and out as the need for teacher-like inputs demanded. For example:

> Nan is playing 'the curious visitor' in the girls' cubby house. They are recounting 'the story so far' and announce the mother has been shot. Nan drops her role momentarily, and tells the girls that that is impossible, because they don't have guns at preshool — even pretend ones. Then, Nan slips back into the role of visitor.

Nan commonly suggested and/or added additional props to extend or elaborate the play. For example, when Julie was setting up a kitchen in the 'brown house', Nan brought a bucket of water, soup bowls, spoons and a ladle. When Alan and several girls were in the interlock house, Nan brought drawing materials and slipped them in.

This pattern of entry and greeting, focusing questions, extending questions or ideas, and the addition of extra props was observed on many occasions with many children. In some of Julie's play however, Nan became involved in a different way. Across the three-week observational period, Nan placed very different meanings on Julie's peer interactions. Initially, Julie's blatantly manipulative interactions with peers were seen as a positive change; an indication that Julie was coming out of her former solitary activity. But just a few days later,

The Human Encounter

Julie's behaviour with peers was interpreted as having reached a worrisome level of domination. By the end of the second week, Julie's behaviour with peers was thought to be approaching an intolerable level. During the third week, the perception was that the problem had declined once again.

During the middle period, Nan was heavily involved in Julie's peer interactions, attempting to elicit more pro-social behaviours. (In Katz's (1984) terms, Nan was trying to break a recursive cycle of domination.) In a very long event (eleven minutes), Nan made a determined attempt to change Julie's interactional pattern:

> Julie and Emma are playing in three drums stacked in a triangle. The girls are birds and they want to use the drums as their nest. Julie is not helping, but is ordering Emma around in an imperious manner. Nan enters and tries to use the content of the play to elicit Julie's help. Nan suggests Julie might enlarge the nest, but Julie counters: 'But we've got a comfortable nest. There's enough room for three.' Emma has been trying to say something, and Nan supports her, but Julie cuts her off, saying: 'That's the mother bird. She's got all the ideas.' When Nan suggests Julie 'listen to the mother bird's idea', Julie again counters, claiming: 'I'm just the baby.' This verbal sparring continues, with both Nan and Julie using the content of the game as a source of support for their positions. Julie is very skilled at this game and after some time, Nan changes her strategy to attempt to goad Julie into helping. She talks of decorating the nest and asks Julie to help. When Julie refuses, Nan says she will ask Emma to help. Julie acts nonchalant. As Emma and Nan decorate with leaves and 'wallpaper', Nan ignores Julie, but Emma does not. As Julie once again gives orders to Emma, Nan intervenes sternly and directs Julie to assist. Julie reverts to the earlier strategy: 'But I'm just a baby bird.' This time, Nan refuses to play the verbal game and becomes angry. She leads Julie from the drums and lectures her sternly: 'If people want to be friends — No, wait a minute. I want you to look at me while I'm talking — If people want to be friends and have friends, they need to help a bit. They help each other. And it's not fair when Emma does all the work in your game and you just sit and watch. And I'm getting a bit cross about that.' Soon after, the lecture ends with Nan asking in a conciliatory tone: 'Is there someone you'd like to include

in your game?' After Julie returns to the drums, she helps for a few minutes, before trouble occurs again.

Over the course of several days, Nan made many other interventions in Julie's peer interactions, to try to foster more desirable social behaviour. These were not noticeably successful and by the third week, Nan was using a different approach, periodically removing Julie for periods of solitary activity, as a respite both for Julie herself and for other children.

Rules

There seemed to be a minimum number of rules governing behaviour in this centre. Most related to safety: for example, shoes had to be removed for music and movement, running was prohibited on the paved areas or indoors, and noise was to be kept to a reasonable level. There were also some procedural rules, such as removing shoes before playing in the sandpit, not bringing toys (especially toy guns) from home, helping at tidy-up time and maintaining a level of decorum during group times. But only the safety rules were enforced vigilantly. For the most part, the rules were 'soft', open to negotiation or exception. For example, shoes were left on in the sandpit when it was cold, and during the music and movement group, when the group size was small. Nan did not often chastise children when rules were broken, but when she did, the recipient was likely to be Dave or Julie:

- When Dave runs across the patio, Nan commands: 'Walk!'

- When Dave fails to sing at music time and creates a distraction with his friends, Nan says firmly: 'Dave, you've been at this preschool a long time now and you know the words. I want you to sing.'

- It is tidy-up time and from the home corner, Julie's voice can be heard, shouting at another child: 'Rubbish! We do so have toys!' Nan calls sternly: 'That voice is too loud for my liking.' Later, the trouble continues and Julie's voice can be heard once again, shrieking in anger at other children. Nan is busy elsewhere, but looks towards them and frowns, saying in a rising tone of warning: 'Julie — ' The noise diminishes.

Developing a Sense of Community

In several important ways, Nan acted to increase the children's awareness of their membership of this community. She made frequent references to the children's connections to others, to their social existence. For example:

- When Tom and Zita arrive at Nan's side, she greets them: 'Hello, you two.'

- As Desmond joins the group getting ready to play a card game, Nan comments: 'We've got another customer. That's good.'

- Earlier, Nan had suggested Duncan and Harry might like to fingerpaint together. Now, she visits them at the fingerpainting table. As she rolls up their sleeves, she says: 'Wasn't it lucky you two were sitting on the drum together?' Duncan responds: 'Yup.' Nan goes on: 'Because I thought to myself — Duncan and Harry were good friends once. They've played some good games together.' Duncan says: 'I know. We are friends, aren't we?' Nan says softly: 'You are friends.'

Frequently, Nan drew children's attention to the actions or achievements of other children. These tended to be simple, brief inputs such as:

- 'Look at Karen's star.'

- 'There's another way to make patterns. Duncan's used his fork.'

- 'That's T-Rex, Alan's dinosaur.'

- 'Eddie, did you see Harry's good idea?'

Basic social skills such as making eye contact when speaking, using other's names and speaking when spoken to, were both modelled and verbally encouraged. Nan helped children to show consideration for others in many ways. She asked children to share materials, help each other, and prompted them to thank others for help received. Nan asked children to clean up after themselves, so others could use the materials. She praised children who showed consideration and chastised those who did not. For example:

- Tom offers to go indoors and bring some cushions out to the cubby house. Nan and the other children speculate on how many cushions he will bring. Will he bring enough for everyone? He does and Nan responds: 'Wasn't he thoughtful? Thank you Tom.' When Zita fails to thank Tom, Nan prompts: 'How about a thank you from you?' Zita says slowly: 'Thank you, Tom.'
- Dave bounces onto the mat where music is about to begin and tumbles Harry, who looks rather surprised. Nan sits beside Dave and says softly but firmly: 'Would you leave Harry alone. I'm not feeling very happy with the way you're being rough with the other people in this preschool.'

Environmental Support of Peer Interaction

As has already been discussed in the previous sections, Nan provided an environment that supported children's peer interactions in many ways. It provided a great deal of space and an abundance of materials, so that overcrowding and scarcity of materials were not sources of peer conflict. With abundant props, many prolonged and highly elaborated dramatic play events occurred.

Nan constantly fine-tuned the environment to attract particular children to specific areas, to aid in the formation of the desired peer goups, to extend children's play and avoid potential peer conflicts. These small changes enabled the children to maintain a high level of interest throughout the session and they never seemed troubled by boredom.

In carefully planning her program, Nan focused almost exclusively on individual children. She placed particular emphasis on their social development, and of all the teachers in the study, seemed to plan for social development in the most specific and deliberate manner.

Concluding Remarks

Nan was vigorous in her work with children. Although she spoke of her relaxation and enjoyment in simply being with the children, her program required a great deal of thought and energy. Nan also gave considerable thought to her own professional development. In neither case, did Nan allow herself to glide. She was actively seeking her own development and continually questioning her interactions with children.

From the beginning, Nan was enthusiastic about participation in this study, which seemed to fit well with her own beliefs about teaching and human development. Nan told of being a little apprehensive on the first day, but then quickly feeling comfortable in the presence of the observer. Nan devoured the written records of observations. She was excited by the feedback on her own actions and the information the observations provided on children. Nan claimed they gave her new insights on some aspects of her teaching:

> There are some things that have made me more conscious, even in the actual doing, before reading over what you've written ... it's made it come alive somehow. That what I'm doing is more meaningful. And then this evaluating it at the same time. Crystallizing thoughts as we've talked over some of the philosophy issues. Perhaps that's happened a long time ago, but it's good to air them again.

Nan was very cognizant of the many links between herself as person and as teacher. She evaluated many of her teaching actions from a very personal measure of what 'felt right' to her. Nan accepted that her emotional state, interests and personal commitments were a powerful influence on her interactions with children and parents.

Through her valuing of authenticity, Nan has shown us that this is a complex and difficult concept. Paradoxically, the very lack of performance; the close connection between Nan's personal identity and her teaching meant that at times, some undeniably authentic actions did not match the idealized image of an early childhood teacher. For example, observations and Nan's comments suggested that the relationship between Dave and Nan was an uncomfortable one. Nan described 'a certain look' that Dave sometimes displayed, that she 'really found hard to take' and there was a series of occasions when Nan's displeasure with Dave was evident.

Nan perceived the diversity of her responses to individuals, and her willingness to display annoyance as well as pleasure, as positive evidence of her authenticity. She saw no reason to 'artificially' homogenize her behaviour. As Moustakas (1968, p. 36) has pointed out, in behaving authentically, one cannot enact only the happy, joyful self. One also must be authentic in times of fear, uncertainty or anger.

Nan

In our idealized images of interactions between teachers and young children, it seems we value authenticity highly, as long as the teacher remains warm, nurturing and happy. When the teacher reflects equally authentic behaviours such as anger, unhappiness or discomfort, we are forced to reexamine our professed belief in authenticity.

Chapter 5

Brenda

The Setting

Brenda's Preschool

This preschool was built in the mid 1970s, with a capital grant from the Australian Government. Its purpose was to provide preschool education for Aboriginal and Torres Strait Islander children. Because of the high proportion of Aboriginal and Islander children enrolled (over 90 per cent), the centre received special government funding and fees were minimal.

This double unit preschool was located in a multi-function centre incorporating facilities for other services such as health programs and community organizations. The preschool section consisted of two mid-size playrooms, joined by sliding doors. A wide covered patio led to a single playground, shared by both units. After a period in which the physical facilities had become rather depleted, the centre currently was undergoing a period of renewal. There were some bright new pieces of equipment and some older, well-worn ones.

Brenda's playroom was brightly painted and decorated with many examples of children's work. Parents' work also was displayed, in the Aboriginal designs painted in bright colours on walls and furniture. The Aboriginal theme was continued in the posters and photographs on the walls. Many of the children's books on display in the library corner reflected Aboriginal content, as did some of the puzzles in the manipulative area. In this building, the acoustics were poor and the sliding doors allowed noise to permeate between units. When staffing shortages occurred, the doors sometimes were left open, allowing the two groups to mingle, But Brenda disliked this practice.

The playground was average in size but rather forlorn. Several pieces of fixed equipment recently had been removed, leaving bald patches. There was little shade and few shrubs, but a large timber climber provided good opportunities for physical play and the shaded sandpit was well used. Moveable equipment such as jouncing boards, trestles and large outdoor blocks added interest, but overall it could not be described as a particularly challenging or aesthetically pleasing environment.

Timing was very flexible in this program. Although the sequence was basically unchanged, segments of the session could differ by up to thirty minutes from day to day and occasionally, the whole-group sessions of language and music did not occur.

8:45	The buses leave to collect children.
9:50 — 9:55	The first bus returns. Brenda greets the children and has a brief group time lasting approximately three minutes, then children are dispersed to free play activities.
9:55 — 10:50	First freeplay time (outdoors one week, indoors the next).
10:00	The second bus returns. Children are greeted in a very brief group time then dispersed to free play activities.
10:50 — 11:00	Tidy up time.
11:00 — 11:15	First group time (language or music).
11:15 — 11:30	Morning tea.
11:30 — 12:05	Second freeplay time (indoors one week, outdoors the next).
12:05 — 12:15	Tidy up time.
12:15 — 12:25	Second group time (music or language).
12:25	Lunch, then rest.
2:00	Children depart on buses.

Activities in this program were similar to those seen in other centres. The children had unrestricted access to the range of materials displayed in the room, and children were able to make choices between blocks, home corner, books, several types of manipulatives, puppets, art activities such as drawing, painting at the easels and collage.

Outdoors, physical activity was encouraged through the use of fixed and moveable equipment. Sand and water play occurred daily and dramatic play was fostered through the use of the outdoor blocks and props such as prams and old chairs. Often, an easel was brought out under a tree, or finger paint, clay or playdough was set up. Sometimes, a mat with manipulatives would be placed on the patio. For the most part, children selected their own activities, though Brenda sometimes organized ball or circle games for all or some of the children.

Children, Families, Staff

The preschool was located in an outer suburb with a large proportion of low-cost and government assisted housing. Although there was diversity in family lifestyles, the community as a whole was typified by low-incomes, high unemployment and the range of social ills that accompany life in an economically depressed community.

Twenty two children were enrolled in this group and their ages ranged from 4.7 — 6.3 years. Only a few children were living in stable two-parent families. The remainder were drawn from families with a range of structures and stability. Several of the children had spent time in foster homes, but at the time of the study, all were living with their natural families. A number of the children had ongoing health problems and were receiving treatment through specialized Aboriginal health services.

Despite their common problems, it would not be accurate to suggest the families utilizing their early childhood program were an homogenous group. Most could be described as Aborigines or Torres Strait Islanders, but within these groups, there were many subgroupings with different origins, traditions and lifestyles. Some of the families were recently arrived from rural Aboriginal communities. Others had been city-dwellers for generations. Some family members were activists, working towards social justice for Aboriginal people. Others were quietly trying to integrate into the white mainstream. In many ways, this was a diverse group.

Both qualified early childhood teachers employed in the preschool were white. The Director (D.) had been at the preschool one year, and Brenda began teaching there only four months before the study began.

The Human Encounter

In both units there were Aboriginal assistants with no formal qualifications, but extensive experience in this centre.

The Teacher

Brenda was approximately 30 years of age, of small stature, slim but well muscled. Generally, Brenda seemed to be in good health, though by the end of some very trying days, she looked grey with exhaustion. Brenda kept her hair short and wore no makeup to preschool. She dressed neatly but casually, in a divided skirt or slacks and a blouse.

Brenda's body movements during the session were varied. She often moved very quickly between children, striding out with purpose. When Brenda made contact with a child, however, her pace slowed markedly. Brenda typically sat on the floor, or squatted on her heels, bringing her face into eye-level contact with the children. At these times, she often was characterized by a stillness that was suggestive of great concentration.

Physical contacts were used by Brenda in a variety of situations. She often hugged children and showed other signs of affection. When children were hurt or upset, Brenda rocked them in her arms, or calmed them by putting her arm around their shoulders and patting them gently on the back. Brenda also used physical contact to help maintain attention. She would gently hold a child's hands while she spoke and maintained close eye contact. At times, Brenda also used physical contact to restrain a child. For example, holding Charles on her knee despite his squirming, until she had verbalized her message.

Brenda could not be described as a particularly vivacious teacher, as so many of her movements and facial expressions were characterized by a calm evenness, but she displayed a very genuine pleasure at children's achievements. Brenda said that she always tried to acknowledge children with a smile, even though she might be totally occupied with others, and this was often observed. At other times. Brenda wore a worried expression, as might be expected in this demanding teaching position.

Brenda typically spoke in a very soft, even tone to individual children or small groups. Her voice was often inaudible to those more than a few feet away. Brenda rarely made announcements to the whole group and, in general, did not have a lot to say. She spoke slowly and articulated carefully. Her responses to children often came after a momentary pause and she seemed to be choosing her words with care.

Brenda's calmness was in marked contrast to the children's behaviour that swirled around her. Even in the midst of a group of boys shouting insults at each other, Brenda exuded calmness and responded thoughtfully, in a very soft voice. On occasion, however, Brenda did lose her cool demeanour. When the situation was an urgent one, such as when several boys climbed over the fence to retrieve a ball from the busy street, Brenda shouted. At other times, under very stressful conditions, Brenda's voice wavered briefly, as she struggled to retain control. She could also sound very firm, as she directed a child to behave in a certain manner (usually after several softer inputs had failed).

Another characteristic speech quality was Brenda's ability to phrase statements in the positive. Very rarely did she make a negative remark about herself or others, and in the classroom Brenda's statements were unvaryingly positive, even under trying conditions.

Brenda did not use pet names or terms of endearment with children, with the exception of the word 'mate'. This expression is not commonly heard from teachers, though it is a part of the Australian vernacular. Although these children frequently used the term, Brenda said that her use of it was not a deliberate attempt to mimic their language. Rather, it had become a natural part of her own vocabulary during the time she had lived and worked with Aboriginal people.

Brenda's Image-of-Self-as-Teacher

General Description: Connections and Continuities

As Brenda spoke of her own development, her beliefs about children and her part in their lives, a sense of coherence emerged. Within her personal beliefs, there seemed to be strong connections and Brenda frequently acknowledged these, so that the connections themselves formed part of her self-image; her understandings about self in relation to world. Brenda spoke of life, now 'fitting together better than it used to', and indeed it seemed that she had found a way of bringing together apparently disparate pieces. Brenda had thought deeply about her own development and although she was aware of some 'ups and downs' in terms of self-acceptance, at least for the present she was at ease with herself. Brenda said she was 'pretty happy with her development thus far'.

As a beginning teacher there had been little distinction between Brenda's personal and professional lives. Since her marriage, there had been a greater separation, yet Brenda still made explicit many links between herself as person and as teacher, as she tried to make sense of her own development and current teaching.

Brenda displayed what appeared to be an almost stereotypic organismic world view. For her, nothing occurred in isolation. Everything was related to everything else and nothing could remain unaffected when one part was changed. Brenda attempted to understand everything in the broadest possible context and for her, the 'big picture' was most important. For example, Brenda believed that in order to interact effectively with children, it was imperative that the teacher understand not only the child, but also the family, the home environment and the community, over a period of time. In Brenda's use of metaphor, there were clues to this organismic world view and a strong sense of the paradoxical. Some examples:

> [You need] a balance of giving and taking.
>
> [You need] to be challenged by the situation, but also contributing to it.
>
> Everyone is different, but ... everyone has both good and bad. You just have to hope the balance favours the good.
>
> There is an ongoing cycle between home and preschool ... They are not two separate worlds, though they are two totally different environments.

The sense of paradox also was evident as Brenda spoke of her actions in the classroom. For example, she described the paradoxical relationship between her concern for individuals and concern for the group. Brenda told of a dilemma where she felt obliged to intervene to protect the rights of group members in the face of a threat from an individual, whilst knowing that the intervention was not in that individual's best interests. Brenda said she could not avoid the dilemma, but managed it by making this type of intervention a 'last resort' measure, to be used only after other strategies had failed.

Brenda's statements suggested that she saw many continuities between herself and the children. For example, Brenda believed that both she and the children were moving along a developmental continuum, and 'talking things through' was a path to understanding, both for herself and the children. Similarly, 'staying calm' was important for all.

Although connectedness was the most noteworthy feature of Brenda's description of her image-of-self-as-teacher, there also were some areas of discontinuity. The most striking of these was the paradoxical issue of culture. Brenda was a white woman who had chosen to specialize in Aboriginal education and for several years had immersed herself in Aboriginal society. During this time, Brenda adopted some of the Aboriginal attitudes to life, integrating these in a way that moved her to a cultural position that was neither completely Aboriginal nor typically white. Brenda had a deep personal understanding and appreciation for Aboriginal lifestyles and culture, yet she was not Aboriginal. This was an inescapable paradox and Brenda's closeness to the Aboriginal people served only to emphasize the gap that could not be bridged. This discontinuity between herself and the Aboriginal community, of which she was both part and not-part, was felt strongly by Brenda and was a major influence on her teaching.

For Brenda, the discontinuity created an ongoing tension in her curriculum. Brenda did not wish to dishonour Aboriginal culture by treating it in a shallow manner in her curriculum, yet she believed it would be 'a desecration' for her to attempt to teach 'authentic' content related to the Aboriginal culture (i.e., languages, old tribal ways). For a white teacher, selecting appropriate Aboriginal content for this diverse group of Aboriginal and Islander children was a long-term dilemma. Brenda described how she worried about it, talked it through with Aboriginal staff members and other teachers in similar setttings, then with no final resolution, set it aside until it came to the surface yet again.

Biographical Aspect

Brenda was the fourth born in a family of seven children. Her older sister was a high school teacher and she interested Brenda in teaching, but because of her small physical size Brenda felt she was not suitable to teach adolescents. When a careers counsellor mentioned kindergarten teaching, Brenda decided 'that sounded about right', so after completing high school, Brenda entered the Kindergarten Teachers College.

Brenda recalled enjoying her time at college, though she had few social contacts. She said she 'kept to herself a lot' and did not socialize with other students outside of college activities. Several lecturers made a positive impact on Brenda, because of their personal interest, openness to her opinions, non-judgmental attitudes and their willingness to allow students to talk through issues. Brenda saw them as 'practicing what they preached' and she felt relaxed in their classes.

The Human Encounter

Although she found child development classes and practice teaching invaluable, Brenda initially said she felt the college program had not done a good job in preparing her for life as a teacher. In particular, it had not provided the skills she needed to cope with the emotional pressures of her first years of teaching. Brenda said the students needed much more time; time to think through issues, time to observe teachers in action and discuss with them the decisions they made in the classroom. Even as Brenda discussed her preservice years, however, she moderated her criticisms by acknowledging that some of the students' human development had to take place in its own time, before college courses could help them further.

During the college program, Brenda became interested in Aboriginal social issues and helped lobby for the establishment of a subject in Aboriginal early education. During her final year at college, Brenda made contact with the government department controlling Aboriginal education, and arranged to do her practicum at a preschool in an Aboriginal community, several hundred miles from the city. Brenda enjoyed the experience greatly and resolved to work in Aboriginal education on graduation.

Immediately after graduation in the mid 1970s, Brenda was appointed to a teacher's position in the same Aboriginal community she had visited the previous year. This experience was to have a profound effect on Brenda's development, both as person and teacher. It was the first time she had lived away from home and as one of a small number of whites in a community of approximately one thousand Aboriginals, the lifestyle was very different from her own family background.

Initially, Brenda lived with a group of teachers from the local primary school, but soon moved into a house in the middle of the community, among the Aboriginal people. Brenda did not attempt to distance herself, as did many of the white teachers, by leaving the community on weekends and during the school holidays. Rather, she immersed herself in community life, even accompanying some Aboriginal friends on their visits to family members in more remote communities. During this time, the distinction between work and non-work did not seem important to Brenda. The boundaries between teaching and living, teacher and person were indistinct.

In this first year of teaching, Brenda at the age of 20 was in charge of a large preschool, with a staff of six. All except Brenda were Aboriginal and some had no experience in preschool education. This was a difficult way to begin a teaching career, but Brenda was able to recall the experience in her usual positive, cheerful way. She said: 'We all learned together'.

Several years later, Brenda was transferred to a more isolated Aboriginal community where she was very unhappy and stayed only a few months. Brenda decided to join some of her Aboriginal friends as itinerant fruit pickers and with typical understatement, said she 'thought it would be interesting and it was'. Although this lifestyle involved considerable hardship, Brenda recalled it as a positive experience that had contributed much to her understanding of life.

Brenda's next move was to a small town, where she became director of a recently established community-based child care centre. Despite the difficulties of starting a new service on a small budget, Brenda recalled this as a happy time, characterized by wonderful support from parents. Many of the parents were itinerant workers and Brenda's experiences as an itinerant worker helped enormously in understanding the lifestyles of these families.

At the end of that year, Brenda returned to the city, to be closer to her fiancé. After an absence of several years and some major changes in her lifestyle and personal beliefs, Brenda was very unhappy in the city. She hated the 'rush-rush-rush', the weak sense of community and the reliance on the clock. Brenda felt a distance had opened between herself and her former friends and colleagues, who could not understand her changed perspectives. Most notably, they could not understand why Brenda retained her interest in Aboriginal education.

In another unusual career choice, Brenda became the director of a commercial child care centre, but this was not an enjoyable position. Part of her dissatisfaction was related to the lack of contact with hurried city parents and at the end of the year Brenda moved once more, to take a position in a preschool for urban Aboriginal children.

In recalling the two years spent at this centre, Brenda said there were 'some good times and some bad'. The community group operating the preschool had deep divisions over social issues such as land rights and goals for Aboriginal education. These emotionally-charged issues also caused divisions amongst the staff and it was not an easy working environment.

After resigning, Brenda became the director of a new mobile kindergarten for Aboriginal children. Despite the demands on her stamina, Brenda remained in this position for several years, leaving it to take up her present position a few months before this study began.

Brenda's career path was unusual, but when it was suggested she looked like a risk taker, Brenda laughed and said that for her, work in an Aboriginal centre represented a degree of safety. She believed that Aboriginal parents' expectations were different from those of white parents in middle class preschools and although there were many things about work in an Aboriginal centre that caused tensions, she understood these. Brenda said she would be much more apprehensive at the prospect of teaching in a white middle-class preschool where she was afraid she 'just didn't know enough about that area at all'.

In commenting on the number of different positions she had held, Brenda explained that her own development was very important to her. She said:

> I've looked to have different experiences. I think I'm still learning ... At every centre that I'm working, I'm still learning. I'm extending myself, and that's important. I feel I'm still developing ... In every centre, I get to a point where I think: oh, nothing more positive is happening, probably in a personal sense ... and I need to look for something more.

Staying Calm

One of the major aspects of Brenda's image-of-self-as-teacher was her calm mental state. She told how she had worked to develop this quality, to the point where she now believed herself to be a 'pretty calm person'. Brenda did not see this as merely a performance of outward calm in the face of stress, but a genuine calmness that had become a part of her, as teacher and as person. Brenda believed she had developed this calm state over many years, in part through her contact with Aboriginal people. She had become more accepting of the unanticipated. Some things happened that were unplanned and undesired, but when this happened, you 'just had to accept it and make the best of it'. In a similarly accepting fashion, Brenda spoke of taking each day as it came, appreciating the present and not being too concerned with the future. (Brenda pointed out that these attitudes are more common in Aboriginal than in white society.)

Brenda described the cognitive and biofeedback strategies she used to induce and maintain a calm state. One of the most important of these was mental preparation. Before the children arrived, she 'talked herself through slowing down ... taking things easy ... consciously acknowledging the stresses ahead' and tried to ensure she was in a calm mental state before the children arrived. When confronted with a stressful situation, Brenda said she 'reminded' herself to stay calm, but if the situation got totally out of hand and her calm state (as well as the children's) was shattered, she attempted to regain it through a strategy of moving herself and the children to a more isolated area, sitting down with them and doing some deep breathing. When a modicum of calm had been regained both for herself and the children, Brenda would speak quietly, 'talking over' the situation, before returning to the mainstream herself and allowing the children to return. (The sequence described by Brenda appeared several times in the observations.)

Brenda's calmness should not be confused with passivity, however. Brenda was alert and fast moving. She was constantly questioning, articulate and able to 'think on her feet' with unusual clarity. Observations suggested that Brenda's calmness certainly existed at a behavioural level and her words indicated that it was an important aspect of her image-of-self-as-teacher. The question remains if it was as integral a part of her person as Brenda believed it to be. At least under stressful conditions, Brenda had to work hard to maintain a calm state. She described how, at the end of a difficult day, she felt absolutely exhausted. She said: 'It feels like there's nothing left inside'.

Sense of Time

Brenda believed that from her experiences with Aboriginal people, she had developed a different attitude to time; one that had little to do with the clock. (In Hall's (1976) terms, this had been a change from 'monochronic' to 'polychronic' time.) When she first went to live in the Aboriginal community, Brenda was shocked to discover that time, as measured by the clock, meant little to Aboriginal people. Brenda would set up a meeting for a certain time, but people would show up two hours before or after the nominated time. The general atmosphere was relaxed and slow moving, and people 'took one day at a time'.

After the initial shock, Brenda began to realize how much her own life had been controlled by the clock. If she was to cope with life in this society and if she was to avoid making unreasonable demands of the children, Brenda believed she needed to adopt a similar attitude to time. So the process began, but Brenda reported that 'it took time' for her to give up the clock.

After she left the Aboriginal community and went to work in a small town, Brenda's altered sense of time still was compatible with that setting. She faced a new period of adjustment, however, when she moved back to the city. Brenda described these changes as 'having to change to one extreme and then sort of come back in again.' Despite the 'coming back in', Brenda's sense of time seemed to have retained some of the 'P-time' (Hall, 1976) qualities.

In her understanding, many things had their own time schedule and Brenda believed it was futile to try to hurry them along. For example, because of her own developmental timeline, her preservice teacher education program could achieve only so much. After the passing of time, and with some experience, she was able to say: 'Oh! So that's what they meant.' Given time, she could 'make the connections'. As a young teacher, it 'took time' for her to really grasp an understanding of children and teaching, in the broadest context, and with each new group, it had 'taken her time' to really know children and their families.

Brenda saw the changes in her sense of time as being a very positive influence on her teaching. She thought it futile and needlessly stress-producing for children and teachers to try to achieve goals related to the clock or the calendar. She pointed out that clock time meant nothing to young children. Brenda's determination not to rush children was expressed many times. For example:

> At tidy up time, if ... things are taking a long time to be tidied away and you're sort of plodding on, bit by bit, you start to get a bit frustrated inside and anxious ... that things are taking so long, but you can't push it. You've got to keep going with the children at their pace.
>
> On the mobile [kindergarten] everything had to go away. That had to be done and it had to be part of the program, that putting away ... [But] we just had to [say]: Take your time. Without sort of rush-rush-rush.

Brenda seemed particularly conscious of the changes in pace throughout the session and although she emphasized the importance of a relaxed pace, she recognized there were times when fast action was needed. She saw the early part of the session as problematic, because of its conflicting time demands. After a long bus ride, the children arrived disoriented and Brenda felt they needed time to adjust, to collect their thoughts. However, she also acknowledged that after the confinement of the bus they needed to move fairly quickly into a more active mode — but of course, 'without rushing'.

The Cognitive Aspects of Teaching

Brenda seemed particularly aware of the intense cognitive demands associated with teaching and suggested several distinct types of mental activity. As mentioned above, Brenda believed mental preparation was important, because if she was already calm and thoughtful, she did not rush into interventions, but was able to take time to consider her response before acting. Even so, Brenda acknowledged there were some situations that required immediate intervention, without time for deliberation.

On-the-spot decision making was probably the most frequently mentioned of Brenda's mental activities. She called it 'the quick think' and several subtypes were identified. One of these involved interpreting children's actions before deciding how to become involved. For example, Brenda described how some of the children's movements and verbal actions with peers looked aggressive, but really were 'just an assertive form of greeting'. She explained that her response would be different if she interpreted the behaviour as aggression, rather than an assertive greeting. Observations supported the point, as very different behaviours were seen from Brenda in these behaviourally-similar situations.

For Brenda, an important aspect of on-the-spot decision making came in children's peer conflicts, when she had to switch from attempting to facilitate the children's own resolution of the problem, to giving directions to solve it. Brenda spoke of this as specific 'point'. She described how she would try facilitative inputs for a period, before reevaluating the situation. If necessary, she would then resort to more directive strategies. Brenda described the many factors she had to weigh, in order to make that decision. She explained that the turning point had a lot to do with demands on her. Facilitating children's own resolution of a problem typically took a lot of time. Sometimes, there were other constraints, that meant the time was just not available. Another factor to be considered was the children's willingness to devote time to the process. Sometimes, they were happy to do so. At other times, they were impatient to get on with what they were doing. Finally, sometimes it just seemed the children were not making progress in resolving the problem themselves.

Another type of on-the-spot mental activity Brenda described was guessing what would happen next within a group of peers. During free play, these predictions had to be made, as Brenda decided whether to move on to another area of the room, or stay with a group of children.

This decision was especially critical at those times when Brenda was the only adult in the room.

A third type of mental activity might be labelled post-hoc thinking. After the end of the session, Brenda thought through the events that had occurred, questioning herself and sometimes doubting the wisdom of her actions. She reevaluated some of the decisions she had made on the spur of the moment and thought about how she might handle situations in the future. Reflection about the day also led to formulating plans for the next day. For example, Brenda explained how in one of these periods of reflection, she had thought about Charles, and recalled all of his problems with peers in that week. On the basis of these reflections, Brenda decided to change the nature of her interventions.

Respect for Children

Brenda spoke of children with great respect. She did not expect them to obey unquestioningly. Her emphasis on 'explaining why' she acted as she did, was a major aspect of her image-of-self-as-teacher and one that appeared many times in the observations. As well as providing children with rationales for her own actions, Brenda said she commonly asked children to verbalize the reasons they were doing something or asking for something. Brenda saw this as a way to help children elaborate their thinking. As Brenda spoke of her willingness to 'explain why', she made explicit another connection she saw, between 'explaining why' and the importance of 'talking things through'. Brenda believed that much of her own learning had come about through being given the opportunity to 'talk things through' and she valued this highly for the children. Brenda spoke of the usefulness of 'explaining why', in helping children make their own connections. For example:

> I often find with the children, they'll say: I want to do this, or I'd like to go there. And you point out a reason why this can't be done and they'll say: Oh, that's right. You see it click in their faces: Yeah, that's right. That extension is needed a lot.

In her respect for children's abilities, Brenda believed that children were quite able to accept that sometimes different rules would apply for different individuals, and understand the reasons why this was so.

Another way in which Brenda's respect was evident, was in her ready acceptance of children just as they are. Brenda did not talk about children in terms of their deficiencies or problems, but spoke positively about their actions — in the context of their lives. It seemed this contextual knowledge helped Brenda understand their sometimes less than desirable behaviour. For example, Brenda was aware that in some of the children's homes, there were no toys a child could call his/her own. For Brenda, this helped explain why these children were very rough with equipment. She continued to worked with them, to develop a more caring approach, but in the meantime expected less of them and did not become unduly upset by rough handling of equipment.

Brenda's understanding of the children in the fullest context also helped her to appreciate their achievements, without the need to measure them against some external scale. This enabled Brenda to enjoy a glow of achievement when even a small milestone was reached. Held against an external measure, the achievement might fade into insignificance, but taken in context, it gave Brenda a boost that helped her to carry on.

Brenda's respect for children and her sensitivity to their feelings was evident both in her words and actions. Some of the strategies she discussed displayed great subtlety. For example, Brenda spoke of how she encouraged children to help each other, but not before first checking that the helpee was comfortable being helped by a peer. Brenda said she gave the helpee the right to refuse help if s/he wished and pointed out that asking for help from the teacher, then having to accept it from a peer, could be two very different things for a young child. With similar sensitivity, Brenda explained that when she spoke for a child who could not manage to verbalize his/her needs to a peer, she tried to continually monitor the reactions of the child for whom she was speaking, to make sure she was saying what the child wanted her to say.

Another way in which Brenda showed her respect for children was in her willingness to be the one to change, when her perspective was at odds with the child's. For example, Brenda discussed the importance of postponing her plans in order to allow children to continue observing an insect:

> I'm happy to [set my intention aside] because that is what the child is interested in at that time ... They were still there watching and they were still interested in it. They wanted to continue on and I think that's important.

The Human Encounter

Description of the Program for Children's Social Development

Within her program for children's social development, Brenda was attempting to increase children's awareness of others' actions, ideas and feelings, and build a sense of community. Brenda explained that when she arrived in this centre, the group had seemed to be a collection of individuals who 'did their own thing', and in many cases seemed quite oblivious of their neighbours. There was a sense of paradox in Brenda's emphasis on developing a sense of community, yet at the same time operating a highly individualized program.

To help children develop an awareness of others, one of the techniques Brenda described, was a verbal interpretation of peer situations. This was used particularly with children such as William, whom Brenda believed might otherwise not understand the nuances of a social situation. Another strategy was encouragement for children to make direct positive verbal contact with peers, rather than directing messages through an adult, as the children tended to do.

Brenda's extensive knowledge of the children's social contexts enabled her to make sense of their sometimes traumatic peer interactions within the preschool. Brenda explained that when she intervened in peer conflicts, she tried to keep her intervention on a process level. Whenever possible, she wanted the children to retain ownership of the problem and its resolution.

Brenda acknowledged that she needed to intervene at times, to protect a child from peers, but this 'protective capacity' clearly was not a major aspect of her image-of-self-as-teacher. Brenda saw her involvement in children's peer interactions as a means of helping a child move along a developmental continuum. At least in part, her choice of strategy was determined by her judgment of where the individual was located on the continuum. Brenda named Gary as a child who still needed her to accompany him to a peer and speak on his behalf. Because Brenda believed that Gary currently had a limited capacity to understand social situations and little patience for involved sequences of social problem-solving, she said she used more directive inputs with him, rather than the facilitative ones used with other children.

In discussing her decision making about involvement in children's peer interactions, Brenda described a particularistic child-centered approach, rather than a matching of child behaviour with a fixed set of standard responses. For example, when discussing her response to unkind laughter (derision) between peers, Brenda claimed she did not have a 'hard policy', but took her cues from the 'victim's' response. If the victim was upset by it, as was Peter when his block building fell, she became involved. If the victim was responding to the laughter with good grace and not appearing upset, she remained uninvolved. Brenda's constant attention to monitoring children's responses was an important part of her low-rule, particularistic program approach. In such an approach, the teacher has to be very sensitive to children's responses to specific situations, and in her words and actions Brenda displayed this sensitivity.

Actions in the Preschool

Contextual Factors

Any description of Brenda's actions in the preschool could not be complete without a description of the children. Brenda described them as 'living life in the fast lane' and 'the most demanding group' she'd ever had. Amongst this group, which was a little older than other preschool groups observed, several children exhibited problem behaviour (although Brenda never labelled the children as 'behaviour problems'). William and Charles dominated the group and Gary was noteworthy because of his poor social skills with peers and general unresponsiveness to adults.

The distinctive peer behaviour between the older boys, that Brenda described as an 'assertive type of greeting', involved shouting insults at each other, making threatening gestures and engaging in apparently heated verbal exchanges. Yet despite this sometimes alarming behaviour, they rarely came to blows. (Corsaro states: '... threats ... often build solidarity within groups while at the same time generating tensions between groups' (1985, p. 277).) The older boys' play was often physically competitive — with much chasing and wrestling. Their play seemed to be a display of their fitness and daring and this added to their domination of the whole group. Brenda's time was heavily taken with these boys' often unruly behaviour, so the quieter children received less teacher attention.

Even with two staff members this was a very demanding group, but the demands were even greater during the frequent absence of the assistant. A. found it difficult to adjust to my presence and despite efforts by Brenda and myself to put her at ease, she stayed as far as possible from me. In practice, this meant that she was out of the playroom for much of the observed time. Brenda's handling of this situation provided many insights on her coping strategies, but I battled feelings of guilt and discomfort for much of my time at this centre.

The Human Encounter

Calmness and Self-control

Brenda explained that her knowledge of these children in context suggested their interests would best be served by a calm teacher, one who did not rely on loudness of voice to retain control. She wanted to model alternate ways of problem-solving and to help children with the process of working through their conflicts. Observations suggested that Brenda's actions were in keeping with these stated aims. Even though the group was sometimes in uproar, Brenda maintained a calm, steady and incredibly positive manner almost throughout.

On a few occasions, Brenda's calmness was threatened and this was evidenced initially through a change in voice. She sounded harassed, cross or even angry, and then uneven in tone. For example:

> In the block corner, tidy up time has been chaotic, with blocks being dropped, a great deal of noise and little work being done. Charles has tried Brenda's patience sorely in the last few minutes, resisting her attempts to get the blocks away. Charles kicks over a stack of blocks another child has placed ready to put away. Brenda grasps his arm and as she leads him from the area, says angrily: 'I've asked you three times to tidy away the blocks!' A few minutes later, chaos breaks out in the block corner yet again. Brenda directs the children out of the block area, and tells them to sit on a nearby mat. She sits near them and in a commanding, but uneven, voice says: 'Now, take a deep breath. Breathe in — and out — and just settle down.' Brenda also takes several deep breaths and then speaks more calmly, explaining the danger of the situation and what she wants them to do. The children return to the block area in a much calmer state and the blocks are quickly put away.

These brief lapses of calmness were rare and came only after many provocative incidents. For the most part, Brenda demonstrated enormous self-control, in some highly stressful situations. Brenda's self-control also was apparent in her ability to delay her response until she was able to observe the child's reactions to an event. For example:

> Paul is trying to link his building with Michael's. Both are finely-balanced, delicate structures that extend high above the children's heads. As Paul carefully places a block between the buildings, both structures collapse. Nearby, Brenda stands

immobile, and watches Paul closely. Time seems to stand still, then Paul smiles ruefully. Brenda smiles a little too and says softly: 'You were trying to add one block to join them and they fell.' Almost immediately, Paul begins work on the new version of his building. Brenda helps.

This incident had a special quality; a moment shared between Brenda and Paul. Although the situation was in one sense a failure, it was also a celebration of Paul's acceptance of a challenge.

Non-authoritarian Stance

In the observations, three aspects of Brenda's interaction with children suggested that she was not in any sense authoritarian: her 'soft' directives, habitually positive speech, and the very low profile accorded to rules.

In some situations Brenda made use of directives, but these usually appeared only after several non-directive strategies had been tried and failed. There were many gradations of directive in Brenda's repertoire, ranging from a very softly-worded request to a hard 'no-nonsense' order. Brenda moved through these in sequence, beginning with the softer forms. The hard phrasing was used only after the softer had failed, or in situations that Brenda interpreted as dangerous and needing quick compliance.

One of the softest directives was categorized as an 'interpretation' because the directive was only implied. For example, Brenda said[1]: 'Michael, Gary would like a turn now.' Another relatively soft phrasing might have been a request: 'Michael, could you please give Gary a turn now?' A phrasing that seemed to be in the middle of the range was Brenda's expression of personal desire, for example, 'I'd like you to give Gary a turn now, please.' Brenda's way of hardening these directives was to drop the 'please' and add at the beginning, a flag such as: '*Right*. I'd like you to give Gary a turn,' or: '*Right*. Could you give Gary the hose now?' The hardest phrasing observed by Brenda was a blunt 'Stop', but as mentioned above, concise orders were rare.

Many times, children complied with Brenda's directives even though they were very softly phrased, but on occasion they did not. When Brenda was determined to gain compliance, she moved quickly from soft to hard and by the time the 'Rights' appeared at the beginning of her statements, the children generally complied. It should be pointed out, however, that on a few occasions, Brenda avoided an ultimate confrontation, pursuing a request some distance, before backing away. In a discussion of one such incident, in which she had accepted Michael's non-compliance with her direction to return a wig to home corner, Brenda identified two salient aspects of the situation. Firstly, she said she was unsure of her position, because she had not seen who had actually brought the wig from home corner. Secondly, when it became clear that her persistence would lead to an escalation of the confrontation, she hesitated, because of her knowledge of Michael. This child's family was in turmoil and Brenda believed he was under immense pressure at home. She said she had no desire to add to his stress level at this time.

Brenda's non-authoritarian stance also was reflected in her speech, which was characterized by habitual use of positive statements. This was evident across every area of Brenda's interaction. Some examples:

- When Charles tries to balance standing on two blocks, Brenda says, 'Blocks are for building, Charles.'

- When Marian and Valerie are struggling for possession of a piece of paper, Brenda says, 'This is Valerie's, Marian. Yours is at the easel.'

- When William turns on the tap as Barry is carrying the end of the hose to the sandpit, Brenda says, 'When Barry is at the sandpit, you can turn it on, William.'

On only one occasion was Brenda observed to voice a negative statement and even this was added to the end of a positive remark: After telling three boys repeatedly and positively, that she would like them to steer their cart *around* the equipment, Brenda says in exasperation, 'Go around the equipment please. Not through it!'

Resolving Peer Conflict

The most noteworthy aspect of peer conflicts in this centre was their sheer frequency, with the block corner being the most common site for conflict during indoor play. Conflicts usually began soon after the arrival of the children and continued throughout the session. For example, Carl arrived on the first bus and often was already at work in the block area when Charles arrived on the second bus. Typically, Charles rushed through the door straight to the block corner, where his first act was a provocative one, such as flicking Carl in the face with his gloves. Sometimes, this 'assertive greeting' was accepted as such by the boys already in the block area, but on other occasions, it marked the beginning of peer conflict for the day. When Brenda judged an interaction to be mock-conflict, she usually opted for a quick distraction strategy, to move the children's attention back to the task at hand. Typically, Brenda's distraction was simply to comment on the block building or ask a question about the children's play.

Another noteworthy aspect of conflict events was the amount of time Brenda devoted to them. Many of these events involved prolonged sequences of interaction, sometimes lasting four or five minutes. Brenda's willingness to remain in the conflict situations for such a protracted time, often at the cost of her involvement elsewhere, reflected the high priority she accorded children's learning of conflict resolution skills. On a few occasions, Brenda demonstrated she could end conflicts promptly, with a swift application of a distraction or ruling on the situation, but these strategies were rarely used.

In talking of her involvement in children's peer conflicts, Brenda saw a clear distinction between the so-called facilitative strategies, where she wanted children to retain ownership of the problem resolution and the directive ones, where she ended it herself. Some of Brenda's actions could readily be categorized as 'facilitative'. For example, Brenda often prompted one child to make direct communication with a peer:

- When William snatches a block from Michael's structure, saying that he needs it, Brenda says, 'Yes, but Michael and Paul were using these blocks, so before you just take one, ask them first.'

If a child was reticent about contacting a peer, Brenda would accompany the child while the contact was made:

- Dianne complains that Cathy won't give her more paint. As Brenda accompanies Dianne back to the fingerpaint table she says, 'You can ask Cathy to share if you'd like some. She mightn't know that you'd like some more.'

When a child appeared unable to communicate a need to a peer, Brenda would assist:

- Gary mutters to Brenda that the others won't give him any water. When he fails to respond to Brenda's prompt to ask

Lyle to fill his container from the hose, Brenda says, 'Lyle, Gary would like some water in his can, please.'

When Brenda raised a possible solution, she stood back to see if the children would accept it. If they did not, she would restate the idea or raise another possibility. The acceptance or rejection of solutions was largely in the children's hands, at least through several cycles of this process.

Brenda's use of questions was particularly interesting. Although answers to some questions provided Brenda with information, many of her questions seemed designed solely to focus children's attention on a problem or possible solution. For example:

- When children squabble over placing another chair at a table, Brenda asks, 'Is there room for another? Where will it go?'

- When several girls argue over roles in a dramatic play scene involving a 'train', Brenda asks, 'Who is collecting the tickets?'

- When Paul and Charles try to carry their long chain of plastic manipulatives, but fail to include Michael, who also had helped with the construction, Brenda asks, 'Do you think two people will be enough?' (And later suggests Michael could help.)

An interesting aspect of Brenda's questions and interpretive statements concerned their variation across a range of neutrality. Judging the neutrality of a question or statement often was problematical. For example:

- When Charles takes a car that William has been using, Brenda says, 'He took your car.'

This could be considered a neutral behaviour description, but Brenda's utterance of it suggested at least an element of support for William's case.

- When Gary knocks William's building down, Brenda says to Gary, 'He's very sad you smashed it down.'

This interpretation contained a subtle apportioning of blame. Brenda's use of the emotive and intentional word 'smashed' rather than a more neutral 'knocked' or even 'bumped,' which might have suggested the possibility of accident, was telling.

These certainly could be considered 'facilitative' strategies when a neutral position was maintained, but often the questions and interpretations contained an arbitrary element that subtly communicated the teacher's favouring of one point of view. It seemed extremely difficult for the teacher to maintain a strictly neutral stance in these conflicts. Brenda, like the rest of us, had no divine gift of impartiality. Although she strived to be non-judgmental, she had to 'call them as she saw them', and often a statement by Brenda had to display only a hint of her favouring one claim over another for children to act upon it. The teacher's support (or lack of it) seemed to hold great weight for at least some of the children.

When Brenda's long conflict resolution sequences were plotted in terms of facilitative and directive strategies, there was indeed an overall pattern of repeated facilitative strategies, followed by more directive ones, but in between there was a good deal of recycling between neutral and arbitrary variations of questions and interpretations. This suggested Brenda's turning point between facilitative and directive inputs may not have been quite as clear cut as her words suggested.

It was interesting to note the importance of individuals in Brenda's selection of some strategies. For example, of all the conflicts plotted, only three times did the process end with Brenda physically removing a child, and in each case the child was Charles. With William, another interesting pattern emerged. Brenda usually began with scrupulous neutrality, but in the face of William's persistent non-cooperation this was difficult to maintain. For example:

> Charles and Jason are together in the block corner, and William is working nearby, when a noisy dispute arises over ownership of certain blocks. William calls to Brenda, saying the others will not give him any blocks. Charles and William are shouting angrily at each other as Brenda arrives and questions the boys about the situation. After ascertaining that William has taken blocks from Charles and Jason's stockpile, Brenda makes arbitrary remarks in support of Charles and Jason's position, such as 'Charles and Jason need those blocks over there,' and 'You might have to think of a different way of making your building, William, if they are using all of the small

blocks.' William refuses to accept any of her points and in slow motion drops a block lightly on his foot, then howls in full voice with shuddering sobs and wracking cough. For several more interchanges, Brenda retains her pro-Charles and Jason stance, as she tries to console William, but he continues to make an inordinate amount of noise. At this point, Brenda alters her stance and asks, 'Charles, do you need *all* of those blocks? ... Can William use a few of them?' As soon as Brenda switches her arbitrary statements to favour William, the other boys surrender their case. Immediately, William stops crying and Brenda thanks the boys for sharing.

Concerns could be raised about the morality of the strategies in this event, but in the context of the classroom at that time, survival was the issue. Brenda was needed elsewhere, she had already devoted a great deal of time to this peer conflict, William was intransigent and of course, Charles and Jason *did* have a large number of blocks stockpiled.

When all else failed, Brenda finally resorted to strategies that clearly were directive, such as rulings, directions for an action, or physical removal of a child from the scene. Of the twelve times these strategies were observed in peer conflicts, only once did Brenda then recycle to more facilitative or arbitrary strategies. When Brenda used a directive strategy, the end of the conflict resolution process was at hand.

Rules

In the interviews, Brenda said she preferred to place individualized limits on children rather than rules for all and this was borne out in the observations. There were some group rules related to safety issues but Brenda typically made only oblique reference to them. For example:

- When Gary waves the hose through the air, Brenda says: 'Gary, can you keep the water in the sandpit, please?'
- When a child throws sand, Brenda asks a focusing question: 'What happens when you throw sand?'

Typically, Brenda explained the reasons for behaving in a desirable way, rather than focusing on compliance with a rule. For example, she explained at some length why running inside was dangerous.

An interesting exception was the 'Three-Block Rule'. Brenda instigated it 'on the spur of the moment', at tidy-up time on a 'bad day'. There had been recurring trouble in the block corner, with children carelessly carrying large loads of blocks and dropping them on other people's toes. Brenda already had been called in several times and later described her motivation for instigating the rule as 'wanting to save myself these dramas.' When Brenda had to enter the block area yet again, she called the children together and explained the dangers of carrying large loads of blocks. She told them that three was the most they could carry with safety. Later, when children took larger loads, Brenda reminded them of the rule, though still in rather oblique ways. For example, she asked: 'Why did I ask you to take three? There was a reason? How many is three?'

In the following few days the rule made many reappearances, sometimes as a straight forward statement: 'Remember we are only carrying three, in case someone gets hurt.' After fourteen days, Brenda was reminding children of the rule only when the situation looked threatening. At other times, she largely ignored children carrying more than three blocks.

Brenda later described how she reflected on this rule and came to realize that it was overly simple for a complex situation. It did not take into account the size of the blocks carried, the ability of individuals to carry large loads, the destination of the load, space around the block shelves, or the mood of the individual. It created other problems too, because Brenda felt bound by it and found limiting her own load to three blocks was a serious impediment to the progress of tidying up.

The final demise of the rule came shortly after my observations finished, but Brenda described the scene. It was 'a good day, a calm day, when the children were able to sit and listen'. Brenda and William had been discussing the safety of a large load of blocks stacked on a toy truck, when another child pointed out to Brenda that really, he could carry five blocks quite safely. A general discussion on block safety ensued and this led to a decision to drop the 'three-block rule'. Brenda said she was pleased to see the rule go, as there were times she had regretted instigating it, but in typically positive fashion did not berate herself for an error of judgment.

Developing a Sense of Community

Brenda's emphasis on helping children become more aware of the shared nature of their social experience within the preschool was evident in several major areas of her interaction. For example, she frequently drew children's attention to the social dimension of their actions:

- Stephen and Martin are taking turns at setting in motion a line of blocks arranged in a domino pattern. Brenda says, 'You built this together and now you're taking turns.' When Stephen works beside Paul at the Lego, Brenda says, 'You've been sharing this with Paul, have you?'

In trying to develop a sense of community, Brenda often encountered the dilemma of trying to balance conflicting needs of individuals and the group. For example:

- When William has some (unusual) success with a Mobilo construction, he wants to leave it intact, but others need to utilize the component pieces. Brenda compromises by allowing William to keep the construction intact for a few minutes, then insists the pieces are returned to the box for the use of others.

As mentioned earlier, the dilemma also occurred as Brenda recognized not only Charles's need to work through problems in his interactions with peers, but also the threat his behaviour represented to others. By the final day of observations, Brenda judged that the risk to other children was simply too great and began to remove Charles from the group at the first sign of trouble.

Brenda's dilemma in balancing the rights and needs of one individual with another frequently appeared when a child offered help to a peer and was rejected. This was a common event with the older boys and it suggested that they might have seen acceptance of peer help as incompatible with their bravado. If a would-be helper was rejected, Brenda usually suggested another location where the willing child could help, but if this offer also was refused, Brenda would support the willing child with an interpretive (arbitrary) remark. With this added pressure, the helpee usually conceded.

In many ways, Brenda tried to imbue in children a sense that this was a shared physical environment, where one had to act with concern for others. For example:

- Brenda explains that cars and blocks are not to be used out in the traffic way, where other children could trip.
- When Carl builds an obstacle course from outdoor blocks,

Brenda points out that it is too close to the shed door and could be a nuisance to others trying to get into the shed.

Frequently, Brenda ensured that individual achievements were brought to the attention of other children. For example:

- Brenda escorts a small group of children (including Michael) to the block area, to admire Paul's recently completed building. Brenda gives quite lavish praise, and after consideration, Michael pronounces sincerely, 'Yes, I *like* it.'
- When Charles makes some (rare) achievements with a matching game, Brenda quietly brings this to the attention of several other children saying: 'Charles has been doing this difficult puzzle, where he has to match shapes and sizes. Charles has matched all the balls.'

Brenda tried to make children more aware of other's perspectives through the use of focusing questions and interpretive statements, but statements referring to other's feelings were less common. When a child failed to treat with due respect, the achievements of another, Brenda sometimes responded with a series of statements that might be termed a 'shaming trilogy'. These statements highlighted how hard the other child had worked, how special the object was to her/him and how hurt her/his feelings were. An example:

- Charles has just knocked down Carl and William's cubby house and William is crying. Brenda arrives on the scene and says to Charles, 'Carl and William have worked very hard making this special cubby house. William's really sad about what you've done.'

When children approached Brenda with tales to tell against other children, Brenda listened to the story. Sometimes, this was the means by which she entered peer disputes, but at other times, Brenda downplayed the complaint. For example:

- Martin approaches Brenda and points to his face as he says, 'Look what Paul done!' Brenda says, 'Mmmm. Purple paint. It will wash off.' Martin still looks very angry and Brenda asks, 'Did that upset you, Martin? Didn't you want paint on your face?' Martin says, 'No', and runs off.

The Human Encounter

An interesting way in which Brenda tried to develop a sense of community was to disclose some of her personal life to the children and to emphasize the personal dimension in other events. Some examples:

- As she introduces some new Aboriginal artifacts, Brenda focuses not on the items themselves, but the craftsman who made them. She reminds the children they have met him several months before and talks about who he is, his family connections and where he is from.

- As Brenda chats to several boys building trucks with Lego, she talks about her husband and his truck. She tells them about getting a new tyre for her car and complains about how much it cost. (The conversational quality was such that a mother passing by joined in with a complaint about the cost of her new tyres.)

Helping Children Gain Access to Peer Play Groups

Brenda had very little involvement in this area, perhaps because so much of her time was given to the pressing demands of peer conflicts. One of the few examples observed, was an incident in which Brenda helped Gary gain access to play group of the older boys:

- Most children have gone into the adjoining room for music with D., but a group of older boys have stayed behind to pack away the blocks. Brenda moves between both rooms. On one trip to check on the progress of the boys, Brenda is accompanied by Gary. She says to the blockpackers, 'Gary has come to help. Is there something special he can do?' Within a few moments, Gary has been accepted into the group.

This brief interaction displayed many of Brenda's skills. Had Gary ventured into that situation without her support, he may well have been refused access. Gary rarely spoke (although his speech was quite understandable) and it seems unlikely that he could have talked his way into the group of bigger boys. Brenda didn't ask, 'Can Gary help?' which would have given the others an opportunity to refuse.

Instead, she used the very positive statement, 'Gary has come to help', that made it clear she was in favour of his helping. Then, she put the ball back in the boys' court by asking them to decide how he might be useful. Given that recognition, they soon found a job that he could do.

Although Brenda had only moments in which to select these words, they reflected her commitment to facilitating children's social contacts without taking away their ownership of the interaction, and her awareness of these children's penchant for refusing help. This event seemed to evidence that blend of examined and spontaneous elements, that together compromise teacher action. Brenda had a set of general guiding principles, and an ability to read and respond to a particular social situation with great sensitivity.

Environmental Support of Peer Interaction

Brenda's use of the environment to support peer interaction was more curative than preventative in nature. The arrangement of the indoor environment was not particularly supportive of harmonious peer interaction. For example, the positioning of the block area next to a major traffic way created situations where Brenda had to intervene to ensure separation or children with incompatible needs. But Brenda often suggested environmental solutions (such as creating greater space between children, or drawing attention to other materials) when children were in conflict.

Outdoors, the scarcity of equipment seemed to be working against harmonious peer interactions. The chasing, wrestling, provocative behaviour of the boys might have been lessened had there been a wider choice of challenging things to do. Even so, Brenda found ways to accommodate activities that sometimes are banned in preschools. For example:

- When Marian squirts water at other children, Brenda suggests she should leave the sandpit and squirt water at the garden. Marian seems happy to comply, and the squirting continues where it will not bother others.

- When Charles makes balls of wet sand and throws these very close to others, Brenda suggests he move to where there are no other children nearby. He does so and continues to make and harmlessly throw sand balls against the rear wall of the sandpit.

The Human Encounter

Involvement in Children's Dramatic Play

Brenda seldom became involved in children's play, apart from those occasions when she was needed to help resolve a problem. One example:

> Roslyn, Gary and several other children are playing roughly with the hand puppets. Brenda enters the play, saying sadly, 'Poor Platypus [puppet], lying on the floor.' Roslyn says cheerfully, 'They're dead!' Brenda responds, 'Dead?! How did they die?' Roslyn replies, 'They fell off the stage.' Brenda suggests, 'Oh, poor things. Do you think you could take them somewhere and fix them up?' Brenda continues to use the puppets' needs to promote more careful handling, but it is to no avail. Finally, Brenda abandons this strategy and explains in a straightforward way that the puppets should be handled carefully.

Concluding Remarks

Brenda was an introspective young woman, who had thought deeply about her place in children's lives and the paths she had taken in her personal and professional development. Participation in the study was welcomed by Brenda as a chance to further this introspective process. She found it interesting to reflect on her development and ponder the origins of some of her present-day beliefs and actions. Brenda said this opportunity had helped in 'reviewing and thinking about how she approached different things.' Brenda believed that from the time of our initial meeting, some four months before observations began, she had been more aware of the social dimension of her teaching and expected that this would continue into the future.

Brenda's high level of self-awareness extended to scrutiny of her everyday teaching. She told of spending time at the end of each day, thinking over what had happened and reevaluating her actions. It seemed there was nothing in the observation transcripts that took Brenda by surprise, though, as described in Chapter 2, she sometimes felt the observation transcripts did not fully convey her emotional state in highly stressful events.

Brenda's actions in the classroom were very much in keeping with the statement of beliefs and the descriptions provided in the interview sessions. Part of the sense of coherency may have been related to the flexibility Brenda seemed to exhibit in her image-of-self-as-teacher.

This enabled her to accommodate with ease, actions that might otherwise have appeared as inconsistencies. Brenda seemed to have incorporated her survival-based actions into her image-of-self-as-teacher, as well as her ideals. As Brenda spoke of the times she acted from a survival base, she did so without regret or apology. It apparently was a matter-of-fact issue for her, that sometimes things happened, and she just had to deal with them as best she could. If she felt her actions were not always as wise as they might have been, then that also was a situation that could only be accepted.

As Brenda described the connections that she saw between herself as person and as teacher, it was clear that these connections themselves formed an acknowledged, integrated part of Brenda's image-of-self-as-teacher. As she read through the observations with me and we talked about them, she sometimes became excited as she saw new connections. I shared that excitement, as the many connections between person and teacher were surfaced.

The stress that existed in the periods when Brenda was without adult help, was a tangible element of this classroom. It could not be said that this was a normal situation, yet in a paradoxical way, the situation seemed to bring us together. We both struggled through those times; Brenda trying to maintain her inner calm and me feeling guilty for having brought so much stress to bear on her.

To adopt a little of Brenda's philosophy myself; this stressful element of the situation would not have been my choice, but it was not within my power to change. Therefore, my only course was to accept and appreciate that this situation also had something positive to offer in my coming to know Brenda. As Moustakas has said:

> To know what it means to be ... a teacher, or any of the other labels we attach to men, we must know the person as an integrated human being, through his own perception, his desires, hopes and fears, his beliefs and his values. We must know him in the real places of his living — in the hours when he sits alone, defeated and in despair; in the days when he knows vitality, excitement, and beauty ... (1968, p. 7)

Note

1 Note that only the first of these statements was actually observed verbatim. The others have been concocted to illustrate other of observed forms directives.

Chapter 6

Kathy

The Setting

Kathy's Preschool

This was a very well established centre, located in a quiet cul de sac in a middle-class suburb. Although older than most, the building was not unlike other Australian preschools, with a large playroom opening onto a wide covered patio. Careful maintenance had kept the centre in good order and only a few clues such as old-fashioned home corner furniture and light fittings attested to its age.

The most noteworthy feature of the preschool was the large, aesthetically pleasing playground, lush with shade trees and flowering shrubs. Kathy was a keen gardener and took great pride in her preschool garden. The beauty of the environment was not lost on visitors. A mother who came to enrol her child wandered in awe through the playground, then commented, 'This place is like a magic garden'.

The centre offered a full day program from 9:00 a.m. to 2:30 p.m. In the three-day group (in which observations were carried out) there were twenty-five children aged 4.9 to 6.0 years. (Several of the older children had been eligible to begin school this year, but their parents opted to keep them at preschool.)

During the observation period, which concluded one month before the end of the school year, substantial differences in timetable and program were observed. During the first week, Kathy began the program with a group session, then directed children to complete certain activities, before offering children a wider choice. Kathy explained that previously the children had been allowed free access to both indoor and outdoor areas throughout the session, but the routine had been changed to accustom children to the demands of formal schooling, which they would be entering in the new year. During the period of observations, however, the timetable gradually reverted to the earlier pattern, with children having virtually unlimited access to both indoor and outdoor areas for the entire morning. The timetable that follows is indicative of this freeplay indoor-outdoor program.

9:00	Arrival.
9:00 — 11:10	Free play time.
11:10 — 11:30	Whole group time (roll marking, news, usually music).
11:30 — 11:45	Morning tea.
11:45 — 12:40	Free play time.
12:40 — 1:00	Tidy-up time.
1:00 — 1:25	Whole group time (usually language).
1:25 — 1:55	Lunch.
1:55 — 2:15	Rest.
2:15 — 2:30	Departures.

In several ways, this was an unusual program. The length of the first period of free play time was noteworthy and the lateness of lunch (and consequent short rest time) was another distinctive feature. Rituals were unusually important in this centre. For example, the checking of the roll was a ceremony marked by an unchanging sequence of actions including the ringing of a handbell, the carrying of the rollbook and the relaying of numbers to the mother on roster in the kitchen.

Children, Families, Assistant

The mother roster was able to function well because none of the mothers were engaged in full-time paid employment, although almost half did some part-time work. Only one child needed regular substitute care and this was provided by a grandmother. Kathy described the clients as 'normal average' families, with only two children living in single parent households. The fathers' occupations included sales representative, clerk, civil servant (government employee), company manager and medical practitioner.

Kathy was assisted by A., a mature-age mother who had been the assistant at the centre for five years. She had completed a certificate course as a teacher's aide several years earlier.

The Teacher

Kathy was approximately 43 years of age, tall with a trim figure and always immaculately dressed. Kathy often looked pale and tired, and although she was observed to move swiftly in emergencies, Kathy's usual pace was unhurried.

Kathy did not initiate a lot of affectionate physical contacts with children, but responded warmly when a child approached her. There were few hugs, but several instances when Kathy held children's hands gently, or put her arm around a child as she spoke. Kathy made some use of controlling physical contacts, such as firmly holding a child's hand or arm to prevent the child running away or physically leading a child to a different location.

For the most part, Kathy spoke softly and slowly, often with a dreamy quality in her voice; an impression enhanced by Kathy's frequent use of generic terms such as 'love', 'darling', or 'dear' rather than children's names. Yet Kathy also was able to convey her disapproval in a firm no-nonsense tone. A common form of address heard in this context was 'm'boy'. Some examples:

- Adrian is angry after a dispute with another child. He glares and mutters as he leaves the sandpit: 'I'm ready for war.' Kathy matches his tone: 'And I'm ready for war too, m'boy!'
- When Aaron fails to collect the buckets as asked, Kathy says: 'My patience is wearing a bit thin with you, m'boy'.

At other times, Kathy's messages to children could be rather ambiguous. For example:

- Kathy has ruled that the large blocks cannot be used today. When she refuses Conrad and Lyle's request for them, Kathy says: 'I'm sorry. We are all inside today and I can't hear myself think.' After she leaves the scene, Conrad asks Lyle: 'Why can't we use them?' Lyle responds: 'I don't know.' Neither child asks Kathy for clarification.

The Human Encounter

Kathy's speech sometimes underwent rapid change as she moved from one child to another, in some cases as she moved from girls to boys. As the girls generally were more cooperative in completing assigned tasks, Kathy often was positive in her responses to them. The boys were less compliant and they were usually the recipients of the 'no-nonsense' tone. For example:

> Kathy is visiting the easels, where the children are to create 'gum trees'. Marian's mother is presiding. As Kathy arrives, she says to the mother in a loud voice: 'Mrs. M., these boys are not to leave here until they've done really good work. Some of them are . . .' Charles interrupts: 'This is a shady one.' Kathy frowns and says: 'I'm coming around to see your work. It's got to be nice and grown-up and sensible.' As Kathy moves past Marian's easel, Marian says: 'Look at my tree.' Kathy looks at Marian's work and smiles as she says warmly: 'Ohhhh, you've used the tissue, Marian. Oh, that's lovely.' Kathy talks to Marian about gum trees, then looks at the paint pots and asks in a changed tone of voice: 'Boys, are you putting these back in the right containers?' This pattern continues for some time, until Kathy leaves the area.

In short, whilst some aspects of Kathy's teaching work were difficult for the observer to fully comprehend, what was clear was the impression that this was a teacher who was tired and experiencing some difficulty in teaching.

Image-of-Self-as-Teacher

As described in Chapter 2, Kathy's teaching was under considerable stress at the time of the observations — a situation she described as 'being burned-out'. The circumstances surrounding Kathy's participation suggest that the interview data should be treated with some scepticism. Kathy appeared to be in an emotionally fragile state and used a variety of verbal strategies to avoid responding to some areas of probing questions. In the face of these responses, some questions were abandoned, or left in an unresolved state at the end of the interviews.

Kathy usually was guarded in her comments when the tape recorder was running. She was careful not to mention children, parents or the assistant by name. For example, the assistant was sometimes referred to in the plural as 'they', and Adrian was 'that fellow'. During the third interview, Kathy looked particularly pale, with dark circles under her eyes. She told me she was 'just counting the days until the end of term'. Although Kathy made no mention of any additional personal distress at that time, later that week it emerged that on the day of the interview she had been extremely concerned about a friend's son who had been injured in an accident. Perhaps because of her distress, Kathy seemed less guarded in this interview. Her remarks were much closer to those heard off-tape on other occasions.

Kathy came to the first conversation session not having read any of the observation transcripts. At the time of our final meeting, she still had read only first day's observations, so our discussion of specific incidents was sparse. On the basis of that one day, however, Kathy expressed considerable dissatisfaction with her actions.

For Kathy, the dominating issues of the moment were her unhappy relationships with the assistant, the 'problem' children and their parents. These issues recurred many times and at the end of the interviews, I knew a great deal about Kathy's perceptions of these problems, but little about other areas of her image-of-self-as-teacher. The emotional power of Kathy's accounts were in keeping with Ball and Goodson's statement: 'The psychological stress and the critical significance of these experiences (with students) are clear in the symbolic power and delivery of the stories the teachers tell' (1985, p. 17).

General Description: Confusion or Ambivalence?

The most pervasive impression as Kathy spoke of her beliefs about teaching, was her confusion or ambivalence. At the end of five interview sessions, the image-of-self-as-teacher that Kathy presented remained a shadowy outline. At times, strong statements emerged from Kathy's bland commentary, but she often retracted these statements or softened them in successive remarks. Frequently, it was impossible to tell whether Kathy's thinking was confused, or whether it was only the communication of complex ideas that suggested confusion.

Occasionally, Kathy's voice would fade into silence as she put an opposing view to an earlier position, but for the most part she gave no sign that she was aware of contradictions in her statements. Kathy often gave multiple positions on a single issue, though not in a way that suggested an awareness of paradox. She did not claim that apparently opposing statements were falsely dichotomized positions; that the difference was no difference. She simply stated she believed one thing, then, soon after, another.

One of the major areas in which this confusion or ambivalence was evident was in the complex issue of Kathy's principles about what was right for children, in the face of increased societal demands for early achievement. This arose many times in discussion and Kathy took several positions in relation to it. For example, Kathy said that she was forced by parents and societal demands to place pressure on children. In this mode, she said this 'went against her grain', and she regretted the loss of power to follow her own principles. Given her choice, the preschool would be a 'haven of rest, rather than [have] this tremendous urge to achieve.' At other times, Kathy's statements suggested a willingness to adjust her principles to meet these external pressures. For example:

> Lifestyles have changed a bit today and we have to move with it and give a bit.

> It's so much more pleasant and positive to take the other tack, but maybe this is part of a change in society too.

> It's so much more positive to do it the other way, but I mean, I just think you have to accept life as it is.

A related strand running through Kathy's statements was a belief in 'moving with the times':

> I think you have to grow with changes and I just hope that I'm not harking back to the old days when life was probably different. I hope I've been able to accept the different expectations of people. I feel I've had to bend a little, to reach their expectations.

Yet in the same interview, Kathy said she was holding out for her beliefs; that her methods of allowing children freedom were at least as successful as the 'pencil and paper stuff' the parents were demanding.

A third position was suggested, when Kathy stated that children today often had to be coerced into worthwhile activity. At least some of Kathy's statements seemed to suggest that her beliefs, as well as actions, had been influenced by societal demands for increased pressure on children. When this possibility was raised for her comment, Kathy disagreed, returning to the earlier position that her beliefs had not altered, and her changed behaviour with children was 'being forced ... by the parents'. Kathy went on to give a justification for this increased pressure in terms of the children themselves; their lack of self-discipline; their unwillingness to apply themselves to learning tasks.

The interviewer also was left with an unclear picture of Kathy's relationships with and feelings towards parents. At times, Kathy spoke glowingly of the parents, how appreciative they were, how cooperative, how 'normal'. On other occasions she was less positive. Frequently, Kathy spoke of her 'professional relationship' with parents. The need for 'maintaining professional distance' was emphasized and she was critical of the assistant for relating to parents at a 'chit chatty' level and using their first names. Kathy said 'the whole standard of the place fell' when this happened. She was careful to honour the no-first-name rule between staff members and with parents, even though she enjoyed very long standing and personal relationships with some families. She had lived in this neighbourhood virtually all her life and had known many of these people for decades. Several of the current families were her neighbours and others attended the same church. Kathy had several close friends who now happened to be parents in the preschool. None of these personal relationships were evident as Kathy maintained 'professional distance' in her day-to-day interactions with parents and only in the final interview did Kathy acknowledge that more personal links existed with some families.

Biographical Aspect

Kathy was the elder of two children. She went to local schools, then enrolled in University to study an applied science. But Kathy did not enjoy the course and after one year transferred to the Kindergarten Teachers College. Kathy had not had a lot of experience with young children and, in retrospect, could recall no particular reason for her choice. She said it was just a 'stab in the dark', and it had 'appealed at the time'.

The three years Kathy spent at the college were remembered as happy ones. For Kathy, one of the best things about the college experience was the many friends she made. She also enjoyed the practice teaching and some of the practical classes in music and art. Kathy did not recall the theoretical subjects as having particular value, except for child development, which was 'a revelation'. However, she said the college program had done the best it could in preparing her for teaching:

The Human Encounter

> I think you have to develop as a person yourself. You can't rely on the college to make you a whole person ... They have to equip you for the job you're going into — but it's more than just a job. You have to equip yourself for other situations; the tangents.

After graduating in the mid-sixties, Kathy worked for several years in a large early childhood centre, a very supportive professional environment, before spending several years teaching nursery school in London. This experience with West Indian families, in an economically depressed part of the city, was still a vivid memory for Kathy. She spoke at length of the 'deprivation' and the poor physical conditions under which she taught. Kathy described her program as 'not so much educating, as compensating', but she valued this experience highly.

On her return to Australia, Kathy spent a short time teaching in a country town, before returning to the city, where she accepted her present teaching position. During the fifteen years in which Kathy had been the only teacher in this centre, she seemed to have suffered some ill effects from professional isolation. (Measor, 1985, has written of the ill effects that result through some teachers' non-involvement with peers. She believes this isolation can lead to feelings of insecurity, status panic and promote a form of alienation called self-estrangement in which meaningful connections between the worker and work are lost.)

Unlike Nan, parent contacts had not been a stimulus for Kathy's development. Further, her belief in a strictly superior-subordinate relationship with her assistant did not allow the emergence of a professionally stimulating dialogue. Kathy joked in a self-derogatory way, about her lack of inspiration and lack of mentors. She said she couldn't think of any person who had influenced her teaching and although naming three professional libraries to which she had access, said she didn't use of any of them. Over a considerable period of time, Kathy had initiated little in terms of her professional development, yet, as she discussed this, only once acknowledged that her own development might have stalled. She said pensively: '... maybe I'm in a contented rut. And the record just keeps going round and round.' Characteristically, immediately afterwards Kathy retracted this statement, saying: 'I'm not *really* in a rut.'

It was difficult for Kathy to talk about her development as a teacher, perhaps because the extraordinary pressures of the present year overpowered her ability to reflect on her development over the previous twenty years. She said she might be more confident and perhaps more understanding than she was as a younger teacher, but went on to describe how she was less positive and tolerant now. She said there had been 'no great milestones along the way' and finally concluded, without conviction, that she supposed she was 'still the same old being' as she had always been.

Self-concept

Kathy's self-referencing statements consistently suggested a poor self-concept. The interviews were punctuated with remarks about her participation in the study such as: 'Am I your problem child?'; 'I doubt I'll be any use to you.'; 'You have to listen to this interview again? What a drag.'; 'I'm not being very good here, am I?'

Kathy was critical of herself on many levels. For example:

> I'm a bitty sort of person. No inspiration. (off-tape)
>
> Do you suppose I haven't got any inspiration at all? Just a robot walking around?
>
> Doing further study must be wonderful for a teacher, but I couldn't do it. No motivation. (off-tape)

Many of Kathy's statements about self suggested she was being taken advantage of by others. For example: 'I'm the sort of person who doesn't delegate a lot of duties ... and sometimes I take on more than ... I should, and sometimes people are quite happy for you to keep going.'

Kathy was critical of the assistant's competence, and said A.'s lack of attention to supervision meant she (Kathy) was not able to sit with a few children without having to worry about the remainder of the group. Kathy said she had to deny herself 'the pleasure of working with small groups, this whole year'. A little earlier, she had said: 'It is just so frustrating, to have to sacrifice everything like that, because she likes to sit down and sew and do carpentry and things like that.'

Often, Kathy's words were tinged with a sense of powerlessness and frustration. When Kathy described the effects on her own development of this very difficult year, she spoke with bitterness and irony. She said:

> I've learnt. I'm just very accepting ... too accepting, but once I've been ridden over ...

> I've just learnt so much this year. I've grown ten feet this year. I'll have a completely different attitude next year as far as (*sigh*) being a softie. I'll just have to brace myself ... I'll be strictly professional next year and I will play by the rules and not be as flexible as I have been.

Although Kathy described herself as 'a softie', someone that others 'took advantage of', this did not fit well with other comments suggesting Kathy had a clear sense of the power of her leadership position. For example, Kathy said she expected parents to be interested in and helpful towards her efforts with children. In describing the parents she worked with in London's East End, she praised them and said they had been 'very appreciative for all that was being done for them.' Kathy also expected children to be appreciative and obedient. For example:

> Next year [at school], I don't think [the children] are going to be cajoled to, asked three or six times to do something.
>
> I can't think of any reason to say: Lovey-dovey-darling, how about carrying this over here?
>
> How can I enjoy undisciplined children?

From the assistant, Kathy also expected acknowledgement of her position and was critical when A. did not give her the respect to which she believed she was entitled.

The third major area that emerged in Kathy's self-referencing statements was her perception of self as being burned-out. But this state was not perceived as being all-encompassing. Kathy limited it to the three-day group in the present year and did not expect any lasting effects once the 'problem group' of children had gone. Kathy made several statements indicating the difference she saw in the quality of her life between the three-day and two-day groups: 'I'm in a sane state on Thursday and Friday.'; 'We just say, "Vacation time!" on Thursday and Friday.'

Kathy made brief reference to the satisfaction she gained from watching children develop and pleasure she felt in interacting with parents, but it was the holidays from teaching that Kathy identified as most important to her perseverance. They 'revived' and 'refreshed' and the long summer holiday each year was a 'major plus of the job'. Kathy debated with herself whether she still found enjoyment in teaching, but reached no firm conclusion. There was no doubt, however, that her teaching of the three-day group currently was not a source of joy.

Some of Kathy's statements on her burned-out state used powerful metaphors (although typically, she tended to retract these immediately afterward). Some examples:

> It's been like a dripping tap. I've just been worn down through the year.

> There's just no let up, no faith. So you steel yourself to carry on.

> Sometimes I think I'd just love to be bashing away at an inanimate object, like a typewriter, and just cut off from the rest of the world ... You interact so much with human beings and ... that's why you appreciate so much, the breaks that you get.

> I'm at such a low ebb now. In another situation, I'd be completely different in the way I deal with situations ... I just feel at the moment there is so much bearing on me, I just can't get on with the job.

In these poignant statements, Kathy was exhibiting many of the characteristic symptoms Wagner describes as 'being caught in a knot' (1987, p. 168). Certainly, Kathy could not see any way out of her 'terrible position', other than trying to survive as best she could until the end of the year, when many of the perceived sources of her problems would move on to school.

In remarks across several contexts, it emerged that Kathy did not place high value on introspection. She said she did not look back, or forward. As she had difficulty recalling past experiences and the impact of those experiences on her development, Kathy wondered, 'Do you suppose I'm too ancient to look back?' Kathy said before participation in the study, she had never had cause to think back over her work experiences: 'The trouble is, you never think about [these issues], do you? You know, philosophically, as you're going along through life. It just all seems to snowball.'

After trying to decide if she had changed as a teacher, Kathy finally suggested it would be better to ask someone else if they thought she had changed, because it was not for her to judge. After a few second's thought, she added, 'We're probably assessing everyone else, instead of assessing ourselves.'

The Human Encounter

The Cognitive Aspects of Teaching

As she discussed teaching, Kathy made few references to the associated mental activities. She acknowledged that her professional thinking might be stimulated by more reading, but somehow, 'never got around to reading', apart from activity-oriented teacher newsletters. In terms of the children, Kathy believed it really was best to 'take them at face value'. They were 'pretty straight forward', and if you thought too deeply about them, 'it just made you look for problems where none existed'. Kathy espoused a similar approach to the curriculum. She thought it best to 'take each day as it comes'. Apart from 'bracing' herself to face Adrian and the other difficult boys, Kathy made no mention of mental preparation.

Speaking of her actions during the program, Kathy made little mention of her on-the-spot mental activity and tended to play down the importance of her decision making. In discussing one event she did say:

> I suppose it depends on the situation. Sometimes, I suppose you go in quite firmly and say what you have to say, because you know that they know right from wrong. But other times, you might take a softer approach, a more indirect approach. [You] probably sum up the situation before you do that.

Kathy also made only scant references to the post-hoc mental activities associated with teaching. During one conversation, as she spoke about Adrian, Kathy seemed surprised to realize that he had made progress in his social skills. She spoke in general terms of evaluating children's skills and planning activities to enhance them, but it seemed the mental activities associated with teaching were not a central part of Kathy's awareness of her work.

Respect for Children

As in other areas, it was difficult to distil a clear picture of Kathy's beliefs about children, as her statements suggested varying positions at different times. In the card sort, Kathy rapidly categorized the given philosophical statements, seemingly in accordance with a set of ideals. She did not attempt to reconcile her comments with her actions in the classroom, or the particular children in her group. Kathy made this quite explicit, by acknowledging the discrepancy she saw between her stated beliefs and her actions. She said: 'These [comments] are completely negative to all the observations you've done in this centre.'

Although in discussion of the given statements, Kathy suggested that she thought children very competent, deserving of trust and generally to be held in high regard, statements about her own group of children gave a more diverse picture. For example, Kathy made many statements about the four boys, with whom she had difficulty coping. They were referred to as 'the wild men from Borneo' and 'the bombastic charging boys'. They were 'undisciplined — lack control'. They had 'no respect for other children' and 'monopolized the trolleys and the shovels'. Kathy saw some positive qualities, however. She said these boys 'knew right from wrong, even though they didn't always chose the right', and on another occasion said: 'They're fairly skilful, those fellows. Even though they're wild, they have got common sense.'

Kathy spoke of some other children in the group in very positive terms. She believed they were very efficient with 'their cutting and their skills and their representative painting'. Lewis was singled out for particular praise. Kathy said:

- '[Lewis] has come good. I just have such respect for him',
- 'I've got great admiration for Lewis's achievements.'

Many of Kathy's statements suggested she doubted these children's judgment. On four occasions, Kathy said that she found it necessary to insist that children tackle a task, even though they may dislike it. Kathy said although a child really disliked something now, 'he might come to like it later', so she felt she must insist. She called this 'putting the thumb on them' and believed that without her guidance, the children would not spend their time wisely. On one occasion, however, Kathy acknowledged that her own directive actions sometimes were counterproductive to succesful implementation of her principles. She said:

[I try to] stand by my principles with preschoolers-letting them move at their own age, at their own level of development. And cultivate their interests and develop their positive self-esteem, which you can't always do if you're being very directive — directing children into things that they're not that keen to do.

Kathy's statements about children suggested an external perspective, rather than a sense of her seeing events from the child's point of view.

The Human Encounter

For example, she spoke crossly of the child who 'just hammered in a few nails and took off', even though the carpentry activity had been planned just for him. (What remained undescribed was the child's engrossment with other things that were clearly more important to him at that time.) Neither did Kathy speak of commonalities between herself and the children. She spoke of children only in ways that suggested they were unlike herself.

It seemed external measures, particularly chronological age, held significant importance in Kathy's understandings about children. In offering justifications for increasing the pressure for achievement on children, Kathy said: 'These children are nearly six years old.' (Implying: it is time they were pressured.) 'I expect a child of six to do as he's told.'

Kathy seemed to have a list of skills that was used as a measuring stick for children's development. These did not appear to be as formal or as fine-grained as a checklist, but included 'cutting and fine motor skills', 'ability with puzzles' and 'representative painting'. Little is known about this area of Kathy's decision making, but it seemed that when children were judged to have reached some appropriate level, Kathy deemed they were 'well-rounded' and 'ready for extension'. ('Extension' was used by Kathy in this unusually specific way, almost as a synonym for an introduction to more formal learning. She did not use this word to describe the incidental extension of children's ideas.) As these points were explored, Kathy gave the example of Adrian's painting. She said that when he painted all over his paper at the beginning of the year, it was acceptable. It became less acceptable by mid-year, because 'it was time he painted representationally'. Kathy decribed how she began intervening in a very directive way, to bring about. She said she stood beside him and made suggestions, told him what to paint. Now, '. . . he can paint quite well, when he puts his mind to it.'

Description of the Program for Children's Social Development

In the discussions, Kathy assigned some importance to the 'social side of development' in her program, comparing it to fine motor skills in its impact on school readiness. It seemed Kathy did not have a set of clearly articulated goals or strategies for enhancing children's social development, but decided her input in social situations as the need arose. She spoke of 'saving peer situations before they collapse', 'keeping the peace', helping the boys out of some 'pretty strong situations', and 'helping Lewis out of a bit of a plight that he might have gotten himself into'. With the exception of the first remark, these comments are in keeping with the strategies Katz has described as 'putting out the fire' (1984, p. 8).

Kathy mentioned some concerns related to the harmonious operation of the group, including helping the boys learn that monopolizing equipment was simply 'not on' and helping children curb impetuous behaviour for the common good. She said:

> [Charles] is impetuous. Just go-go the whole time. And if you can just settle [him] a little bit and be sensible in his actions and perhaps think a little bit as he goes, for the good of the group — all would be well.

The importance accorded the social development program was linked to Kathy's understandings of individual chidren's needs. Kathy believed that most of the children were already very skilled in the social domain and described their peer interactions as 'lovely, a delight.' She explained that these children were ready for 'extension' (into more formal learning).

The child who was the most frequent topic of discussion was Adrian. He was noteworthy in Kathy's eyes particularly because of his low level of social skills and his aggressive behaviour toward peers. Kathy said she tried to monitor his peer interactions and intervene before the play collapsed. Her interventions were sometimes to 'try and suggest a more positive way of interacting' or remove him completely. But in the face of this 'constant job — vigil', Kathy was not always able to be on hand. She explained that Adrian received 'more than his fair share' of her attention and in some cases, 'battles were fought out in the peer group'. There also were times when Kathy decided to take no action, because she felt that other children were quite able to overlook his misdeeds, and she did not want to be continually chastising him. Kathy's flagging spirits were clearly evident in the following desription of Adrian:

> [Adrian] hasn't quite got a cooperative spirit yet as far as, well, interaction with peers go or assisting in any way. And I mean, we have gone for twelve months and tried and tried as positively as we can, but I mean, you're only human, aren't you?

Under pressure from what she perceived was a very trying group, Kathy believed she was not as positive or as tolerant in her interactions with children, as she once was. She said: 'Now, I draw the line.'; 'I'll try a negative attack now.'

In this very difficult year, Kathy's image-of-self-as-teacher seemed to be in a precarious state. Kathy believed this to be entirely due to factors outside of herself — the pressures she was experiencing from children, parents and staff. Kathy said she 'had no grey hairs at the beginning of the year, and by the end of the year, there were fifty thousand'. This numeric picture seemed to summarize Kathy's perspective on her current 'burned-out' condition. It was not the result of a gradual accumulation, over a long period of time, but rather a problem that had occurred suddenly: 'I just think I've been so lucky for so long, just to have had really smooth, uninterrupted, relaxed teaching. It just seems to have been the perfect environment and then just to have everything — reach a climax this year'.

From the outside-in perspective of the observer, however, it seemed that these factors may not have been solely to blame for Kathy's distressed state. Over a long period of time, Kathy had worked in isolation from other teachers, giving much to her teaching, but making few deposits in terms of her own professional renewal. When these difficult circumstances arose, Kathy had few resources to draw upon.

Actions in the Preschool

Kathy's Program

To understand Kathy's involvement in children's peer interactions, they must be considered as part of the whole program. Taken in isolation, the strategies Kathy used in her involvement in children's peer interactions were not unlike those observed in other preschools. The differences lay to a large extent in the events in which Kathy did not become involved. Sometimes, it was questionable whether Kathy was aware of situations, but at other times it was clear she was aware, but had chosen not to become involved. For example, an interesting situation developed between four boys, with Kathy in very close proximity:

> It has been a difficult morning with a series of children's disruptive, angry peer conflicts. Now, Kathy is planting grass runners in a bare patch close to the treehouse and the sandpit. In the treehouse, four boys have been involved in a long dramatic play event. Kathy directs the boys to come and help

with the grass planting. The boys discuss the problem of leaving the treehouse unattended, because they are afraid the girls (particularly Rosanne) will take it over. Throughout the boys' conversation, Kathy continues planting, making only one comment: 'It doesn't sound like Rosanne, wanting to take over the treehouse'. The boys decide that Aaron should stay in the treehouse as a guard. The other three join Kathy at the grass planting. After a few minutes, the three boys move into the sandpit and start a new game. Aaron stays in the treehouse a little longer, then leaves his post to move to the sandpit. The other boys are alarmed, especially when they notice Rosanne and several other girls moving towards the treehouse. The boys turn on Aaron, demanding that he return to his guard duty. Aaron refuses, saying he doesn't care 'if the girls *do* move in'. After further argument, the boys finally acquiesce and allow Aaron to stay in the sandpit. The treehouse apparently is forgotten. Kathy continues to plant grass.

This was an intriguing peer interaction sequence because of the interesting social issues it raised. To the observer, it seemed to offer several opportunities to discuss issues, verbalize alternate positions and negotiate solutions. Equally, of course, it could be argued that the children did not need Kathy's intervention, as they did resolve it satisfactorily in the end. Kathy's low level of involvement in this sequence, however, was in keeping with observations over time that suggested that social development, particularly children's skills in interacting with peers, was not a high priority in Kathy's program. A much greater emphasis was placed on task completion and the promotion of children's contacts with materials.

Several common threads seemed to run through Kathy's interactions with children and were interwoven to provide a relatively consistent texture, even across days of changing organization and routine. One of the strongest was Kathy's distinction between work and play, a second was her use of control strategies, and the third was the relatively low priority accorded strategies for fostering independence.

Work vs Play

Although Kathy did not use the labels 'work' and 'play', through her actions a clear distinction was made. Each day, certain activities were

The Human Encounter

designated as 'work', by Kathy's insistence that children should complete them. Many (though not all) of these designated activities were 'closed' (i.e., they required a set of fixed actions from the child for completion) and revolved around a current theme. During the first two weeks, the theme was Aborigines and the 'work' activities included painting within a given outline of a lizard, weaving lengths of grass into a cardboard frame and making cardboard 'shields'. At the same time, more open-ended activities continued to be available, but were not stressed equally. Despite Kathy referring to the products of the 'work' activities as 'your' lizard, or 'your' shield, many of the children (particularly the boys) showed little interest in them, and at times demonstrated ingenuity in avoiding them.

Many of Kathy's interactions with children centered on completion of these activities. When she noticed one of the designated activities had few children participating, Kathy sometimes 'rounded up customers'. At times the children were reluctant, but Kathy did not acknowledge their lack of enthusiasm. Children who came to Kathy for help with entirely different matters were at risk of being redirected to the designated activities and they sometimes behaved defensively. For example:

> Kathy is visiting the boys in the sandpit and she begins to speak: 'Brian ....' Before she can continue, Brian interrupts: 'I already got some glueing'. Kathy does not comment on his response, but continues with her statement (that is quite unrelated to 'glueing').

Control Strategies

Kathy seemed aware of the power of her very presence, to bring forth acceptable behaviour in children and she commonly used this as a control strategy. Kathy would frown at a child from a distance or draw the child's attention by calling his/her name. For example:

- When Aaron does not acknowledge Kathy's call to begin tidying away, Kathy calls in increasing volume: 'Aaron — Aaron! — AARON!!!'

In many cases, this reminder of Kathy's attention was effective in stopping a child behaving in a certain way. On other occasions, Kathy made it more explicit. For example:

Adrian and Gavin are throwing small lumps of soil at each other. Kathy is some distance away, chatting to a parent. Kathy calls: 'Gavin — Gavin —' Gavin looks towards her. Kathy frowns, shaking her finger and head. Adrian also looks up at the sound of Kathy's voice, and she confirms: 'Yes, Adrian. We're watching.'

Kathy also used the threat of her presence as a deterrent when children reported other children's misbehaviour. For example:

Aaron comes to Kathy on the patio, with a complaint that Lewis is spoiling a block building. Kathy says: 'Lewis will be out here in a minute if he's spoiling anything. You go in and tell him that, and I'll be in in a minute, on patrol.'

Kathy also used questioning as a subtle means of control. She often asked children about their intentions as a preliminary to redirecting them to one of the designated activities. Several of the boys were adept in this interactional sequence, arguing emphatically for their intentions and, some cases, avoiding a redirection. If the child wavered, however, Kathy was quick to redirect. For example, Kathy encountered two girls washing their hands in the bathroom:

Kathy asks Louise and Colleen: 'Will you two ladies come and do a puzzle, please?' The girls do not respond and Kathy asks: 'Have you finished your work downstairs?' Colleen replies without a lot of conviction: 'No-ooo.' Kathy asks: 'What are you doing downstairs?' Louise responds: 'Working.' Kathy asks: 'Whereabouts?' Colleen giggles: 'I don't know. We forget.' Kathy says: 'I just want you for a little while, to do your puzzles. Because there wasn't room before. But don't just pick an easy one, like a little toddler.' The girls walk slowly to the puzzle mat.

Kathy often was warm in her responses to children, but on only one occasion, was she observed to make direct reference to a child's feelings. This was not in relation to the very strong feelings that sometimes were in evidence in this program, but dealt with a relatively minor event; William's unhappiness at having to put away his toy weapons.

The Human Encounter

Developing Independence

Across the program, Kathy's interactions with children appeared to place little importance on supporting independence. Although the richness of the physical environment (particularly outdoors) provided many opportunities for children's problem solving, in her interactions Kathy was quick to provide solutions. For example:

- When William wants a container to hold his stones, Kathy makes one from a cardboard cylinder.

- When Greg suggests some fireworks might be a nice addition to his block building, Kathy is enthusiastic. Immediately, she decides how they will be constructed, gets the materials from the storeroom and makes the 'fireworks'. Only after she has made ten fireworks, does Kathy suggest Greg might make some for himself.

- Kathy makes a simple fishing line for Gavin, with a stick and length of string. She draws, cuts out and attaches a paper fish for the end of the line.

Kathy appeared to place limited value on children's judgment in the designated activities, where she sometimes criticized children for choosing puzzles that were too easy, and frequently refused to accept a child's judgment that he/she had completed the activity. Kathy often asked children to bring the object to her for approval, before it could be pronounced finished. In painting, children sometimes were asked to rehang their work on the easel and add items that Kathy suggested. Although the boys complained about this, they usually complied. An exception was Lewis, who when asked to add a yellow sun to his painting, said that he couldn't, 'because it was night time'. Kathy had no response, and Lewis was gone.

In other, more open-ended activities, Kathy demonstrated a greater faith in the children's judgment. Two examples illustrate this:

- As Kathy walks past the large tree, Conrad is suspended off the ground, standing with his feet in a small loop on the end of a very thick rope that is hung over a branch. Aaron and William are holding the other end of the rope.

- Kathy does not stop, but says calmly as she passes: 'Lower him slowly'. Kathy does not look back, but the boys lower him slowly and carefully. Kathy is passing the treehouse, where some boys are lowering a wheelbarrow on a rope from the rail of the deck (about four feet above ground level). Other children cluster underneath, ready to guide the wheelbarrow. William hangs over the rail of the treehouse, giving instructions. Kathy says mildly, 'I've noticed how sensible you've been.' William says, 'That's why we've got crash helmets.' Kathy says, 'So long as you're careful. Have you got safety rules?' No one replies and Kathy says, 'That's important', as she leaves the area. The boys lower the wheelbarrow without incident.

Many observations supported Kathy's comments about the burden of supervision, as she was forced to move through a very large outdoor area, dealing with individuals and small groups. At these times, Kathy made very brief inputs to one group of children, then rapidly left for another location. (After scanning the first day's observations, Kathy described this pattern as 'staccato'.) At times, however, Kathy's own actions appeared to contribute to her burden. For example: A group of boys in the block corner are setting up the small blocks in a domino pattern. Kathy says that she wants to be there to see the dominos fall. Then, Kathy moves outdoors and begins legislating the order of turns on the swing. A few minutes later, Kathy suggests to Conrad that he dig the soil off the in-ground lawn sprinkler caps. (He needs her help in locating them.) Thus Kathy had three groups of children, spread over a wide geographic area, all seeking her presence in order to function. Over the next fifteen minutes, the necessity to move rapidly between these three groups was impossibly demanding for Kathy.

Resolving Peer Conflict

Conflicts between children occurred with reasonable frequency in this setting, but Kathy did not always become involved. When children came to Kathy with stories of misdeeds of peers (tale-telling) and/or reports of conflict, Kathy had several characteristic responses. If the tale involved a misdeed, rather than a report of conflict, frequently Kathy rejected the tale completely, such as when she told Conrad she didn't 'want to know about Adrian's naughty word'.

A common response to a report of peer conflict was to deal with the conflict at that point, by interacting with the complainant, rather than going to the scene and becoming involved with all parties. Frequently, she used a consoling or distracting response to downplay the problem. If a conflict occurred towards the end of a free play segment, this seemed to be a standard response. Some examples:

- When Charles complains that Adrian has knocked his building down, Kathy responds calmly: 'Well, build it back up'.

- When Patricia and Christy come with a complaint about another child, Kathy says, 'Never mind. It will soon be tidy-up time'.

A similar response, heard on several occasions when children reported others disrupting their play, was Kathy's suggestion or direction to go and play somewhere else. For example:

Patricia and Wayne come to Kathy, to complain about Adrian and/or Gavin. Patricia says, 'Adrian kicked me — um, I mean Gavin.' Wayne begins to speak, 'And . . .' but Kathy is already speaking. She says, 'Well, listen, what about you two just keep away? What would you two like to do? Neither child replies and after a second or two, Kathy goes on: 'Can you think of some ideas? I might even get some paper in a while, for some kites, and you might like to do some rubbing and make your own kites. It's a beaut day for kites.' Patricia refers again to the problem with the boys. Kathy responds: 'Patricia, try and keep away. You and Wayne go and play in a nice little spot where you'd like to play. I tell you what. Patricia, go for a walk into the rainforest, and you'll probably find some interesting things there after the rain.' Kathy turns to talk to another child and Patricia and Wayne wander off in the direction of the rainforest.

In some cases, playing elsewhere was a reasonable solution, when the disrupted play did not involve a particular location or group of props. In other cases, however, it suggested a lack of appreciation for the complexity and importance of the physical environments children created for their dramatic play. This seemed to support the suspected assumption (seen in many of Kathy's activity-based interactions) that children's self-selected activity was not considered as important as other teacher-nominated aspects of the program.

Kathy

As with other cases of undesirable behaviour, Kathy sometimes responded to reports of peer conflict by threatening to intervene. Less frequently, she accompanied a child to the location of the conflict, and actually became involved. Another means of entry came as the conflict developed around Kathy or as she observed a problem and entered of her own accord.

In many cases, Kathy tried to end these conflicts as quickly as possible, with the application of a quick ruling or a directive. An example:

> As Kathy arrives in the sandpit, several children are in turmoil, accusing Adrian of various misdeeds. Judy says, 'Adrian hit me.' Adrian denies it: 'No, I didn't!' Judy continues: 'And he tipped some sand out of that.' Barry says to Adrian, 'Yes, you did.' Kathy enters: 'Well, if Adrian can't play nicely with his friends ... ' Judy adds: 'And he took the cup off me.' Kathy goes on: 'We'll give him one more chance and if he can't play with his friends sensibly, I'll ask him to move away.' Adrian hangs his head and plays alone. Kathy leaves the sandpit.

When children were in conflict over the order of turns, as happened frequently, typically Kathy ruled who was next. These conflicts were quickly resolved, but often broke out once again, as soon as Kathy left the scene. A typical example:

> On the tyre swing, a struggle breaks out between Anna and Colleen. Anna is in the tyre, but Colleen is trying to pull her out. Both girls are squealing. Kathy looks up, claps her hands and calls: 'Anna! Colleen!' Both girls speak at once. Anna says: 'I haven't had my second turn!' Colleen says: 'She's had her turn!' Kathy speaks over the girls, saying: 'No — No. (To Anna:) Well that was after someone else had a turn. You hop off and give Colleen a go and then we'll give you another turn. We just go one at a time.'

Kathy also used many pronouncements, including injunctions to share or 'be friends' and an interesting strategy that seemed to contain an element of shaming. Some examples were:

- When Anna and Kaye complain about other children fighting them for possession of dramatic play props, Kathy says in a disappointed tone, 'When I went up before, you were all playing so nicely.'

- When Brian, Conrad and Wayne have a water fight, Kathy says, 'And you were playing so good, down there in the box, with the water paint.'

- When several girls argue over possession of the dancing clothes, Kathy says in a sad tone, 'And yesterday you were all sharing so nicely.'

Kathy's use of the more facilitative strategies commonly was limited to a single focusing question or an interpretive statement. Of the interpretive statements noted, several were arbitrary ones, in which Kathy's support for one child's position was clear. Sometimes, Kathy's interpretations contained an implied directive. For example:

- Aaron has been in control of the hose in the sandpit and has been refusing others water. Now, as they argue over the water supply yet again, Kathy says firmly, 'Aaron will give you some water.'

- Marian becomes very officious in organizing other children to take turns with her pet ducklings. When the children complain about her heavy-handedness, Kathy says, 'Marian *will* share the ducks. She *will* give other children a turn, because she will have them all night.'

The emphasis in Kathy's statements was unmistakeable. It was almost as if she had omitted the words 'or else' from the end of the statements and after hearing such positively-worded statements about themselves, Aaron and Marian could hardly continue to be obstructive.

Use of neutral interpretive statements in peer conflict situations was rare, though they did appear in one long, facilitative sequence of conflict resolution involving Adrian, Gavin and Conrad. This was a mysterious situation. Adrian, Gavin and Conrad had been playing in the treehouse, when Adrian came to Kathy with a complaint that several butterfly nets had been taken from them by a group of boys now located in the small playhouse.

As Kathy accompanies Adrian to the small playhouse, she asks, 'Where are the nets?' Adrian points to the playhouse, where several boys are watching their approach and he says: 'It could be there. They're the ones who stealed them.' Kathy says, 'There's enough to share, Adrian.' As they arrive, Kathy says to the other boys, 'We've just come to see what's happening with the nets.' Kathy asks if the nets are here and the boys say they have two, though none are in sight. Kathy suggests to Adrian that they go and look for the other missing nets, but before they can leave, Wayne accuses Adrian: 'He said a naughty word.' Adrian starts confidently, 'Miss K. said ...' As the others look to him, his voice dies and he says only, 'Ummm ... Ummm ...' Kathy says in support, 'Adrian *did* get the nets first.' With renewed confidence, Adrian says, 'Yes. And you steal them from us!' An argument breaks out between the boys and Kathy interrupts with an injunction to share, then again suggests they look for the missing nets. Kathy and Adrian go back to the treehouse, where Gavin is playing. They find two nets there, but Adrian insists he needs another, because there are three boys in the game. Kathy rules that two nets will be sufficient and advises Adrian, 'You enjoy yours while you can. Get all your fish, then when Conrad comes, you can give him a turn, if he hasn't got one.' By the end of this sequence, Adrian is unusually cheerful and he engages Kathy in a lively discussion about where they will be having lunch today.

Both within peer conflicts and in other interactions, Kathy rarely attempted to promote direct contact between children. For example, when a child complained that another would not give him/her a turn, Kathy ruled a solution, rather than suggest the children talk the problem through. The pattern was typically: Child One → Kathy → Child Two, rather than Child One → Kathy → Child One → Child Two.

Rules

Formal rules had a low profile in this centre. Some basic safety rules were enforced, such as not running indoors and not throwing sand or stones, but procedural rules were few. The most evident of these was for children to gather when the signal was given for grouptime, but Kathy was never heard to make reference to this. The children's compliance was total. Sometimes, Kathy made short-term rules, for example banning the use of the hose in the sandpit for a day and

The Human Encounter

limiting access to outdoor activities during the first block of freeplay time.

When rules were made or enforced, Kathy sometimes gave explanations, though on occasion, these were less than clear. For example, Kathy wavered over a rule that the girls were not to take paint from the easel to add to their tins of water (used with a brush to 'paint' outdoor surfaces):

> As the girls add the paint to their tins, Kathy says, 'Yesterday, you made it too watery. You put so much water in there, it ruined the paint for the easels. So I was really going to say today; no paint at all, because you'd spoiled it so much. So do you think — just have one little go, please.' A child painting at the easel points to the paint saying, 'Very watery, that.' Kathy responds, 'Well, if the girls add too much, it ruins it.' She says to one of the girls, 'Just use the tap today, sweetie. You just use that because it's going to ruin the easel paint. If you want coloured water, you'll have to go and get some ochre and grind that up and make your own paint like the Aborigines. I'll get you some chalk to grind up.' (The girls experiment with grinding chalk and other things to make paint and it becomes a fascinating activity for them.)

Whilst the emphasis on rules was limited, Kathy used directives that carried a clear expectation that children were to obey. Kathy's phrasing of directives ranged widely. At times, they were blunt commands, such as: 'Come down and tidy up' and particularly in the designated tasks, could be strongly worded. For example:

- When Aaron is told to add 'grass' to his painting, he says, 'I can't do grass'. Kathy says sternly, 'Well, you can try, m'boy!'

At other times, directives were worded very softly, occasionally even as questions. For example:

- 'Colleen, could you lend a helping hand here, please?'
- When Anna protests at the tidy-up time announcement, Kathy says, 'Oh well, Anna, it's just very late now, darling. We've got to do a bit of tidying up.'

Kathy

Developing a Sense of Community

In several ways, Kathy tried to instil in children an awareness and concern for others. Most frequently, Kathy directed children to perform acts that were for the common good. For example, she directed children to tidy up the mess they had left, put the blocks down gently, so as not to disturb others, leave the soap in the washing bucket, and leave the shovels behind, so others could use them.

Kathy made frequent injunctions to children to act with care, in a wide range of situations. Often, she made reference to other children as part of these statements:

- When the girls' actions threaten the boys' dam, Kathy says, 'Oh girls, you mustn't break their dam down. They spent ages building that.'
- When a boy suggests demolishing an abandonded block building, to give his team more room to build, Kathy says, 'On no. You could build it over here. Someone was working very hard. You just look after his and continue with your own.'
- When Conrad carelessly brandishes a shovel, Kathy says, 'Conrad, when you're digging close together, just take it easy with your shovel. Go gently.'

Kathy made some reference to the social aspect of experiences, in positive statements such as: 'If we do it together, it won't take long', but such remarks were not common.

Although Kathy encouraged children to work together in the open-ended 'play' activities, in the designated 'work' activities, it seemed Kathy placed greater value on solitary work. If children chattered or played together as they worked, Kathy would try to refocus them on the task or direct them to 'concentrate'. Kathy did draw children's attention to the achievements of others and actively promoted helping interactions. Some examples:

- Kathy suggests Gavin and Lewis go and find worms for the ducks. Lewis runs off, but Gavin stays behind. Kathy says, 'Go with Lewis, love. He knows where the worms are.'

- When William and Conrad show Kathy the rocks they have found, Kathy asks William, 'Will you go with this fellow and show him how to make a stone axe?' (Later, it was Kathy who made the axe.)

A notable feature in many of these helping relationships was that they were not initiated by either child. No one had expressed a desire to be helped or to help. Kathy was the initiator.

In another version of the helping relationship, Kathy often nominated one child to a superior position over peers. Some examples:

- At tidy-up time in the block corner, Kathy says to Colleen, 'You're in charge of the cars. Barry will help.'

- When Kathy leaves the duck enclosure, she asks, 'Marian, can I leave you in charge of the ducks?' (As detailed above, Kathy later was forced to intervene, when Marian became officious towards other children.)

Kathy rarely brought details of her life outside the centre into the program. On only one occasion was she heard to make reference to her family, when she responded to Aaron's comment that he wished he were a bird, by telling him, 'That's like my mother. She always wished she could be a bird too.'

Helping Children Gain Access to Peer Play Groups

Kathy was only minimally involved in the formation of peer play groups and in helping children gain access to them. She was much more active in the interruption of peer play groups, so that one or more of the members might work on designated activities. Typically, Kathy did not suggest that all members of a particular peer play group might work cooperatively on a designated task, but redirected only one or two individuals from the group.

When children protested at being removed from their peer group play, Kathy downplayed their complaints, telling them not to make a fuss, because they 'had all day to do that' and could always 'come back to it later'. In reality, however, Kathy often kept children at the designated activities for a considerable time and the cooperative play between the remaining members of the group frequently broke down. Once again, the suspected assumption that teacher-designated 'work' was more important than children's self-selected 'play' was supported.

Kathy

In the following example, there appeared to be useful opportunities for children wanting to negotiate access and a rare positive social opportunity for Adrian.

> As Kathy arrives at the jungle gym cubby, Adrian is sitting alone inside. Brian, Wayne and Dick hover outside and Wayne is asking Adrian, 'Can we go in the house?' Before Adrian can answer, Brian suggests, 'Let's go over to the other house.' As the three boys begin to walk away, Kathy calls them back saying, 'Brian, you can go over there, but Adrian must learn to share.' Then, Kathy turns to Adrian and questions him about whether he has completed the tasks indoors and put the material away. Adrian says he has finished with the Mobilo, but Kathy says she wants to see what he has made. The other boys have waited through this dialogue, but now announce they will come and play with the Mobilo too. Kathy tells them, 'Well — I think we're packing it away up there now, but we'll put it out again later.' Kathy takes Adrian's hand and leads him towards the playroom. Dick says to the others, 'Look, they're leaving.' Brian calls to Adrian, 'Are you coming back?' He repeats this call, and Adrian looks over his shoulder as Kathy leads him towards the patio and calls, 'Yes.' Brian, Wayne and Dick look at each other, then tentatively at first, move into the cubby house. (Adrian does go indoors but Kathy is distracted and the Mobilo is forgotten. The other boys play together in the jungle gym cubby, not without some strife, until the end of freeplay, some thirty minutes later.)

It would seem in this event, that at least Brian and perhaps Wayne and Dick, were keen to play with Adrian, and with some help may have negotiated an amicable arrangement, but it was not to be.

Involvement in Children's Dramatic Play

Kathy's involvement in children's dramatic play was not extensive. She sometimes offered extending ideas, but frequently these were phrased as a single directive rather than a range of suggestions. On one occasion, a more facilitatory approach was seen when the girls were trying to get organized for the 'Princess' game (a musical circle game involving a number of roles). Kathy helped by asking the participants clarifying questions about who was playing each role. In later repetitions,

The Human Encounter

however, when children argued about turns, Kathy simply ruled on who would play each role and consoled those who did not get the role of their choice.

On the rare occasion when Kathy took on a play role, typically it was a very brief interlude. For example:

> As Kathy passes the block corner, Conrad puts his toy radio to his mouth and says, 'Come in, Mrs. K. — Come in Mrs. K.' Kathy smiles and puts her hand to her mouth, saying, 'Coming in. Yes?' Conrad does not respond and Kathy drops the role, but admires the toy radio.

On the two occasions when Kathy had a more prolonged involvement with children in dramatic play, she adopted a fringe role that enabled her to slip in and out of role easily, though in one case it was rather hard to distinguish between fantasy and reality:

> Rain is threatening as Kathy visits Adrian, Conrad, Wayne and Brian outdoors in the playhouse where their game centres on haunted houses. She says, 'Now listen. If the rain comes down, you've got shelter in there. You'll be alright up in this house, won't you?' The boys engage Kathy in chatter about the ghosts, then Kathy repeats, 'So you can have a sleep in there or have your dinner in there, or anything inside there.' Adrian says worriedly, 'We really haven't got much in here.' Kathy says lightly, 'Oh you've got your blankets and your chairs and your buckets for food and a teapot.' Then Kathy turns to talk to Colleen, who has come to see what is going on. Soon after, Kathy leaves. Adrian still seems rather uncertain, but soon appears less anxious.

On one occasion, when Kathy visited children in a play situation that clearly was not going well, there seemed an almost ritualized quality to her input that did not seem able to break the impasse:

> Kathy approaches the cubby in the jungle gym. Adrian, with a morose expression, is sitting on one side and Dick, equally glum, sits on the other. There is no contact between them. Kathy asks, 'How's this camp going, down here?' No one replies. Kathy makes several modifications, removing a ladder from the top of the jungle gym and taking a broom away. Then, she asks another general question, 'Now are you alright, here in your camp?' Adrian mutters unconvincingly, 'Good.' Kathy responds, 'With

Dick?' There is no response. Kathy continues, 'Well, I'll be here later, to do some work with the bamboo. We might be able to make some musical instruments, like whistles.' Again, there is no response, then Dick asks, 'Is Greg and Barry going to come down?' (Kathy earlier had directed these boys away from the game.) Kathy says, 'In a while. They're going to work in the sand for a little while.' Dick has been holding a cardboard tube 'didgeridoo' (Aboriginal musical instrument) made earlier and suddenly, he throws it to the ground. Kathy warns him about caring for it, then as she prepares to leave, asks again, 'Are you fellows right here for a little while?' Once again, there is no response and Kathy leaves.

Environmental Support of Peer Interaction

There was a marked difference between the outdoor and indoor environments in this centre. Outdoors, a wonderful collection of props and other materials was fully accessible to the children, and provided a rich variety of settings for interactive play. Most of the children appeared to prefer the outdoors and after having enjoyed unlimited access for almost the whole year, many seemed annoyed when asked to stay indoors for part of the session.

Outdoors, the children had many ongoing interests that engaged them from one day to the next. For example, in the large digging patch a group of boys were excavating a 'mine' that had grown to gigantic proportions. These boys liked to work here for part of each day and their play was productive and highly elaborated as they unearthed interesting rocks and other long-lost (and sometimes recently-buried) objects. Similarly, each day the 'Telecom Boys' worked diligently, using a collection of props that included ladders, shovels, a very thick rope, hard hats, a box of discarded telephone equipment and porter's trolleys. The children maintained these strong interests throughout the period of observation.

Indoors and on the patio the environment was structured quite differently. With the exception of the block area and home corner, children did not have free access to materials. The teacher's selected materials for the day were placed on tables or mats. Other items were stored on screened shelves or in a storeroom to which the children did not have access. The materials for the designated activities were present, but if children needed other materials, (for example, containers for found 'treasures' or additional props for dramatic play) they had to ask Kathy. This environmental arrangement appeared to increase both the children's dependence and the number of demands made upon Kathy.

As mentioned earlier, Kathy sometimes made suggestions or directions about environmental adjustments to resolve children's peer conflicts, directing children to search for additional materials, or relocating play away from other children. However, Kathy was not observed adjusting the physical environment in the absence of strife, as a means of conflict avoidance.

In one interesting and prolonged sequence, Kathy worked cooperatively with Dick and Brian, to help them create an 'obstacle course'.

> The boys had a very elaborate plan to attach a long rope to several pieces of fixed equipment and it is clear they will need a lot of adult help to implement their ideas: As construction begins, Kathy consults the boys about the placement of the rope, but for safety reasons, some ideas have to be changed. Despite Kathy's sensitive attempts to involve the boys in the implementation of the modified plan, they gradually lose interest. Kathy now becomes much more directive, keeping the boys on task and issuing instructions on how to place the rope. As the obstacle course is finally completed, Kathy returns to her earlier approach, asking the boys if it meets with their approval.

This event illustrates one of the paradoxical situations that occur between teachers and children in preschool settings. The boys were highly motivated to create a wonderful structure, but were intolerant of the changes that Kathy felt she must make for reasons of safety and practicality. When the ownership of the project passed from them to Kathy, they had no interest in continuing. Kathy had a limited number of options at this point. Should she have allowed the project to collapse even though she could see value in it for others? After the rope was installed, it was enjoyed by many children, but Dick and Brian moved on.

Concluding Remarks

Participation in this study was not a useful or enjoyable experience for Kathy. She said she had been 'uptight' when observed and wished the observations had been carried out in the two-day group, where she was 'much more relaxed and natural'. She said the only value in the observations was to 'give a picture of a burned-out teacher'. It seemed the pressure of being observed had joined the pressures of the children, assistant and parents, as reasons why Kathy's teaching was not as she would have wished.

Kathy looked only briefly at the first day's observations, and as she later related, said: 'Oh my God! Really! Up and down all the time. But that's the tension in the being and que sera, whatever will be, will be.' Her shock at confronting her perceived inadequacy, followed by a hasty shutting of the door, is very close to Morton's description. He writes:

> The person at the same time maintains the affirmation and admits the force of the evidence against it, with a shrug of the shoulders at the discrepancy ... [but] the problem lies as much with the concept of belief as in the person's tangled thinking. (1980, p. 80)

It seemed that Kathy's thinking about self-as-teacher was tangled, but more than this, it seemed that she was not able to examine the tangles, or even acknowledge they existed. Throughout, it appeared that Kathy's reluctance to self-examine may have been a protective strategy. She seemed afraid to think too deeply or look too closely at her own actions. It was as if Kathy had closed down the feedback loops that could have given her information on herself and her functioning. Fiske has written of the 'self-protective' life style that she claims is the most important commitment for numbers of people in mid-life. She says: 'It is as if they must avoid both listening to themselves think and experiencing peace and quiet, that for others offers the maturational processes time to yield their restorative results' (1980, p. 260).

Whether or not Kathy was undergoing a stressful period in her life outside the preschool we do not know, but it seems certain that her life as a teacher was undergoing great stress. And like Sikes' (1985, p. 54) description of those very experienced teachers for whom professional development has stagnated, Kathy's development seemed to have come to a halt.

There were times when Kathy seemed to withdraw from children briefly, even though she was physically present. The most notable withdrawals were the retreats to gardening. Although these seemed to prevent her from entering other, potentially more productive interactions with children, if one recalls Kathy's words: 'Sometimes I think

I'd just love to be bashing away at an inanimate object like a typewriter, and just cut off from the rest of the world', then the brief respite offered by gardening may have been a useful strategy for Kathy, as a way of coping with a high-stress situation.

Despite the pressures she perceived and the stress she was experiencing, there remained many positive aspects of Kathy's teaching. Parents regarded her highly and told me many times how fortunate their children were to have Miss K. as a teacher. The children also continued to greet her warmly and to initiate many affectionate contacts.

Whether or not Kathy was, in fact, a 'burned out' teacher could not be ascertained. The concept of teacher burn-out is such a poorly-defined one, accurate diagnosis is impossible. However, there would seem to be a case for Farber's notion of 'teacher wear-out' (1984, p. 328) as a description of Kathy's condition, rather than teacher burn-out.

Chapter 7

Living Together in the Preschool

Making Sense of Teacher Actions

Paradoxes and Ambiguities

In keeping with other hermaneutic inquiries that seek to understand the meanings of human action and interaction, this study raised more questions than it answered. Both the search for meaning in the teachers' interactions with children, and the deeper realm of inquiry into the relationships between the person and the teacher, were laden with the paradoxes and complexities that characterize human life. This was a source both of strength and of difficulty. Yamamoto has written:

> if *homo sapiens* is reduced to a single dimension for the convenience of our explorations, we are at best dealing with a poor facsimile. Such an artifact does not reveal any paradoxes — those mysterious ingredients that make people so uniquely human. Whether we like it or not, heterogeneity, inconsistency, and unpredictability are part and parcel of this fascinating species. (1984, p. 67)

In its ability to capture some of the complexities, paradoxes and inconsistencies of life in preschool settings, this study was a truly human inquiry. However, the same strength-giving qualities also presented many methodological difficulties, and precluded the distillation of concise findings.

Habermas (1972, p. 309) has written of the importance of the interpreter's own understandings in coming to understand another, Awareness of this inescapable aspect of human inquiry brought about

The Human Encounter

continual recycling between my own perspective and what the participants told of their perspectives. It meant recurrent examination of my own beliefs, scrutiny of my responses to what I was being told and what I observed.

Generations of philosophers and psychologists have attempted to study the essence of our humanness, but it has remained elusive. Neither could this study hope to explore the deepest realms of personhood. It was confined to an exploration of some of the person's beliefs about children, her part in their lives and the connections suggested between the person and teacher. These internal areas were discussed under the rubric of the person's 'image-of-self-as-teacher'.

The surface (behavioural) dimension of the study also exposed many of the paradoxes and difficulties inherent in 'making sense' of human action and interaction. Some affinity was felt with Teilhard de Chardin's words about analysis of human phenomena:

> [Analysis] that marvellous instrument of scientific research to which we owe all our advances but which, breaking down synthesis after synthesis, allows one soul after another to escape, leaving us confronted with a pile of dismantled machinery and evanescent particles. (1958, p. 257)

In this attempt to analyze interactions between teachers and children, a pervasive force was the essentially transactional nature of human with human contacts (Berman, 1973). Taken at a surface level, some teacher actions appeared at first to be quite unambiguous, for example, Brenda's directive: 'Please put the wig away now'. Yet the children's responses clearly indicated that, for them, the meaning of the statement was not as it appeared. They blithely ignored these apparent directives. What is more, subsequent teacher responses to the children's ignoring showed that the teacher, also, did not consider them firm directives. Some statements that could confidently have been categorized as directives or facilitative actions were understood by children as such, but others were not.

Another window on the ambiguities of teacher actions was provided in peer conflict situations, where it was often difficult to decide if a particular question or interpretive statement was a neutral remark (aimed at clarifying the situation for the participants) or an arbitrary one (in which the teacher conveyed her opinion about who was 'right' and 'wrong').

Like all of us, these teachers could see only through their own eyes. It is not reasonable to expect teachers to remain strictly neutral in situations where they have extensive knowledge of innumerable similar situations, and an elaborate knowledge of the children involved. In any case, these teachers also had a vested interest in the outcome. They were not like an impartial industrial arbitrator, allied neither with employed nor employee. They did have opinions about the moral dimensions of the situation, about who was right and who was wrong (Furlong and Carroll, 1990) and their opinions had a way of surfacing, even when the teacher was striving for neutrality. The teachers also possessed an elaborate knowledge of the mainstream cultural and social conventions and were aware that they were preparing children to live within this context. For this reason Silin (1987) argues, educational decision making should not try to emulate the 'objectivity' of positivist science, but rightly belongs in the realm of moral and political consideration.

On a strictly pragmatic level, the demands of these classrooms meant that teachers simply did not have time to minutely analyze their comments and, in any case, the ultimate judgments of neutrality had to be left to the children, who responded very differently to these remarks. For example, when Brenda attempted to help children resolve their conflicts with peers, some children (such as Michael) responded to the barest hint of teacher support for the other child. Others (like William) did not acquiesce in the face of hints, implied support for opponents, or even the most blatantly stated negative opinions.

As I strived to make sense of the participants' understandings of life in these settings, the transactional nature of communication among teachers and children became clear. Although on the surface, some teacher statements appeared ambiguous, children's responses indicated that because of their shared knowledge of the situation, in many cases they knew exactly what the teacher meant and knew what was expected of them. If they misread the teacher's communication, often it was quickly clarified. For example, when Nan made what appeared to be quite ambiguous statements about a game in the sandpit, her remarks were read (accurately) by most of the children as: 'It's time to end the game'. When Harry misread her statement and thought he had the option of continuing the game, Nan clarified the situation for him.

In Kathy's case, the interpretation of some statements remained problematic. For example, in the event when Kathy made a series of tangental remarks about the block play, seemingly to tell the boys it was time to end the play, the boys parried each remark without acknowledging the underlying message. This continued until Kathy resorted to a blunt directive. There could have been several interpretations of this sequence. Kathy's remarks may have been ambiguous to the children; they may simply have been enjoying the verbal sparring; or they may have read her remarks accurately from the beginning, and have been manipulating the situation to gain a few more minutes of play. Without accessing the children's understandings of the situation, there was simply no way to tell. (In preliminary work for this study, videotapes of interactions were used to try to prompt 4- and 5-year-olds to verbalize their understandings of events in which they had earlier participated. Although the data were of interest, the technique was not continued because of many procedural difficulties (see McLean, 1986).)

It would seem that adequate descriptions and categorizations of teacher actions cannot be made without consideration of the meaning the behaviour holds for those who must interpret it in order to function in the setting (Carter and Doyle, 1987, p. 147). Combs *et al.* state: 'attempts to isolate specific methods as "good" or "necessary" for the helping process prove generally sterile. The meaning of the methods as perceived by the persons on whom they are employed, rather than the methods themselves, determine their effect' (1978, p. 6).

Recourse to student perspectives to define teacher actions creates a high level of disquiet in many educational researchers. It would be so much more comfortable if we could rely on unambiguous, concrete, behavioural descriptions. Yet it seems that life in classrooms is not lived according to such neat categorization schemes. To force the complexities of human interaction to comply with such schemes would be to lose the essence of the human teacher touching, and being touched by, the human child.

Because of the detail provided on these teachers' actions, it would be possible for readers to point to occurrences of apparent inconsistency, ambiguous statements, lack of follow through and momentary lack of awareness, and label these as flaws. However, I would posit that it is not these teachers' actions that are flawed, but the idealized view of teaching against which their actions are compared. In Groundwater-Smith's words, analyses of curriculum work as pretext often lead to a 'significant apportioning of "the blame" to teachers ... without seeking to locate them in their own historical and cultural spaces' (1988, p. 96). Teachers themselves also hold an idealized model of teaching and, as Greenberg points out, this can be a burden. He writes:

> Each teacher daily faces the reality of his own teaching behavior ... In addition to this reality ... most teachers also

carry within themselves another reality that can be a nagging, painful burden. This inner reality is composed of myths — over-idealized notions about what a teacher should be like, how a teacher should behave, what a teacher should be feeling or not feeling. (1969, p. 24)

The people in this study were experienced mature teachers, who recently had received recognition within the profession, for the quality of their teaching. This affirmation led at least three of them to renewed confidence in herself as teacher. Perhaps because of their experience and confidence, these teachers did not appear to find their ideals a burden. They showed a ready acceptance of at least some of the shortcomings they perceived in reaching 'the ideal'. Even so, ideals were often referred to by the teachers and it would seem that no understanding of life in classrooms can be complete, unless these ideals are acknowledged and examined.

Ideals and Realities

Perhaps the greatest obstacle to our understanding of what goes on within classrooms is an omission. We approach the social world of the classroom with the view that what happens there is teaching and learning, but this is only part of the story. What happens in classrooms is living. For many hours each week, this large group of people finds ways to live together in reasonable harmony in this enclosed space (Leiberman and Miller, 1978). What happens there some of that time is 'teaching' or 'learning', or, alternatively, 'education'.

'Education', as Peters points out, is a word with many and diverse meanings, but one of the most commonly-held beliefs about education is that it must be focused on some future aim. As Peters states: 'Education implies ... that something worthwhile is being or has been intentionally transmitted in a morally acceptable manner' (1967, p. 3). Fenstermacher says that teaching requires: 'at least two persons, one of whom possesses some skill or other form of content and the other does not, and the possessor intends to convey the content to the one who lacks it, leading to the formation of a relationship between them for this purpose' (1986, p. 38). Greene describes teaching as: 'the living being who is the teacher, intentionally trying to provoke diverse persons to reach beyond themselves, to become different, to enter a state more desirable than the one they are presently in' (1984, p. 284). In all of these descriptions, 'education' or 'teaching' involves a future orientation: an intention by the teacher to assist the students to move to some further and more desirable point on a continuum.

In early childhood education, the traditional focus has been not on change through transmission of information, but through facilitation of development. As Peters and Klein state:

> Assumed is a relationship between early and later development and the malleability of development (for better or worse) through the manipulation of early experience. These assumptions currently are held by early childhood educators no matter what their theoretical or philosophical bent and hold wide currency in society as a whole. (1981, p. 143)

But the teacher's actions, directed towards a movement of the child along a developmental continuum, is only part of what goes on inside preschools. Further, if teacher actions are interpreted only in terms of a narrow future-directed orientation, some acquire a misleading and negative meaning.

The use of the concept of 'living', to describe what happens between participants in classrooms, is not a new idea. Friedrich Froebel made mention of it and it has received considerable attention in the middle of this century, from humanist educators such as Jackson (1968), Richardson (1967), Hughes (1958) and Ashton-Warner (1963). It also has appeared in more recent writing about teaching. For example, in Clandinin's (1986) study, one teacher was seen to be guided by an image of 'the classroom as home', a concept not unlike 'living' in its breadth of concern.

The broader concept of 'living' enables one to move away from the narrow future-orientation inherent in 'teaching' or 'education' and incorporate that other important aspect of life in classrooms — the here and now. The teachers in this study were not concerned solely with the future, or moving children along developmental continuums. They also were concerned with the quality of life in the present: the well-being of their students and themselves. They were trying to find ways for this group of people to live in reasonable harmony, today. As Hosford says: 'We spend much time with our students. It should not be spent, but lived' (1980, p. 50).

The bifurcation of teaching from its parent, living, has been responsible for a proliferation of myths surrounding teaching. Even in early childhood education, where the personhood of the teacher has been the subject of much rhetoric, and close relations between teacher and child have been highly valued, the temptation has been to consider 'teacher' and 'teaching' as something quite apart from 'person' and 'living'.

There is a marked difference in descriptions of teaching grounded in observations of classroom life as it is actually lived, and idealized descriptions of teaching as it 'should be' (Leiberman and Miller, 1978). Real-life accounts such as Ayers (1989), Calderhead (1987), Clandinin (1986), Doyle (1977b), Jackson (1968) and Yonemura (1986), portray the classroom as a complex and often ambiguous working environment. Even the teachers in this study, persons of extensive experience and acknowledged ability, were at times uncertain, confused by complex social events and faced with the necessity of making fast decisions in stressful situations. As McPherson writes: 'No teacher ever does what she thinks is best. We do the best we can in the circumstances' (1972, p. 197).

Many preservice texts in early childhood education paint an entirely different picture; a fully-comprehensible environment in which the teacher, at all times, is in total control. For example, Hildebrand says to beginning teachers: 'You are there, alert, interested and knowledgeable about the situation' (1985, p. 342).

A case could be made for the usefulness of presenting a set of ideals to student teachers as goals towards which they might strive, in much the same way as a code of ethics serves as a personal yardstick against which to measure one's own actions. However, it is questionable whether the presentation of a set of often simplistic ideals helps beginning teachers come to understand the complex realities of teaching. As Wagner suggests, books on teacher education 'abound in imperative exhortations of the teachers-to-be' (1987, p. 175). She writes: 'A good teacher *must* be friendly, fair, kind, knowledgeable, warm, honest ... Sometimes it seems as if we as teacher educators do our best to pile on more and more imperatives' (*ibid.*). When these imperatives are internalized, but then fail to match the teacher's perceptions of his/her own teaching actions, the teacher may become caught up in affective self-conflicts that lead to great personal anxiety.

Respected early childhood education writers such as Beaty (1984), Hymes (1981), Hildebrand (1981) and Spodek (1985) have stressed the importance of consistency in the teacher's actions. In the real world of these classrooms, however, only Rhonda emphasized the value of total consistency. In the other settings, rules often were open to interpretation and selectively enforced. These teachers did not interact in identical ways with individual children and they occasionally made

The Human Encounter

statements only to change their minds, or wavered over ambiguous issues. In short, they were human, and characterized by the same inconsistencies and paradoxes as other members of our species.

According to idealized views of teaching, the teacher's behaviour should be predictably even. She is not supposed to be affected by factors such as mood, stress, or differing degrees of liking for individual children. No one would suggest that adults with poor mental health should work with young children, yet none of us is entirely free from personal problems, doubts and anxieties. That is the nature of the human existence. As Beynon suggests, teachers are not 'cardboard cut-outs' (1985, p. 177), but people with the same range of motives and emotions as other human beings.

In this study, the teacher's mood, the circumstances, the identity of children involved — all seemed to be related to noticeable differences in the nature of the teacher's contacts with children. For example, in most cases, Nan was warm, affectionate and responsive to children. However, on the day when she was worried about her assistant's behaviour, Nan's actions with children became unusually distracted. When Julie behaved inappropriately, Nan became visibly annoyed. Throughout the freeplay period, Nan was clearly distressed, with tense and angular body movement. Only at the end of the grouptime, as Nan handled the beautiful, fragile, leaf skeletons she had gathered from a rainforest, did the lines fade from her brow and her body posture relax. Clearly, Nan's anxiety was a major influence on the nature of her interactions with children on that day. (Later, rather uncharacteristically, Nan berated herself for this loss of control.)

Several of the teachers acknowledged the importance of a calm mental state in working with young children and described their techniques for attaining it, before the arrival of the children. They told how they tried to purge other distracting thoughts from their minds, so as to be tranquil, maximally receptive and moving at a slower pace, appropriate for the young child. (It was a joy to arrive very early at Nan's preschool, to appreciate with her, the dew on the garden, the bird calls and the soft orchestral music on the stereo.) Despite this careful mental preparation, however, there was no guarantee of remaining calm through later events. Brenda placed the greatest importance on a calm mental state, and achieved outward calmness (at least) under very trying circumstances. Even so, events in the preschool sometimes shattered her calm state and left her feeling anxious, angry or drained.

These teachers certainly were not immune to children's negative actions, as Yardley suggests: 'the teacher views each child objectively.

She is not personally affronted by a child's aggressive behaviour; she isn't hurt if a child rejects her; she isn't disturbed when he becomes anti-social' (1971, p. 63).

These teachers were not incapacitated by children's negative reactions to others or themselves, but neither were they totally unaffected. When Julie was acting in a tyrannical manner towards Emma and others, Nan was affronted and told Julie so in very blunt terms. Brenda was visibly upset when Charles added stress to Michael's already highly-stressed life. When Darren failed to assist at tidy-up time, Rhonda was unmistakeably aggravated and communicated her personal displeasure to him.

According to the ideals of teaching, teachers must accept each child equally, without prejudice (Read and Patterson, 1980; Yardley, 1971). Few writers (Greenberg, 1969; Richardson, 1967) have acknowledged that teachers will not form equally-valued relationships with every child in their groups. Yet as Greenberg writes, to suggest this is possibly is to disregard the humanity of the teacher and to deny the uniqueness of persons (1969, p. 27).

Underlying the ideal is a belief in an enormous self-control on the part of the teacher. If the teacher is to match the ideal, she must control, or at least conceal, her emotions, moods and personal feelings towards each child. When teachers feel 'dislike' for a child (Hildebrand, 1985, p. 335), or feel the child is 'less quickly lovable' (Hymes, 1981, p. 97), they are counselled to put extra effort into understanding the child and building a good relationship, regardless of their personal feelings.

As they spoke about teaching, the teachers in this study echoed that concern. Only haltingly did they acknowledge that they had difficulty dealing with one or two children, but said they strived to conceal their feelings and to form a good relationship with all children. Rhonda emphasized this most strongly. She saw it as a 'professional responsibility'.

Despite these good intentions, however, there was a small number of children with whom these teachers were having more difficult relationships. Kathy had many problems with Adrian, a demanding child whom she described in unguarded moments in quite negative terms. Nan identified Dave as a child who was difficult to live with. Although Brenda understood Charles's traumatic history and turbulent home life, and had empathy for his problems, she felt her interactions with him were often non-satisfying. Finally, Rhonda had difficulties with Carmel, a child whose manner Rhonda found rather aggravating.

To some extent, all of these difficult relationships involved children with problematic behaviour patterns. However, this alone could not account for the difficult relationships. Other children in each setting also behaved unacceptably from time to time, but these teacher-child relationships had a different quality. For example, in Kathy's centre, Lewis's behaviour often was a problem and he and Kathy 'crossed swords' regularly. But Kathy spoke of Lewis with affection and admiration (calling him 'Old Lewie') and the disputes between Kathy and Lewis were quickly over. Nan enjoyed a similar relationship with Julie, a child whose behaviour often was problematical. Although she sometimes was annoyed with Julie, Nan showed great affection for her and spoke warmly of the years they had known each other, since Julie had first visited the centre as a new-born.

In talking about their more difficult relationships with these individuals, Brenda and Nan both made reference to 'a sort of look' that the child displayed, a facial expression that somehow made the teachers feel confrontive. As Nan said: 'I really find that look hard to take'. These comments were reminiscent of work done by the French ethologist Montagner (Pines, 1984) who suggests young children develop characteristic bodily and facial gestures that can be categorized as aggressive, pacifying or attaching. He found that pacifying and attaching gestures attracted positive responses from others, whilst aggressive gestures promoted less desirable responses, and even caused some children to be repelled by others. Montagner's work focused on peer interactions, but these teacher's descriptions suggest the possibility that similar, fundamental (almost perceptual-level) interactions may be part of the complex web of interactions that binds those that live together within classrooms.

In traditional early childhood education, the 'instructional' approach, in which the teacher tries to control the learning process by directing the learners' every action, has never been highly valued (Hildebrand, 1981). Instead, the teacher is expected to educate by means of indirect strategies (Montessori, 1974) such as facilitation, enticement and persuasion (Hymes, 1981). For example, Hymes writes of instilling a concern for others:

> You talk. You persuade. You give examples. You do your best to make the case for decency. You are not long-winded, of course ... Words are the essence. You reach for the best way to penetrate a child's mind. (1981, p. 138)

A facilitator does not use the power differential between teacher and child like a blunt instrument, but tries to support the child as s/he resolves a problem for her/himself. The teacher does not assume ownership of the problem, but allows the child to retain ownership. In the interactive events observed in these settings, however, facilitation emerged as a paradoxical and sometimes murky construct, with only a fine line between persuasion, enticement, or 'verbal motivation' (Hildebrand, 1981, p. 93) and manipulation. For example, Nan's attempts to help children gain access to peer play groups involved such apparently facilitative actions as accompanying a child while s/he issued an invitation to another to join in, and speaking for the child to a peer if words failed her/him. However, upon closer examination of these situations, it seemed that on some occasions, Nan might not have been acting in a strictly facilitative way, but might have been subtly manipulating the situation in the interests of the 'outsider' child.

Consider the dilemma of a teacher such as Nan, who believed that non-directive strategies were much more desirable than directives. She wanted to offer children as many choices as possible and have them solve their own problems whenever they could. However, at the most basic level, the success of non-directive strategies relies on the cooperation of the children. If children steadfastly refuse to cooperate, as they sometimes do, what then? Hymes' (1981) advice is to keep trying until the child acquiesces, but in the classroom many other things are happening simultaneously and the teacher does not have the option of staying with a child indefinitely. She has limited options at this point. She can abandon the scene altogether ('unethical' says Katz, 1984), resort to a directive strategy, or introduce an element of manipulation into her indirect approach in the hope of gaining children's acquiesence.

Before we condemn the manipulation as dishonest, unethical or failing to respect the integrity of the child, we would do well to consider Toulmin's words:

> No doubt, the doctrine that we should — in all circumstances, and at all times — perceive, act, and feel, in ways that are strictly realistic and appropriate, is a counsel of perfection. In actual fact, we all have 'touchy' subjects and moments of vulnerability ... In moments of extreme grandiosity, we may 'manipulate' our associates, so reducing them to means in the fulfilment of our goals and intentions. (1977, p. 316)

These teachers were not always able to facilitate, to persuade, to entice. Many factors were involved in their ability to use these desired strategies, not the least of which was the children themselves. And as Toulmin (1977) suggests, the salient factors affecting the teacher's facilitation or lack of facilitation, were not exclusively external or situational. The teacher was also influenced by a complex and influential network of personal factors. Her 'moments of vulnerability', her mood, her longstanding beliefs and priorities; all were included in the complex equations that formed life in these preschools.

A Tentative Model

Theoretical Bases

Much research in the last decade has begun to explore the personal practical knowledge of teachers (Bolster, 1983; Calderhead, 1987; Elbaz, 1983; Lampert, 1985), but although researchers such as Shulman (1987) have acknowledged that the practical knowledge of early childhood teachers may well be different from that of other educators, little is yet understood about their specific knowledge base and how this is used in practice. At later levels of education, traditional views of the teacher's knowledge base have centered on content information and skills, and the means of transmitting these from teacher to learner (Fenstermacher, 1986; Wilson, Shulman and Richert, 1987). But this has never been seen as a useful conceptual model in early childhood education, where knowledge of child development has been considered most important (Silin, 1987; Spodek, 1987).

One of the most commonly heard terms in early childhood education at present is 'developmentally appropriate practice' (Bredekamp, 1987), but much remains to be understood about how early childhood teachers utilize their knowledge of child development and how this aspect of the early childhood educator's knowledge base interacts with other areas of knowledge in practical decisions about teaching actions (Silin, 1987). As Fein and Schwartz (1982) have pointed out, there remains a substantial gap between knowledge of child development and an early childhood teacher's practical knowledge of teaching.

Clandinin (1986, p. 177) has suggested that personal practical knowledge is not modelled on theoretical knowledge and it is futile to attempt to understand practical knowledge by attempting to analyze teacher actions in terms of various theoretical approaches. Certainly in this study, alternate theories of social development or social learning were found to be of very limited use in coming to understand these teachers' actions or the nature of social life in these educational settings. In both words and actions, these teachers were eclectic. They used varying combinations of modelling, positive reinforcement, social instruction and at the same time, placed a good deal of faith in the maturational process.

In its areas of interest, this study crossed the boundaries of many areas of knowledge and considered various theoretical approaches. Humanist psychology contributed to the understandings that were possible through the work done by Combs (1978) and others on the inner lives of persons. But internal aspects such as beliefs, values and attitudes alone cannot account for teacher actions, even considering the more recent conceptions in which belief/attitude and action are seen to be reciprocally related (Kelman, 1974; Nespor, 1987; Theunissen, 1984; Zeichner, Tabachnick and Densmore, 1987).

Clearly, the context in which actions occur is a crucial influence on human interaction and any path to understanding must be able to incorporate contextual features, including both the physical and human environments. The theoretical approach taken by Bronfenbrenner (1979) and other human ecologists, has provided a framework through which to examine the interactive influences on development, and this study has made considerable use of the work of social ecologists such as Day (1983) and Doyle (1977b) in considering the contextual influences on human interaction.

Similarly, the symbolic-interactionist approach has contributed to the understandings that could be generated. Blumer's (1969) notion of shared meanings, a world of constructed realities (Berger and Luckman, 1967), in which participants continually construct and respond to the meanings events hold for them, was found to be a useful way of thinking about and making sense of what happens within classrooms.

Critical pedagogy (Smyth, 1987) takes a broader focus in examining the influences of the social context on the ways in which curriculum and schooling is constructed. Although this study did not make extensive use of this perspective, the influences of the social context on these teachers' beliefs and actions continually emerged. Aspects of the social context were an important influence on the images these people held of themselves as teachers, the priorities they set and the meanings they assigned to classroom events. For example, Brenda's experiences living with and teaching Aborigines had given her a unique understanding of the dilemmas faced by Aboriginal people in an education system that was thoroughly grounded in white Australian culture. Other, less dramatic influences also were apparent. For example, Kathy showed how the demands of the society for early achievement and conservative educational practices impacted on her views and actions in the preschool. Critical pedagogists acknowledge that some of the impact of the social context resides in the person of the teacher and the understandings that person holds about the way classrooms should be, but thus far at least, the major focus has remained on the societal, rather than the personal, the general, rather than the specific. Thus, the broadest social context remained peripheral, rather than central to this investigation.

What seemed to be required to understand what goes on between teachers and children, was a framework that provided for interactions within the internal world of the person; between the internal and external worlds of the person; as well as the interactions between persons in a given social environment. The 'intentionalist' or 'constructivist' models, (Doyle, 1977a; Fenstermacher, 1986; Magoon, 1983) in which the teacher is seen as a person constructing his/her own understandings of events and acting upon them, would seem to come closest to this framework. Ball and Goodson describe this perspective as follows: 'The teacher is seen as involved in the development of creative and strategical responses to societal and situational constraints ... or as resolving ever-present dilemmas through and within their interactions with pupils' (1985, pp. 7–8).

To attempt to examine the perspectives of so many people is a complex undertaking, but this is simplified if the framework is conceived as a wheel, with spokes radiating from a central hub. Each spoke might be thought to represent the internal aspects of one individual in the group. The hub, where all the spokes come together, might be considered the 'shared reality': the jointly-constructed, highly interactive social world of the classroom, in this case, labelled 'Living Together'.

In his studies of disturbed families, Henry (1971) was able to study each individual and every possible combination within the family group. In the metaphor of the wheel, he considered every spoke and every possible perspective on the hub. But in this study, with twenty-two to twenty-seven people in each setting, such coverage was impossible. Instead, the focus was on the internal life of the teacher (one spoke) and the observable interactions within the classroom (the hub).

Because so little is known of the internal lives of the children, the wheel schema has been collapsed to a simple three-part model. All the child factors have been grouped together in a single spoke. This distortion has been accepted as the price paid, in attempting to reduce an enormously complex web of interaction to a simple two-dimensional model (see Figure 1).

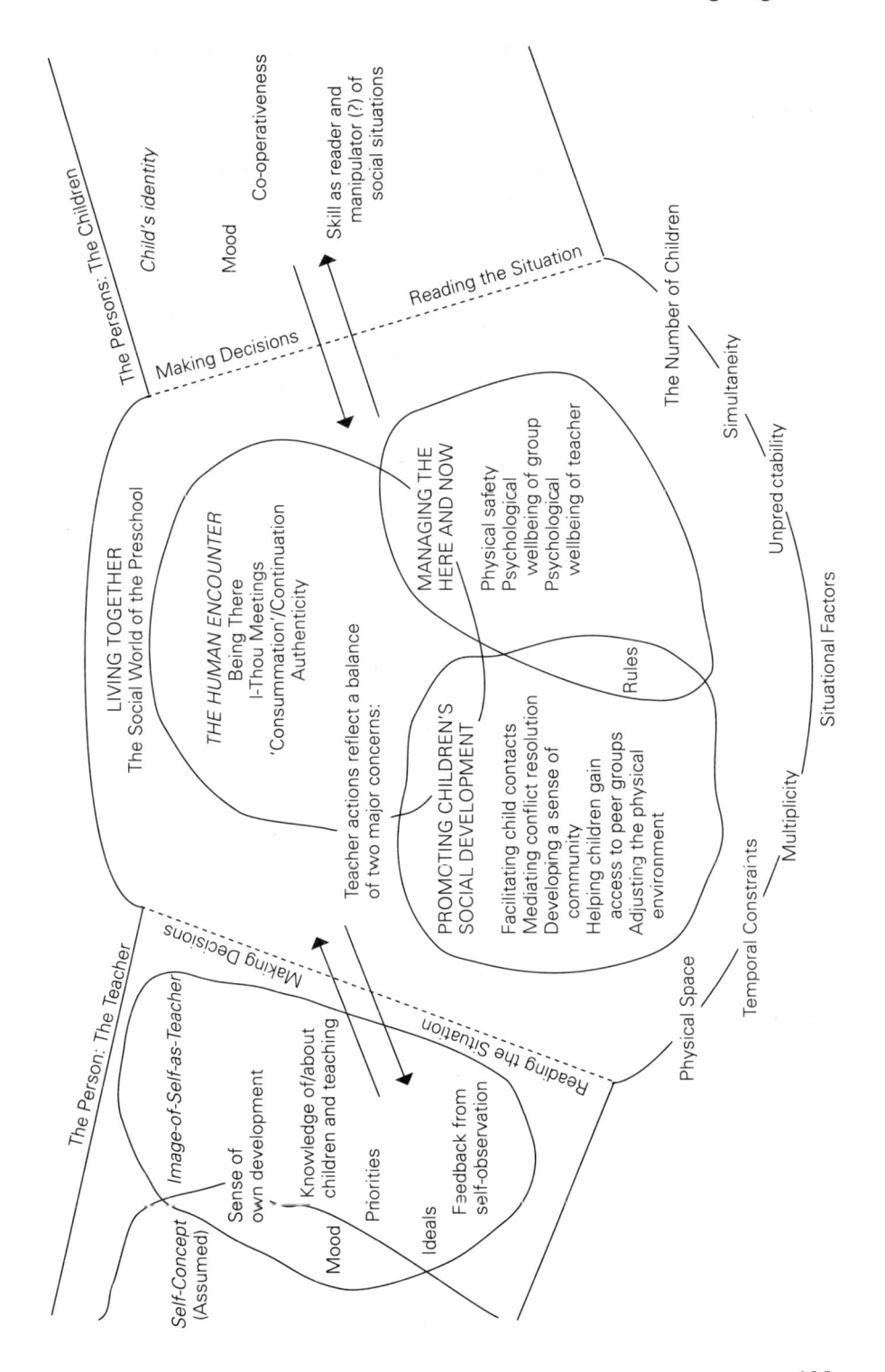

Living Together

The Persons: The Children
- Child's identity
- Mood
- Co-operativeness
- Skill as reader and manipulator (?) of social situations

Reading the Situation

Making Decisions

LIVING TOGETHER
The Social World of the Preschool

THE HUMAN ENCOUNTER
Being There
I-Thou Meetings
'Consummation'/Continuation
Authenticity

MANAGING THE HERE AND NOW
- Physical safety
- Psychological wellbeing of group
- Psychological wellbeing of teacher
- Rules

Teacher actions reflect a balance of two major concerns:

PROMOTING CHILDREN'S SOCIAL DEVELOPMENT
- Facilitating child contacts
- Mediating conflict resolution
- Developing a sense of community
- Helping children gain access to peer groups
- Adjusting the physical environment

The Number of Children
- Simultaneity
- Unpredictability
- Multiplicity

Situational Factors
- Temporal Constraints
- Physical Space

Reading the Situation

Making Decisions

The Person: The Teacher
- Self-Concept (Assumed)
- Image-of-Self-as-Teacher
- Sense of own development
- Knowledge of/about children and teaching
- Mood
- Priorities
- Ideals
- Feedback from self-observation

185

The Human Encounter

It seems that what happens when teachers and children 'live together' in preschools, cannot be understood without some consideration of who those persons are. Equally, however, the person cannot be understood in isolation, without recourse to the others who share that world. This paradoxical situation characterizes not just educational settings, but humans and human interaction everywhere. As Laing writes:

> No one acts or experiences in a vacuum. The person whom we describe, and over whom we theorize, *is not the only agent in his world*. How he perceives and acts towards the others, how they perceive and act towards him, how he perceives them as perceiving him, how they perceive him as perceiving them, are all aspects of 'the situation'. They are all pertinent to understanding one person's participation in it. (1969, p. 66)

Because of this interdependency, the boundary between the internal (personal) and external (situational) factors has to remain highly permeable. One can never say with certainty, where 'self' ends and 'other' begins. As Dallmayr writes: 'Contrary to the assumption of a fixed or easily defined boundary, there is a strong tradition in Western thought ... according to which the linkage between I and Other is not a relation of exclusivity but one of mutual dependence' (1984, p. x). In the interests of clarity, however, it is now deemed necessary to briefly ignore this interdependence and describe the internal aspects of the teacher as though these were a discrete entity.

Image-of-Self-as-Teacher

It is widely accepted that persons carry with them a set of understandings about themselves. Such understandings are variously called the self-concept (Yamamoto, 1972), self-image (Yamamoto, 1972), self-definition (Gould, 1980), or self-identity (Carr, 1983; Laing, 1969). One common feature in writings on the self concept, is the assumption that it is quite distinct from the self. For example, it has been described as a 'story' about one's self, that is told to self or others (Carr, 1983; Laing, 1969) or a map depicting territory (Yamamoto, 1972). Self-concept is believed to be relatively stable over time, with change occurring very slowly through experiences with others. But Morton has cautioned that we should be wary of assigning too much unity or integrity to a person's beliefs about self. He points out that these, no less than other beliefs, could be expected to be complex, ambiguous and contradictory. He writes: 'Our attempts at uncomplicated perception are compromised by our persistently complicated cognition, and our attempts at detached rationality are fouled by our persistently human motivation' (1980, p. 94).

The problems of self-reference are many, and it would seem our beliefs about ourselves are no less paradoxical and ambiguous than our actions. However, the 'stories' we tell ourselves, about ourselves, provide one way of 'making sense', of interpreting our interactions with others and thus influencing our ongoing interactions. As Toulmin writes: 'Self-knowledge in this sense is a product both of self-study and self-creation' (1977, p. 294).

Just as all persons carry with them a set of beliefs about themselves, so might the person who is teacher be thought to carry a set of beliefs about him/herself as teacher. These beliefs might be called the 'image-of-self-as-teacher'. It might be expected the connections between this image-of-self-as-teacher and action would be similar to the connections between self-concept and action; that is, the internalized image might be considered to both guide and interpret action in a reflexive way.

It would be expected that this specialized self-image would not be unrelated to the person's broader self-concept. The person entering a teacher-education program already possesses an elaborate set of understandings about self, education and the world at large. He or she does not begin the creation of an image-of-self-as-teacher on a blank slate. Some parts of the image are already present, in shadowy outline. Therefore, it is suggested that the image-of-self-as-teacher is not a separate entity, unconnected to the broader self-concept, but an overlapping set of beliefs. It would be expected that many connections would exist between the two areas of beliefs about self. Clandinin, in her work on teacher image writes: 'The emotional and moral dimensions of image are the glue which binds together the educational and personal private sides of an individual's life' (1986, p. 131).

In this conception, the image-of-self-as-teacher, although involving an element of personal choice, of 'self-creation' (Toulmin, 1977), would be relatively stable, as it is rooted in the self-concept. Some writers (Greene, 1981; Lampert, 1985), however, have assigned the teacher's 'identity' a much more malleable position. They suggest the person has an almost unlimited breadth of possibility, to decide on a persona as a teacher.

Just as the self-concept is believed to change very slowly, it could be assumed that as the person who is the teacher lives her/his life and moves through a career, there would be a continual interplay of beliefs and experiences. (Clandinin, 1986, calls this a 'coalescence of experience'.) Several writers have seen this interplay as the means of adult development (Nias, 1985), and Gould has labelled it 'transformation', a basically maturationally-driven internal change. He writes:

> I see transformation as the central concept of adult development. If we are to understand the subtle day-to-day changes as well as the large crises in work and love, we must appeal to these central, ongoing processes, whereby each of us is driven by maturational necessity to be more whole, to include within us disenfranchised parts, and to be as internally free as we are capable of being. (1980, p. 224)

Other writers share this view that the interplay of internal factors is not only a change, but a bringing together, a move to greater coherency of self-image. For example, Fiske writes of 'synthesis of ambiguities' (1980, p. 261) as a process leading to internal growth, and Greene says: 'making connections is important too, "bringing the severed parts together" ... creating patterns and syntheses in experience, making our working lives more meaningful' (1981, p. 34).

This study was not able to access the deepest connections and interplay between self, self-concept and image-of-self-as-teacher, yet it was able to surface some connections and suggest others. For Brenda and Nan, some of these connections were well-travelled, familiar paths. These were highly introspective persons who already were aware of many of the connections between their self-concept and image-of-self-as-teacher. Yet even with these teachers, some areas, some connections, remained unexplored and we sometimes shared a sense of discovery, as we found new connections or interesting possibilities. Through this process of joint exploration, and from readings of the literature on the relationships of self and others, several distinct areas of the image-of-self-as-teacher were suggested.

It seemed there existed a strong sense of the person's own development or personal history. This sense of 'where-I-have-come-from' seemed an influential part of 'who-I-am-now', and the teachers often referred to their recollections of past experiences, to make sense of the here and now. For example, after scanning the observational narratives, Kathy commented that she used the word 'love' as a term of address for children, more than she had realized. Immediately, she went on, 'That comes from the time I spent in London. I picked it up from the Cockneys.' Although Kathy's London experience had been almost twenty years before, it remained part of Kathy's 'story' about herself.

As educational researchers have followed Goodson's lead in 're-integrating situational with biographical and historical analysis' (1980, p. 69), a number of writers have pointed to the importance of particular events in teachers' lives that are influential in the ways these teachers act and think about themselves. These events have variously been labelled 'critical incidents' (Measor, 1985, p. 61), 'personally memorable events' (Beynon, 1985, p. 166), or 'watershed experiences' (Clandinin, 1986, p. 147). Measor defines critical incidents as 'key events in the individual's life and around which pivotal decisions revolve. These events provoke the individual into selecting particular kinds of actions, then, in turn, lead them in particular directions and they end up having implications for identity' (1985, p. 61).

As these teachers spoke about themselves as teachers, it was possible to identify several of these watershed experiences. Rhonda's image of herself as 'a practical person' was expressed many times and she gave examples from throughout her teaching career (over almost twenty years) to support this belief. Rhonda's experiences as a beginning teacher in a difficult situation, with too many children and not enough adult help, was still a vivid memory. She told how she survived, by developing practical, 'economical' teaching strategies. These still were part of her teaching actions and her image of herself as teacher. Being 'a practical person' was part of her 'story'; not just a tale of the past, but a way of making sense of the present. Brenda's experiences in her first year of teaching also were a vital part of her story and her sense of who she was as a teacher.

Beynon (1985, p. 66) suggests that these memorable incidents may predate the commencement of a teaching career, and this was the case with one of Nan's watershed experiences, which dated from her childhood. Several times, Nan recalled her unhappy experiences of rejection by other children. This seemed to be not just a story for my consumption, but a way for Nan to 'make sense' of her present-day protective interactions on behalf of shy children. Richardson writes:

> Probably most of us, at times, see in our pupils shadows of our former selves. This can be both a help and a hindrance to us in doing our jobs. If a teacher has an image of himself as a child hovering on the edges of groups ... he is likely to notice and sympathize with a pupil who appears to be having similar difficulties. (1967, p. 64)

Richardson's (1967) words seem to describe Nan's involvement precisely. Whether her personal identification was a help or hindrance is difficult to say, but it was *there*, an important element in Nan's way of managing the dilemma of protecting children from rejection versus encouraging their self-sufficiency. (It is interesting to note that Smith, Kleine, Dwyer and Pruntz, 1985, p. 196 hypothesize that innovative, reform-oriented educators, more than the population at large, internalize strongly the unfinished business of their childhoods.)

Two other areas of the image-of-self-as-teacher that emerged from the data, were the teacher's ideals about children and teaching, and her first-hand knowledge of teaching and children. The relationship between these areas differed between teachers. Nan and Brenda, for instance, both seemed to hold knowledge of children and teaching that was firmly rooted in their own experiences. It seemed the 'conceptual apparatus' (Eisner, 1984, p. 207) or 'vision of worthwhileness' (Greene, 1981, p. 32) they had acquired as student teachers, had been transformed through years of experience, into a much more personal conception. They did not make reference to a set of ideals that was different from their own day-to-day knowledge of children. Their knowledge of children and of teaching was highly particularistic and these teachers felt very uncomfortable when asked to speak of their beliefs in more general terms. Anning reports a similar response when she asked teachers to categorize children. She writes: 'The process of decontextualizing learners from recognizable classroom constructs was not a 'natural' way for ... practitioners to think' (1988, p. 131). It is interesting to note that both Brenda and Nan paid close attention to feedback on their own actions. They scrutinized their interactions with children and continually questioned their specific actions and beliefs about appropriate teaching strategies.

Rhonda also seemed to have integrated her ideals with her personal knowledge of children and teaching, although in content her knowledge base was very different from that of Brenda and Nan. Rhonda's knowledge of children and teaching also differed, in that it seemed to be based more in her accumulated past experiences, rather than her present-day experiences of these particular children. Rhonda saw little value in introspection and appeared not to examine her own actions as closely as did Brenda and Nan. There was a sense that Rhonda's 'story' was completed and now she was following along, with a sense of comfort and certainty about herself and her interactions with children.

Although Kathy's image-of-self-as-teacher remained a largely indistinct form, it seemed a set of ideals was an important part of that image. Somehow, the ideals were maintained as a separate entity, quite distinct from her knowledge of these particular children, and teaching as she was currently experiencing it. As Kathy discussed teaching, her comments seemed to come sometimes from her ideals, and sometimes from the more experiential base. Unlike the other teachers, Kathy was most comfortable when speaking in general terms about her ideals. At least at the time of the study, Kathy gave little attention to self-observation and self-questioning.

The relationships between these teachers' differing knowledge bases and degrees of reflectivity raise important questions about the need for feedback from self-observations and the value of living the 'examined life' as a teacher. A belief in the value of introspection, or the turning of our not inconsiderable powers of observation on ourselves, has been given great importance since the time of Aristotle. Grundy says: 'For Aristotle the goals of morality were not in question. One did not deliberate, for instance, about whether just action was desirable, only about how to act justly. Deliberation is thus an essential element of practical action' (1987, p. 63).

Many thinkers in education have agreed with Aristotle, that the examined life is the only one worth living, or taken further, that examined teaching is the only type worth doing. A number of reasons have been advocated for this belief in the power of introspection. Many believe that it is able to expose incongruities or inconsistencies, so the person can then make the necessary adjustments towards greater consistency both among beliefs, and between belief and action (Bacmeister, 1980; Berk, 1976; Combs *et al.*, 1978; Petkau and Wheeler, 1981; Tyler and Goodlad, 1979; Williams, Neff and Finkelstein, 1981). Others (Fiske, 1980; Richardson, 1967) suggest the value of introspection lies not so much in the power to promote greater consistency, but in the person's ability to identify the ambiguities and find ways to live with them. Most recently, reflection has been seen as a means of coming to understand the nature of a professional's knowledge-in-action (Grimmett and Erikson, 1988; Schon, 1983; 1987). Critical reflection (Smyth, 1986; Van Manen, 1977) has added the social dimension, as a means of surfacing the taken for granted understandings that perpetuate social injustices through educational practices. For example, the critical pedagogists have advocated critical reflection as a means by which practitioners can individually authenticate critical theory about the socially-constructed nature of educational practices (Grundy, 1987, p. 19) and thus move towards an emancipatory curriculum.

Undoubtedly, introspection, self-observation and questioning are valuable qualities in teachers. Such self-examination has worth both for the quality of interaction between student and teacher and for the teacher's personal development. It would seem quite unrealistic, however, to suggest introspection has the power to totally remove inconsistency, ambiguity or injustice from human lives. Unlike Williams, Neff and Finkelstein (1981), I do not believe it possible to move the base of *all* teacher actions from tacit to explicit knowledge (Polanyi, 1967). Neither would we wish to, as such interaction, taken in extreme, would be distinctly non-human. Stripped of all human paradox and unpredictability, the contact between teacher and learner would resemble the interaction that occurs between computer and student.

Introspection, therefore, is not a singular, uniformly positive, clear-cut process, but a difficult and nebulous one. Just as there are many ways of acting in the world, so there are many ways of thinking about it, and many levels of reflectivity (Van Manen, 1977). Rogers describes the examined life as 'an exacting life, a hard life, requiring special knowledge, patience and effort' (1967, p. 65). What he has not mentioned is that living the examined life as a teacher also entails a degree of risk-taking; a willingness to make one's self vulnerable. Under some threatening circumstances, it may be safer not to question one's self too closely or observe one's interaction too minutely; in Fiske's terms, to lead a 'self-protective' (1980, p. 260) lifestyle.

During the time of this study, Kathy felt under threat from many sources, and it seemed for her introspection was simply too great a risk. She appeared to have virtually closed down the lines of feedback on her interactions in the classroom. Kathy seemed to be protecting not only her ability to function at an action level, but also her image-of-self-as-teacher. In her statements about teaching and in the tension she exhibited, Kathy showed many of the 'knots' described by Wagner (1987).

Writers on teacher burnout, such as Farber (1984) and Kalker (1984) make dire forecasts of the outcomes in terms of teacher performance and mental health, when teachers 'wall off' themselves in this way. Greene also sees this as a very negative situation. She writes: 'teachers are likely to become technicians or transmission belts, unable to think about their own thinking or their own valuing, out of touch with their lived landscapes, distanced from the human beings they hope to enable to learn' (1981, p. 36). Writers in human development, such as Gould (1980) and Moustakas suggest the person's own development must surely stop if the 'dialogue with self' (1968, p. 47) ends. But at least for the short term, the shutting down of feedback lines may be a strategy that enables a fragile person to keep going (Henry, 1971, p. xvii).

Although a total sense of coherence (Antonovsky, 1981) in one's beliefs may be more than most humans can reasonably hope for, a minimal level of coherence or 'underlying order' (Morton, 1980, p. 92) in one's belief systems would seem to be a prerequisite for any level of human functioning. In an ideal world, teachers would at all times, be fully aware of their actions and their embeddedness in the social context. In Greene's words, they would have a 'wide-awakeness; an enhanced consciousness of what it is to be in the world along with others, to have a plan of action, to pursue, to mend, to try to achieve' (1981, p. 35). But this is not an ideal world and such heightened awareness could not be claimed as a constant feature of these teachers' everyday lives. Kathy's position may well have been towards the end of a continuum of reflectivity, but even the most robust and introspective of the teachers in this study retained some small areas that were not open to self-scrutiny, some 'illusions'. As Henry (1971) and Fromm (1968) suggest, their continued ability to function in the social world may well depend on such illusions.

The Human Encounter

Readers who have had the opportunity to observe many early childhood teachers at work may have encountered a teacher who interacts pleasantly with young children, but leaves you with the suspicion that there is 'no one at home'. You wonder if children who reach out to him/her also feel they have encountered an empty teacher-shell, from which the person has somehow escaped. But what is it, that makes some interactions between teachers and children seem 'real', vital and alive, and others appear empty and hollow? When one's interest lies not in the surface level interactions between teachers and students, but in the fundamental person-with-person contacts that occur in educational settings, what does this mean? What is 'the human encounter' and can it occur in preschools, where the differences between the teacher and the taught are so marked?

Buber writes: 'The fundamental fact of human existence is neither the individual as such nor the aggregate as such ... the fundamental fact of human existence is man with man' (Moustakas, 1968, p. 35). Meetings between people, Buber (1965) believes, are the essence of the human condition; this is the truly 'human encounter'. Yet the coming together of teacher and children in preschools is no guarantee of the best of human contact, only the possibility of it. Paradoxically, in our humanness, there is the capacity for both the best and worst of human interaction. Fromm writes:

> Many qualities are various possibilities of being human. In fact, they are all within each one of us. To be fully aware of one's humanity means to be aware that, as Terrence said ... I am man and nothing human is alien to me; that each one carries all of humanity within himself — the saint as well as the criminal. (1968, p. 59)

In Buber's (1967) terms, the pinnacle of human-with-human contact is the 'I-Thou' relationship, but there are many aspects of teacher-child interactions that make the 'I-Thou' unlikely in preschool settings. For example, Buber believes that for this relationship to occur, both parties must encounter each other of their own free will, yet young children typically do not have a choice about attending preschool. They are enrolled because it is their parents' wish and they do not have the option of walking out if it is not to their liking. To a lesser extent, the teacher also has little choice in the matter. If she wishes to stay in employment, she must arrive each morning and remain through the appointed times, even though on some occasions (and with some groups of children) she might rather be elsewhere.

Buber (1965) emphasizes that for the more mundane 'I-It' relationship to become an 'I-Thou', the persons involved must be characterized by equality. Theunissen states that there must be a community in which no one disposes the other: 'a relationship of mutuality. Without mutuality, there is no dialogical relationship' (1984, p. 275). One of the most pervasive features of early childhood classrooms is the differential power of children and teacher. Although the children are by no means powerless, the teacher is larger, stronger, more articulate and carries the weight of authority, thus mutuality rarely occurs in teacher-child relationships.

Buber also emphasizes that the 'I-Thou' relationship cannot occur whilst it is seen as a means to an end: 'Between I and Thou there is no end, no greed, no anticipation ... Every means is an impediment. Only where all means have fallen away can the meeting come about' (Theunissen, 1984, p. 275). It is ironical that this pinnacle of human contact can occur in classrooms settings, only when one of the most central aspects of teaching is foregone. For a teacher to meet a child in an I-Thou encounter, at least for one moment in time the teacher would have to give up the desire to use this interaction as a means of achieving a goal. Both teacher and child would need to approach the meeting in a state of 'grace' (Buber, 1965, p. 98; Theunissen, 1984, p. 280), with a willingness to open him/herself to the other, a genuine desire to take on the other's perspective and a surrender to the immediacy of the moment.

Given these requirements, it is clear that contacts between teachers and young children only rarely will conform to Buber's (1965) description of an 'I-Thou' relationship. Yet these rare contacts still may be exceedingly powerful. In their criticisms of research on effective teaching, Doyle (1977b) and Fenstermacher (1978) agree that there is little evidence to support the assumption that the most frequent interactions between teachers and children are necessarily the most important ones. And as Moustakas has said:

> No matter how complicated or restricted or frightening life appears to be, the opportunity for encounter is always present. However heavy the pressures and responsibilities of life, there is nothing that can completely prevent genuine meetings between teacher and child. (1966, pp. 29–30)

In this study, note was taken of those times when teachers seemed to share a special moment with children. Caldwell and Honig's (1971) observation instrument uses the term 'consummation' to refer to those times when a teacher makes a comment to a child, recognizing the successful completion of a task. As observed in these settings, such 'consummations' had a celebratory ambiance. They often involved praise, but the interaction was not simply positive reinforcement. The child was not 'given' praise, but rather the teacher helped the child to appreciate some cause for celebration in the child's own achievements. It became clear that such joint recognition of a special moment did not require task completion. Sometimes, it occurred even in 'unsuccessful' situations. One of the most noteworthy examples was Brenda's interaction with Paul, upon the collapse of his block building. Amidst the noisy turmoil of the classroom, Brenda and Paul seemed to share a moment of pure communication and joy in his attempt at mastery — despite the immediate failure. (It was interesting that many of the consummatory interactions noted in Brenda's classroom involved Paul. Just as some teacher-child relationships are more difficult than others, so it seems that some may have special qualitites that make them a source of particular pleasure for teacher and child.)

Humanist writers such as Moustakas (1966) and Laing (1969) have written of 'confirmation'; the behavioural manifestation of a valuing of the child — trusting the child's inherent wisdom and seeing the child's presence as enriching. The teachers in this study often were confirming. The very structure of their curricula, which allowed children to make many of their own choices, both in selecting activities and deciding what to do within those activities, was a source of confirmation. In each setting, the teachers often 'blatantly listened' (McLean, 1986) to children, showing through their body posture and verbal responses, that they were attending to the child's communication and treating it in a serious manner.

These teachers' respect for children and their ideas was evident across many situations, yet the degree of confirmation (Laing, 1969, p. 82) in interactions varied considerably. Ironically, the highest level of confirmation was seen in Brenda's centre, where the children were the most vigorous, argumentative group observed. Despite enormous situational pressures, Brenda continued to listen to children, acknowledge their points of view and check their feelings or ideas before giving directions that would involve them.

Confirmation also was seen in these teachers' facilitatory teaching strategies, where they recognized the child's agency by allowing him/her to retain control of the outcome. Even in interactions that were not necessarily gratifying to the child, such as when a request was refused, these teachers acknowledged the child's existence. Recognition of 'other' was an almost constant feature of Brenda's, Nan's and Rhonda's interactions. They were 'mentally present' and did not make distracted or mindless responses. Nan was particularly concerned with the need for mental alertness in her interactions with children — a concern that was evident in her encouragement for children to make their own judgments about their work. She condemned the mindless 'That's-lovely-darling' responses she sometimes observed in other adults.

Even with these three teachers, however, there were occasional interactions where confirmation was low. For example, when Nan was angry with Dave after a sustained peer conflict, she would not allow him to voice his version of the event. Similarly, as Rhonda was attempting to get the girls' dance recital underway, and Carmel repeatedly raised objections, Rhonda's lesser confirmation was evident in her responses.

In these low-confirmation interactions, the teachers seemed under pressure to deal with stressful situations. If the degree of stress teachers felt was related to the degree of confirmation of their actions, one would expect that Kathy might display responses low in confirmation and this was borne out in observations, where across a range of situations, Kathy's actions were low in confirmation as she refused to accept children's judgments. There also were times when Kathy was rather vague in her response or when she responded 'tangentally' (Laing, 1969, p. 85), with a statement unconnected to the child's earlier remark. Although, of course, there were periods when Kathy was warm and responsive to children, the frequency of low-confirmations suggested a picture of a tired teacher, for whom each day was a struggle.

Buber has written of another aspect of the human encounter, 'being there' (1965; 1967). These deceptively simple words encompass a wealth of meaning for Buber and other humanists. They convey the 'being-ness' — the immediacy and availability of this person to the other; the mutuality — this person is a human being as the other is a human being; and finally, the ability of this being to experience the other's being. As Buber says: 'The man whose calling it is to influence the being of persons ... must experience this action of his ever anew from the other side' (1965, p. 100). Fromm calls this ability to take on the other's perspective 'empathy or compassion' (1968, p. 79), and Moustakas (1968) emphasizes its importance for teachers.

This willingness to step into the other's shoes, to see things from the child's perspective, was often seen in the teachers in this study. Nan had a particularly strong sense of her connection with children and seemed to be saying, 'I am as they are'. Nan wanted many of the same things for herself and the children, most notably, to be relaxed in each other's company and to enjoy the experience of being together. In making judgments about children and her interactions with them, Nan trusted her feelings and personal experiences. (A similar personal base for teaching decisions was described by Talley, the teacher in the preliminary study, as 'feeling right'. Talley might 'try on' new teaching strategies for a time, but ultimately a decision would be made about whether to include them in her repertoire based on whether they 'felt right' to her (McLean, 1985).)

Unlike Nan and Brenda, Rhonda saw a stronger distinction between herself as teacher, and the children. As the legislator of rules, Rhonda was single minded and sometimes did not display an awareness of the child's perspective. In interviews, however, Rhonda's comments suggested that she may have been aware of the children's differing perspectives, but deliberately purged this awareness from her actions in the interests of behavioural consistency.

The notion of teaching as a performance, in which the teacher plays an artificial role to motivate children, has never been part of the traditional early childhood philosophy, where children's interests have been highly valued and gimmicks have been dismissed as trivial and unnecessary (Carini, 1986). The notion of teacher authenticity, as explored by humanist writers (Hawkins, 1974; Moustakas, 1966) would seem a much better fit with traditional early childhood concerns, yet in the real world of these preschools, authenticity was found to have some paradoxical aspects.

All of the teachers expressed a desire to 'be themselves' in their interactions with children. Although Rhonda and Brenda gave examples of occasions when they did perform, the notion of teaching as a performance was not a comfortable one for them. Performing was seen as 'something that you sometimes have to do', rather than a description of what teaching is, or should be, about.

Nan expressed a strong aversion to the concept of teaching as performance and placed the greatest emphasis on authenticity, a concept to which she had devoted considerable thought. As Nan described it, her self-concept did not see a single unified self, constant across all situations, but something constructed between self and others. This acceptance of the 'between self and others' aspect, enabled Nan to acknowledge very different behaviours as being equally authentic. As she adjusted her responses according to the identity of the other, she did not see some actions as a distortion of her 'authentic self', but as a different manifestation of an equally authentic self.

Nan strived to make her contacts with children 'real', and was not perturbed if her feelings showed. Particularly in the case of the robust children, when Nan was displeased she gave quite blunt feedback. Unlike the common early childhood ideal, Nan was not always evenly tempered and warmly accepting. Sometimes she 'lost her cool'. As Buber writes: '[The teacher] need possess none of the perfections which the child may dream he possess; but he must be really there' (1965, p. 98). Nan was very much *there* for those children.

Yet even Nan had difficulty being totally open and authentic with children all of the time. As discussed in an earlier section, her 'facilitative' interactions sometimes contained a subtle element of direction, in which she manouevred children towards an outcome she valued, without acknowledging this to the children. Because of her knowledge of individual children's insecurity, she sometimes concealed her negative feelings, and because of her practical knowledge about how to maintain reasonable harmony and order in group life, sometimes acted in ways that were not necessarily a full reflection of her present emotional state. Thus the enactment of the notion of teacher authenticity takes on an aura of myth. The best of human encounters may be characterized by the teacher's authenticity, but there are many other types of interactions between teachers and children in the course of living together in preschool settings.

Situational Factors

Any attempt to understand the human interactions between teachers and children must of necessity consider the backdrop, the texture of classroom life, against which such interactions occur. In these settings, the physical environment was found to exert a powerful influence on the social world that was constructed within the preschools. These were large and challenging environments in which children often were widely dispersed. A group of twenty-five children could be actively engaged with a wide range of materials and with each other, for the most part, without overcrowding, but the sheer size of the environments meant that teachers and children were not always in close contact. It was not unusual for a teacher to greet a child well into the program: 'Hello. I haven't seen you today. What have you been doing?' (This was not true of Brenda's centre, where the environment was smaller and children rarely were out of her sight.)

The human environment also was part of the backdrop against which teacher actions took place and from which they drew meaning. Ethnographic and ecological studies of elementary school classrooms have suggested that three common features of the human environment in classrooms are multidimensionality, simultaneity and unpredictability (Doyle, 1977b), and these features also were found to be powerful descriptors of life in preschool settings. Erikson writes: 'One of the most salient ethnographic "facts" about life in classrooms [is] that there always seems to be more than one thing at a time happening' (1977, p. 67). In these preschool settings, it seemed the extent of multidimensionality might be even greater than that encountered by researchers in elementary school classrooms. These groups were dispersed over a much larger area, often using indoor and outdoor spaces simultaneously, and were involved in a huge range of activities. At times, there were almost as many different activities as there were children.

Doyle's (1977b) 'simultaneity', in which the teacher was needed in many places at once, was a particularly salient feature of these settings. Sometimes children would cluster around the teacher (a feature also described by Jackson, 1968) waiting for help with a problem. Many demands were made concurrently and the teacher had to find ways of dealing with these dilemmas. It was not possible for the teachers to meet every request that was made of them. If they occasionally failed to follow through, forgetting a commitment in the press of subsequent events, it may have been because there were times when the situational pressures simply overpowered the teachers' ability to deal with them. It should be taken as an indication of these teachers' skills that such incidents happened so infrequently.

A common feature in all of the settings was the intertwining of multiple interactions. If the interactional events of the session could be graphically displayed in a temporal sense, they would not appear serially, like beads on a string, but as overlapping and intermittent. For example, a teacher might begin to interact with a group of children in one location, only to be diverted by the arrival of another child with a more urgent need. Often, teachers were obliged to leave interactional sequences partway through, to attend to more pressing demands elsewhere. Sometimes, the teachers returned to earlier situations and picked up the threads of their interaction, or cycled between three or four groups in relative proximity. Seldom did teachers have the luxury of completing one series of interactions before another began.

The teachers' awareness of and opportunity to interact with quiet children (the 'invisible children', (Byrnes, 1984)) often was conditional upon the momentary demands of the total group situation. When the group was noisily demanding, and the teacher was needed in many places at once, these children missed out, as they did in Brenda's classroom when the boys were in conflict. When the group was reasonably settled, teachers did have an opportunity to interact with the quiet children. For example, Nan was able to enjoy some very facilitative interactions with Richard during these periods of calm.

Doyle's third factor, 'unpredictability', also was found to be a salient feature of these settings. Although all of the teachers planned aspects of their programs, these plans often were substantially modified or discarded entirely, during the course of the session. Flexibility seemed an essential component of these teachers' skills. Although life in these settings was often unpredictable, these teachers were required to make a constant series of short-term predictions. Decisions had to be made every few minutes (sometimes, every few seconds) about whether to stay with one small group of children or move on to others. This seemed to be a common dilemma for the teachers. If they left too soon, a conflict could break out once again or a fragile dramatic play group fall apart. At the same time, they knew that other children would benefit from their presence. Sometimes, the teachers were able to stay nearby, to observe the results of their input before leaving the scene, but on most occasions they were busy elsewhere within a few seconds of completion of an interactional sequence.

This highly complex network of situational factors was the context in which living, teaching and learning were embedded in these preschool settings. It is interesting to ponder to what extent these situational factors existed by virtue of the teachers' deliberate choices and to what extent they were the unintended consequence of other values, other decisions. Certainly Rhonda made a deliberate attempt to address these factors by reducing the demands made on her and thus freeing her to work with individuals — a high priority in her program. But the degree of control that characterized Rhonda's program would have been unacceptable to Brenda and Nan, who seemed to enjoy the vitality, flexibility and spontaneity of their programs, even if this brought greater unpredictability and uncertainty. As Jackson says:

> [Teachers] come to know that the path of educational progress more closely resembles the path of a butterfly than the flight of a bullet. Moreover, the majority of teachers seem to enjoy working under these [unpredictable] conditions and actually look forward to having their plans spoiled by the occurrence of unexpected events. (1968, p. 167)

One of the most fascinating aspects of studying teachers in their real-life teaching contexts is the reflexive nature of their activities. Many Australian preschool teachers operate outside of the social or administrative structures commonly associated with schools (Nias, 1985), and although not free from constraints, have a considerable amount of scope to create the sort of educational program they desire. But the social world within the preschool is not created in the first seven days of the school year, then left untouched. It is continually being renegotiated, tested, acted upon and reacted to — constructed — by all of the participants. Although the teacher is not the only decision maker in this process, her personal needs and preferences exert a powerful influence on the social environment that is created.

Teacher as Decision Maker

The situational factors described in the previous section were highly influential in determining what was and was not possible for these teachers, but even more important were the teachers' own interpretation of events in context. They made sense of their perceptions of the immediate situation by drawing on their knowledge base — not only their long term beliefs and knowledge about children and accumulated experiences of similar situations, but also their shorter term, highly particularized knowledge of these individuals in this immediate context. Leinhardt defines this 'situated knowledge' as 'a contextually developed knowledge that is accessed and used in a way that tends to make use of characteristic features of the environment as solution tools' (1988, p. 146). Grundy describes this as a form of hermaneutical interpretation and says it is not a strictly technical form of decision making, but a highly sophisticated act of discernment, that 'makes full use of the teacher's knowledge of situations and children' (1987, p. 61). Such a complex and sophisticated decision making process suggests a teacher paralyzed, lost in thought, whilst analyzing the situation and weighing options. But, of course, these teachers frequently had to interpret situations and make decisions about their own actions almost instantaneously — a process Brenda described neatly as 'the quick think'.

Several strategies these teachers used to cope with this complexity and the need for rapid interpretation and decision making, were suggested from the data. Particularly in high stress conditions, the teachers seemed to focus on just one or two of the most salient elements of the situation and ignore other aspects. In keeping with Doyle's (1977b, p. 53) conclusions, it seemed this strategy might be less than optimal since it sometimes came at the expense of missed opportunities. For example, in the interactional sequence in which Nan was trying to meet Julie's need for positive peer contacts, she had to work hard to entice Zita to make contact with Julie. In focusing on Julie's need, however, Nan failed to note Zita's reluctance and the subsequent peer interaction did not meet Zita's own needs well. Similarly, when Carmel and several boys were engaged in noisy play in the block corner, Rhonda swiftly removed Carmel, without explanation. The intervention certainly reduced the noise level indoors and *may* have strengthened Carmel's appreciation of consequences when a rule was infringed, but opportunities for other areas of learning were passed by. During those stressful times, however, when the teacher is faced with an overload of demands and conflicting needs that are threatening her immediate well-being, this strategy may be a way to continue to function, even though at a less-than-optimal level.

Another strategy for dealing with the multitude of factors seemed to centre on the importance teachers placed on the identity of the participants (Doyle, 1977b calls this 'differentiation'). In many of the observed sequences of interaction, the identity of the children involved was clearly a major influence on the nature of the teacher's decisions. For example, Brenda used physical removal of a child as a strategy to end peer conflicts *only* when Charles was involved. In her own words, Nan 'pussy-footed' (i.e., proceeded gently and cautiously) or 'roused' (i.e., chastised) depending on whether the child involved was the fragile Richard or the robust Dennis.

To make complex decisions swiftly, several teachers seemed to have developed strategies that tried to create at least a few seconds' space for thought before decisive action was taken. In Brenda's highly particularistic program, where rules were few and teacher actions frequently were decided on a situation-by-situation basis, time to read the situation was critical. Brenda tried to ensure this by mentally preparing herself, using what was almost a biofeedback routine, to slow her responses so there was time for thought before action. When entering peer conflict situations, Nan often asked a lot of questions of children, but seemed to pay little attention to the answers before decisively ending the conflict. It seemed this also might have been a strategy for 'buying a little time' before acting.

For these experienced teachers, it seemed the well-established nature of certain patterns of interaction also helped them make rapid decisions. Yinger reports from cognitive research, that repeated practice enables the individual to chunk information and thus 'reduce the strain on short-term, or working, memory and increase the ability to do more things simultaneously' (1987, p. 301). This is one of the characteristics of 'the expert' practitioner. Similarly, Leinhardt (1988, p. 146) has suggested that a highly proceduralized and automatic form of knowledge is an important part of the teacher's expertise in solving specific teaching situations.

For the teachers in this study, certain familiar, and often used, strategies did not seem to rely as heavily on a detailed reading of the immediate situation and thus allowed the teachers to make some decisions without a lot of conscious deliberation. For example, Nan was surprised and pleased to see in the observational narratives, her frequent use of open-ended questions. She said there had been a time when she was trying to alter her speech patterns to include this form of questioning, when she had to 'stop and think' before every utterance. But at the time of the study, she no longer thought about it. Both Brenda and Nan suggested their statements to children were a combination of these almost automatic responses and other, more consciously reasoned components. They indicated that they had to consciously consider the key elements of their statements, but many other components were not really thought through, but simply uttered. Yinger has described a similar type of problem solving as a 'stored pattern' (1987, p. 312), that is used as a base around which contextually-sensitive modifications occur to form a creative design.

Nan's description of the long period of conscious, active commitment that was required to incorporate new teaching strategies in one's repertoire, before they reached this level of automaticity, was in keeping with the process described by Talley, the teacher in the preliminary studies (McLean, 1986).

These then were some of the ways in which these teachers as persons were connected to the interactive social world within the preschool, as they interpreted situations and made decisions about their own actions. The study managed to bring to the surface some of the complexities and paradoxes of early childhood teaching, and suggested that teaching might be described as a never-ending series of on-the-spot decisions, involving an impossibly large number of constantly-changing contextual factors and often conflicting concerns. Yet these teachers were able to make sense of it and function within their settings, with considerable skill.

Living and Teaching: The 'Here and Now' and 'Promotion of Development'

Just as one might debate whether the cup is half full or half empty, one could highlight either the similarities or dissimilarities amongst these teachers. To an observer familiar with preschool settings, the dissimilarities were powerful. These teachers were individuals, who in interaction with diverse groups of children in different social and physical contexts, had created quite different social worlds within their preschools. To use Berman's (1973) term, there was a 'texture' to life that was unique to each setting. Despite these differences, however, in all of the preschools the teachers appeared to be balancing two common concerns. The promotion of children's development was of great importance to these teachers, but they also experienced pressing demands related to the other major concern — the management of the here and now (Carter and Doyle, 1987).

Managing the Here and Now

'Survival' is not a pleasant word. It carries many negative connotations in education, where teachers are expected to do far more than ensure their own survival and that of their students. Survival in the classroom

Living Together

commonly is equated with 'coping', a synonym for poor teaching (Verma and Peters, 1975). Only with preservice or beginning teachers has survival been an acknowledged and accepted part of a teacher's concerns (Doyle, 1977b; Fuller and Brown, 1975; Katz, 1972; Petkau and Wheeler, 1981). Experienced teachers generally are thought to have moved beyond survival issues to more future-oriented concerns; to have moved from 'comfort' to 'criticism' (Russell 1988, p. 19). Yet survival issues of several types remained visible and important aspects of life in these settings.

When twenty to twenty-five children under the age of six years streamed into the preschool, a heavy responsibility settled on the teacher. She could not assume that the children would act in ways that would guarantee their own physical survival or that of their peers. The children rapidly scattered over a large geographical area and teachers were obliged to arrange adequate supervision, to ensure children's physical survival. There were many ways in which teachers managed this important aspect of the here and now. Some had firm policies on placement of staff members. Others made adjustments in staff placements as the session progressed and children flowed indoors and out. But supervision remained a constant concern. Even when working with individuals, these teachers had to remain cognizant of the whereabouts of other children.

Teachers relied on their assistants to share the supervisory duty and when the assistant was absent from the room (as in Brenda's case), or perceived to be unreliable (as in Kathy's case), supervision became an enormously heavy burden for the teacher. Under these conditions, the teacher had to remain constantly on the move. She could afford only a brief interaction with individual children before moving on.

The maintenance of children's physical safety seemed to involve quite complex interpretations that took into account the teacher's beliefs about appropriate degrees of challenge and risk, knowledge of individual children and knowledge of the finer details of the physical environment. Definitions of what was safe and unsafe were seen to vary both within settings and between them.

Rhonda had the most consistently-applied safety rules, but for all teachers the identity of the children was important. Actions could be considered safe for one individual or small group, but unsafe if different children were involved. For example, Kathy said she 'trusted *those* boys, because *they* had common sense'. Similarly, Rhonda moved quickly to forestall Tom, 'because *he* doesn't yet have a sense of when it might hurt somebody else'. Child identity apart, there were widespread variations in what the teachers generally considered safe and unsafe. Brenda worried about outdoor blocks left under a tree, just in case children climbed the tree and fell onto them. Kathy was aware, but not unduly worried by a child suspended three feet off the ground by a rope, or leaning over the threehouse rail.

Just as with physical safety, psychological safety cannot be assumed when a large group of preschoolers is confined in one location for several hours. At least a minimal level of organization is required to protect the psychological well-being of both adults and children. In all of these programs, there was an underlying structure that tried to ensure a reasonably harmonious existence for all. Even in Brenda's and Nan's low-structure programs, where formal rules were few, there were procedures for maintaining a level of decorum. Although some observers would consider the noise level high, limits of conduct did exist and the teachers acted to maintain those limits. Nan explained that 'organization for psychological survival' was a taken-for-granted aspect of life in her preschool. She had never thought to discuss it with her assistant, it was simply there.

In Rhonda's centre, the organization for psychological survival was more visible and readily acknowledged. Rhonda did not rely on incidental, 'as-they-seemed-needed' interactions with children to maintain conditions for psychological well-being. She legislated for it in advance, with an extensive rule structure that produced quite distinctive patterns of teacher-child and child-child interactions. For example, Rhonda referred children to pre-existing rules to resolve their social problems, and the children frequently quoted the rules to each other (or threatened to report rule violations).

Although psychological survival is important to all participants, the extent of the teacher's personal well-being emerged as a particularly influential factor in teacher-child interactions. As Hughes writes: 'The teacher is a person with unique experiences and needs. His behavior, like that of children and other adults, is influenced by his efforts to meet those needs' (1958, p. 461).

As previously discussed, Kathy's sense of well-being appeared doubtful during this period and many of her interactions with children reflected the stress she was experiencing in her day-to-day working life (Lazarus and Cohen, 1977). Brenda, although showing great resilience to situational stress, still reached a point when her calm demeanour was shattered and her facilitative actions ceased. For each of these teachers, their ability to facilitate, persuade, and entice had definite limits. When that limit was reached, the balance tipped from attempting to promote development in facilitative ways, to resolving the situation *now*, as much for the teacher's well-being as that of the children. A clear indication of this personal need to quickly resolve a situation was given in Brenda's account of the introduction of 'The Three-Block Rule'. When children continued to carry large loads and dropped blocks on each other's toes, despite a long series of (unsuccessful) facilitative interventions from Brenda, she introduced 'The Three-Block Rule' — a strategy that was most unlike her usual actions. She explained her decision: 'I wanted to save myself all these dramas'.

Carter and Doyle state: 'learning in classrooms is embedded in a complex matrix of events and forces that must be managed first if students are to be brought into contact with the curriculum and thus afforded an opportunity to learn' (1987, p. 157). In these settings also, it seemed the promotion of children's development was a less fundamental concern than the management of the here and now. If the group was reasonably settled, if no one was in physical jeopardy, if the demands on the teacher permitted, and if the teacher was maintaining a reasonable level of personal well-being, then the promotion of development became the dominant concern.

The tipping of the balance between management of the here and now and the promotion of development seemed to depend heavily on the teacher's interpretation of situations in context, and these teachers 'read' situations in very different ways. For example, Nan interpreted almost all peer conflict situations as needing rapid (teacher-initiated) conclusion, even when (to the observer at least) there appeared to be few other demands. As chaos erupted around Brenda, she continued to read conflict situations and the general group context, as allowing prolonged facilitative interventions. If the group context alone was considered, then Brenda's situation was much more pressing than Nan's, but the most salient factor was not the contextual factors themselves, but the teacher's reading of them.

In the graphic representation of this framework (see Figure 1), the two major areas of concern are shown as overlapping, because some teacher actions concurrently could be promoting development and managing the here and now. For example, the teacher's involvement in a conflict event might at the same time be facilitating several children's development of conflict resolution skills, lowering the noise level for all present, and preserving the physical safety of the children involved.

In examining the place teachers might hold in negative incidents between children, Katz (1984) suggests that the teacher's use of these situations to facilitate development is 'professional' teacher behaviour. If the teacher simply 'puts out the fire' (a concern with managing the here and now), this is 'unprofessional' teacher behaviour. Observations in this study suggest the picture is rather more complex than Katz implies. Whether the teacher becomes involved in ways that attempt to facilitate development, or whether she acts in ways that reflect her concern for the immediate present, depends on a complex interpretive process that encompasses both situational and personal factors.

Regardless of these teachers' beliefs, priorities or commitments, situational pressures sometimes led them to act in ways that were outside their normal (and preferred) range of behaviours. For example, over several days, as Charles' behaviour toward peers became increasingly threatening, Brenda's actions remained essentially facilitative. There came a time, however, when she resolved to remove Charles from his peer play group at the first sign of trouble, and acted accordingly. This strategy was alien to Brenda's preferred ways of interacting with children, but she deemed it necessary. A similar situation was seen in Nan's centre, when despite Nan's repeated facilitative attempts, Julie became increasingly tyrannical with her peers. At that point, Nan decided that everyone needed a respite and Julie was removed from interactive play situations to work alone.

The teachers were aware that, in these situations, often the needs of different children were incompatible, and whatever action decided upon would not be in everyone's best interests. Dilemmas such as these have been recognized as being at the core of teaching (Berlak and Berlak, 1981; Lampert, 1985; Leiberman and Miller, 1978). With the exception of Kathy, these teachers managed such dilemmas with an acknowledgement of the problem, followed by an acceptance of the situation. They were aware that teaching was, as Jackson has said, an essentially 'opportunistic process' (1968, p. 166). They did not hold idealized views of their actions, but recognized that situational factors limited what was possible at any given time. They also were accepting of many of their own (very human) limitations.

In their acceptance of the vicissitudes of classroom life, these three teachers were reminiscent of Mr. Gumpy (Burningham, 1970), a character in a well-known children's story. Mr. Gumpy was a knowledgeable but optimistic character, who, despite his misgivings, allowed a motley mismatched group of passengers aboard his boat. When the inevitable happened and all ended up in the river, Mr. Gumpy made no recriminations, but simply said: 'It's time for tea'.

These teachers also were knowledgeable about life in their settings. For them, this was not the complex and sometimes confusing place it might appear to an outsider, but a coherent environment that they understood, in a very personal and down-to-earth way. Like Mr. Gumpy, their attitude was realistic. Their first-hand knowledge told them that sometimes their plans would go awry; sometimes they would not be on hand when they were needed; sometimes their actions would not be perfect; sometimes children would be uncooperative. Yet despite this knowledge, they retained a sense of optimism. Although paradoxically, they held high expectations for themselves and the children, when things did not work out, they did not berate themselves, the children or the situation, but like Mr. Gumpy, said, 'It's time for tea', or perhaps, 'There's always tomorrow'. In their philosophical acceptance of limited success, these teachers did not see 'failures', but looked foward to the opportunities that tomorrow would bring.

Unlike many of their colleagues in other levels of education, these preschool teachers were not constrained by deadlines for children's achievement. They had no fixed syllabus and no testing program to impose temporal constraints. Their major deadline was the child's entry into primary school. This low level of temporal pressure was reflected in their timetabling decisions, where very large blocks of time were given to children's freeplay activities and the timetable as scheduled often bore little resemblance to the enacted program. Contacts between people in Western cultures are almost always bound by temporal constraints (Henry, 1971), but the low level of time constraints in these preschools made them quite distinctive social and educational settings.

Promoting Social Development

An important part of life within these settings was the teacher's concern for the quality of life in the present, but it was the promotion of children's development on which the programs' claim to be 'educational' rather than 'custodial' was based. Studies of child development have provided much information on young children's social development and patterns of interaction with peers (Asher, 1983; Asher, Oden and Gottman, 1977; Grusec and Lytton, 1988; Hartup, 1983; Honig, 1982; Moore, 1981), but few researchers have attempted to enter the life-worlds of children (Corsaro, 1985, p. 286) or examined the outcomes of various types of teacher intervention on children's peer interactions in naturalistic settings (Chafel, 1987; Marantz, 1988). In any case, the translation of research findings into practical teaching actions in real-life contexts is more than a simple matter of application.

These teachers' attempts to foster children's social development did not occur in isolation, but were embedded in a dense network of contextual, personal and transactional factors. One of the most distinctive aspects of working with young children is that the children's current abilities are themselves a compelling feature of the context in which the teacher makes decisions about how to promote children's development. Regardless of the teacher's skill, young children are not able to interact with each other with the same fluency as adults. A measure of social discord, of challenge, social failures as well as successes, are part of life in a group of preschoolers (Corsaro, 1985). This is the context in which the early childhood teacher works.

Across these programs, children's social development was accorded varying levels of importance. Brenda and Nan gave it the highest priority, whilst Rhonda and Kathy saw it as occupying a lesser position. Within the broad area of social development, each of the teachers focused on some aspects of children's peer interactions, rather than others. If the researcher were to dismantle teacher behaviour into small enough pieces, it could be said that there was a basic repertoire of micro-level behaviours that were common to all these teachers as they tried to help children acquire and practice social skills. To say they shared a common repertoire, however, would be akin to saying that Michaelangelo and Picasso shared the same colours of the spectrum. The ways in which these teachers combined the behaviours created patterns that were theirs alone.

Whether some teacher actions were more effective than others in promoting children's social development could not be ascertained in this study. It seemed, however, that these teachers did not select their preferred strategies objectively, on the basis of recent research. Their preferences had a great deal to do with themselves as persons, their beliefs about children and teaching, and the way in which they perceived the current needs of this group of children. As Combs says:

> Good teaching is not, it seems, a question of right methods or behaviors, but a problem-solving matter, having to do with the teacher's unique use of self as he/she finds appropriate solutions to carry out the teacher's own and society's purposes. (1978, p. 558)

Each of these teachers had her own ways to solve those problems.

Conflict situations: Conflicts between children were observed in every setting, though with differing frequency and intensity. In Brenda's centre, for example, the recurring conflicts within a small group of boys demanded a great deal of attention and dominated Brenda's pattern of interaction with all children. In Rhonda's centre, conflicts between children were much less frequent and Rhonda rarely became involved.

Many people feel uncomfortable with conflict and act to avoid it whenever possible. Similarly, those who work with young children may act intuitively, to end conflicts between children as quickly as possible. But Corsaro (1985), Minuchin and Shapiro (1983) and Ward (1985) suggest that fast conflict resolution by the teacher is not necessarily synonymous with the development of children's conflict resolution skills.

Conflict events, as they were encountered in these preschool settings, were found to be highly transactional situations, in which teachers and children appeared to continually read the other's responses and make adjustments in their own actions. It was clear that the shape of these events reflected both the teacher's and children's inputs. For example, it seemed that the extent of Brenda's involvement in peer conflicts was largely a function of the children's established patterns of interaction with peers. There was an imperative quality to these situations. When conflicts erupted, they did so with noise and pending violence, and Brenda was compelled to intervene.

The nature of her involvement, however, reflected Brenda's commitment to allowing children to retain ownership of their problems and solutions. She could have ended the conflicts quickly with a directive strategy, but in most cases opted for a long sequence of facilitative attempts to encourage children to verbalize the problem and generate solutions (Rogers and Ross, 1986, p. 16). Only if the conflict persisted was a turning point reached when Brenda took responsibility from the children and ended the conflict.

It was clear that other teachers 'read' conflict situations differently and the nature of their involvement assumed quite a different shape. For Rhonda and Kathy, conflicts between children were unfortunate distractions that took children's attention from other important tasks. Rhonda's low level of involvement reflected a conscious choice to stay out of children's conflicts because, like Hill (1982), she believed it was in the children's best interests to work them through without adult interference. On the rare occasion when Rhonda did become involved, after observing protracted peer conflicts, she quickly took control, resolved the conflict and refocused the children's attention on the substance of their play.

Kathy's relatively low level of involvement may have been a protective device, to reduce the level of personal stress she was experiencing. Kathy downplayed children's problems with peers and attempted to distract children from such situations. When she did become actively involved, Kathy typically used a directive to end the conflict promptly and restore the equilibrium of the group as quickly as possible.

Nan's beliefs about and actions in children's peer conflict situations surfaced the complexities of attempts to promote children's social development. She saw children's interactions with peers as a central province in which she could and should act as a teacher. Nan was very skilled in her use of the physical environment to support children's interactions with each other and she used this 'indirect strategy' (Hildebrand, 1981) to reduce the likelihood of conflict. At a personal level, Nan held strong convictions about world peace and nuclear disarmament (and made this known to parents as she explained why war toys were banned in her preschool). Although expressing a belief in the importance of children developing conflict resolution skills, when faced with children's conflicts, Nan seemed very uneasy and usually acted to end the conflict as soon as possible.

Even for these very experienced teachers, conflict situations among children were not easily handled. Although all showed they had within their repertoire of teaching actions the necessary strategies to quickly end the conflict, their sequence of actions reflected complex patterns of interpretation and decision making. Perhaps more than any other area, conflict situations seemed to best illustrate the dual nature of the teacher's task. Their actions reflected their own attempts to balance the management of the here and now with facilitation of children's social development.

Helping children gain access to peer play groups: Although many parents claim that a major reason for preschool attendance is to 'help children make friends', the role of the teacher in promoting children's friendly relations is not always a clear one. Helping children access peer play groups does not have the same imperative quality as peer conflicts. Sometimes children will ask for assistance, but more frequently the teacher must decide whether intervention is appropriate (Chafel, 1987), and these situations often pose dilemmas for the teacher.

One of the fundamental difficulties is whether a child's solitary state is a situation that needs remedying. Should all children be actively engaged with peers? Moustakas (1968) thinks not, and argues that solitude, as much as gregariousness, is a part of man. Asher (1983), in reviewing experimental research on children's peer interactions, also questions the assumption that low levels of interaction indicate low social competence and thus the need for adult intervention. In early childhood education further support for non-intervention comes from a tradition suggesting the teacher would be wise to stay out of children's social relationships (Montessori, 1964).

But there also has been concern with young children who are neglected or rejected by their peers, or who seem to lack the necessary skills to make positive contacts with others (Buzzelli and File, 1989; Byrnes, 1984). Extensive research using sociometric techniques has categorized young children according to their degree of popularity, rejection or neglect by peers (Asher, Singleton, Tinsley and Hymel, 1978; Hazden *et al.*, 1984; Peery, 1979) and suggested strategies teachers might use to help neglected or rejected children gain a higher level of acceptance by peers. Such strategies range from the use of games, literature and puppets (to demonstrate alternate forms of interacting), to arranging for two children to work together on a project (Rogers and Ross, 1986). Even with skilled teacher intervention, however, there is no means of ensuring a child's acceptance by peers, as Moore states: 'Teachers and parents can support the child through trying times, but in the last analysis, status in the peer group must be earned' (1981, p. 106).

Deciding to intervene, to assist a child in gaining entrance to a peer play group, is only the first difficulty. The nature of the teacher action also is problematic. Studies by Corsaro (1979; 1981; 1985) suggest that children's own strategies for gaining entry to peer play groups are quite different from those adults might advocate. Corsaro found that direct verbal strategies such as asking 'Can I play?' were used infrequently by children, who made much more use of indirect nonverbal strategies, such as circling and observing. Even so, the failure rate was high and, as Corsaro says, 'I soon learned that access into peer activities was a fragile process, and that one must be prepared for overt rejection' (1979, p. 323).

In some situations observed in these preschools, children's actions made it clear they very much wanted to be part of a particular play group. On other occasions, children's desires were much less certain. Their hovering on the fringes of peer play groups may have been a sufficient level of involvement for them at that time. There was also the question of what eventuated after a child had gained entry to the group. With teacher support, some children could enter, but this was no guarantee of harmonious, just or kindly interactions with one's peers, after the teacher had left the scene (Ross and Rogers, 1986, p. 15).

These access situations were highly ambiguous, and in making sense of them teachers made different decisions about the extent and nature of their own involvement. For Nan, this area was the highest priority and featured heavily in her program planning during the period of the observations. At the other end of the scale, Rhonda strove to stay out of access situations as much as possible, because of her belief that her mediation in peer interactions would increase children's dependence. Yet for both Rhonda and Nan, the identity of the children involved and their perceptions of those children's needs, was a particularly salient aspect of their decisions about whether to become involved and how to become involved. For example, Rhonda was observed to become involved in this area only when Cameron, a shy child, was needing assistance. This focus on helping specific children to coordinate their understandings of social situations with peers is in keeping with the approach suggested by Chafel (1987).

Brenda and Kathy also displayed low frequencies of this type of involvement, though on one of the rare occasions when Brenda did become involved, she seemed to have read the situation carefully and made a very sensitive and successful bid to help Gary gain entry to a play group of peers.

As discussed in an earlier section, Nan's extensive involvement in this area seemed to have been motivated, at least in part, by memories of her own experiences of childhood rejection and her desire to protect 'fragile' children from similar rejection. Nan had developed an extensive repertoire of strategies to help children gain access. They included prompting the outside child; suggesting ways s/he could fit in; encouraging children within the group to issue invitations to outsiders; acting as a 'public relations' person to verbalize the outsider's fine qualities; negotiating a child's entry; and fine-tuning the physical environment to entice selected children into interactive play. Through reminders about caring for other members of the peer play group, Nan also tried to ensure that once a child gained entry s/he remained a member of that small group.

It was interesting to note that of these teachers, only Nan deliberately and systematically planned her program to promote certain groupings of children in play activities, to meet what she perceived to be their individual social needs, a strategy described by Rogers and Ross (1986, p. 16). For the other teachers, their involvement in helping create peer play groupings was spontaneous, dependent upon the unforeseen interactive events that occurred.

Involvement in children's dramatic play: Some recent research has suggested that the preschool teacher's involvement in children's sociodramatic play is a powerful way to facilitate their development. In this study, although none of the teachers displayed the same high level of involvement as described in Perry's (1986) event based program approach, all participated in children's dramatic play.

On occasion, however, these teachers unobtrusively observed children's dramatic play, then decided to move on without becoming involved. When they did participate in the play, several different intensities of involvement were noted. The lowest level of intensity seen in this study seemed to be an almost ritualized quality of interaction between teacher and players. For example, Rhonda and Kathy sometimes visited play sites and expressed their interest, but did not attempt to influence the play in any way. They simply made a 'social call'. The problem of an adult fitting into the micro-world of children has been vividly described by Paley who says, 'often I drift around the edge of their knowing without finding a place to land' (1986, p. 131).

A greater level of intensity occurred when the teacher took on a fringe role in the play, then used that role to introduce a new idea or guide the children's behaviour. One of the most common fringe roles — used by all teachers — was what might be termed 'the curious visitor'. In this role, the teacher could observe, ask clarifying questions and offer some extending ideas, but then slip out of the play easily, without disturbing the game.

A third level of intensity occurred when the teacher took on a central role in the play, then used the role to elaborate the play and promote certain types of interaction among the players. Nan was observed most frequently in this level of involvement and her actions followed one of the most stable patterns encountered in the study. Nan tried to observe the play briefly before entering, then asked many focusing questions, to help the children think through their actions within the game and their relationships with other players (Buzzelli and File, 1989, p. 73 describe this strategy). Nan then would offer extending ideas or suggest environmental modifications, before leaving the play scene. Unlike many other types of interaction, this pattern seemed largely unaffected by the identity of the children involved.

An exception was the long interactional sequence in which Nan became involved with Julie and Emma in their bird's nest play. This intriguing event showed the essentially transactional nature of life in preschool settings, and was almost like a chess game in Nan's and Julie's move and counter move. Nan wanted Julie to help her companion Emma with the construction tasks, rather than act as supervisor, but Nan did not use her power to decree this. She allowed Julie to use the substantive content of the game to justify her refusal to assist with the tasks, just as Nan used the content to argue the opposing position. Julie was amazingly skilled in this verbal game, however, and even after a long sequence, Nan was unable to convince Julie by logic, that she should help.

Nan's initial selection of a non-directive strategy, to try to help Julie understand why she *should* help in the play, was in keeping with Nan's preferred range of facilitative teaching actions. However, as Nan's frustration grew in the face of Julie's refusal to cooperate, the here and now demanded satisfaction, and Nan switched to increasingly directive statements. The escalation culminated in a strategy that reflected Nan's power in this setting: she lectured Julie about her unacceptable conduct. Julie's recalcitrance had pushed Nan beyond the range of teacher actions she preferred. Once again, it was the interaction of many factors both within the teacher and the child, and the context in which the interaction occurred, that gave meaning and shape to this observable interactional sequence.

Rules: Research on the relationship between rule structure and children's peer interaction is not extensive, but at least some educational and developmental research suggests that social competence is enhanced in highly structured environments (Moos and Moos, 1978; Mitman, Mergendoller, Ward and Tikunoff, 1981). On the other hand, Minuchin and Shapiro (1983) suggest that peer contacts are more positive in low-structure classrooms. Similarly, Huston-Stein, Friedrich-Cofer and Susman (1977), in a study of economically disadvantaged children, found that children in high-structure classes had less frequent prosocial peer interactions. It would seem, then, that the relationship between degree of classroom structure and interpersonal climate is not well understood (Grusec and Lytton, 1988). Marantz, in reviewing experimental research on disciplinary practices and young children's prosocial development, can only tentatively conclude that: 'Insistence on proper behaviour must be clearly stated and delivered with sincere strong affect' (1988, p. 31).

Of the preschools in this study, Rhonda's program held a unique position in its reliance on an extensive and consistently enforced rule system. This reflected Rhonda's belief that a consistent rule structure gave children a secure base from which to operate and thus increased their competence with peers. For Rhonda, rules were both a means of managing the here and now and a way of promoting children's development. Her conviction was based not in her knowledge of recent research on classroom structure and social competence, but in her own way of looking at the world and her personal experiences with children. As Grundy (1987, p. 21) suggests, this teacher may have been acting in ways *congruent* with a theoretical position, but not *because* of the theory.

For the other teachers in the study, rules were seen as something that was necessary for the management of the here and now, but that had little direct value for children's social development. These teachers minimized the number of rules and enforced them somewhat selectively, according to their reading of specific situations and the identity of the children involved. In the low value they placed on children's ability to conform to rules, these teachers probably would reject Furlong and Carroll's assertion that indoctrination is appropriate for young children because 'they are being initiated into the reflective community and must learn not only general principles, but maxims and practices' (1990, p. 163).

Environmental support for peer interaction: In keeping with many Australian early childhood centres, these preschool programs were located in large, diverse physical environments, rich with materials for children to use in interactive ways. These teachers had many resources at their disposal and used them in various ways to support children's peer interaction. Of course, all provided the basic physical requirements such as long freeplay periods in which children could play together, interesting items to chat about, extensive collections of dramatic play props and groupings of chairs, tables and outdoor equipment that encouraged children to talk with each other (Rogers and Ross, 1986, p. 13). Paradoxically, these environments also supported the development of children's social competence with peers by allowing children to temporarily escape the control of adults — to provide children an opportunity to 'get on with' their self-appointed tasks in the peer world (Corsaro, 1985, p. 275).

In peer conflict situations, all teachers used some on-the-spot modifications to the physical environment that were 'curative' in nature. For example, the teachers often suggested children spread out, to increase the physical distance between them and thus lessen the likelihood of conflict. Similarly, they added materials or tools to an activity area, where children were waiting for turns. In some cases, there also were 'preventative' adjustments to the environment. Nan seemed particularly aware of the ways in which the physical environment impacted on children's interactions and often made adjustments before conflicts could arise.

Nan's fine-tuning of the physical environment, to promote certain combinations of children and promote certain types of interaction, was not the only strategy used to attract the focal children. The 'behind-the-scenes' (Hymes, 1981, p. 133) facilitation was supported by Nan's interpersonal contacts with children, when she made sure they were aware of the modification and often verbalized her reason for devising it.

Traditional early childhood education has emphasized the importance of the physical environment in challenging, engaging and supporting children. For example, early childhood practitioners generally have believed that scarcity of materials or tools leads to children's peer conflicts and that sharing cannot be forced upon children. As Lindberg and Swedlow state: 'An understanding of sharing cannot be legislated suddenly; it must be developed in an environment where a child feels that many things that he needs will be available to him, although he cannot have everything he wishes' (1985, p. 220).

Although the teachers in this study occasionally made injunctions to share and supported children in taking turns on equipment, they appeared to support Lindberg and Swedlow's (1985) view. Multiples of the same equipment (such as scissors, pots of paste, shovels and buckets) were common, and whenever possible children were directed towards other materials, rather than waiting to take turns with a single piece of equipment.

An alternative view has long existed in the Montessori approach, where materials purposely have been limited, in the belief that this helps children to learn to share (Krogh, 1984; Krogh and Lamme, 1985). It should be noted, however, that the emphasis in the Montessori approach is on productive individual work rather than harmonious group activity. A similar view is taken in Chinese preschools, where some studies (Sapon-Shevin, 1980) suggest that scarcity of materials actually promotes sharing. It would be interesting to explore the connections between the wider economic and social context and beliefs about how best to develop young children's ability to share. It would seem likely that these beliefs are rooted in differing cultures and economic realities.

Developing a sense of community: Extensive work by Corsaro (1979; 1981; 1985), examining the peer culture of nursery school children, suggests that young children are capable of sharing a group identity and a sense of community (Corsaro, 1985, p. 279). In each of these settings, the teachers acted to develop this sense of community. Some of their actions were highly visible, others were more subtle. As with the other areas of involvement noted, this area was of more importance to some teachers than others and each teacher had preferred ways of interacting. In Rhonda's and Kathy's centres, for example, ritual and routine were an important part of life. In Brenda and Nan's centres, ritual played a very small part and routines such as greetings and grouptimes showed considerable variation from day to day.

It has been stated (Pendleton, 1980) that learning to live in a group is one of the major tasks a preschooler faces, and for Rhonda an important part of living together was good manners. Ironically, few manners-related interactions were actually observed in this centre, perhaps because the children already were extremely well-mannered. In the other centres, although children were expected to treat each other and the staff with some respect, formal manners were not heavily emphasized. In every setting, the adults provided a good model, habitually using 'please' and 'thank you' in their interactions with children.

As they interacted with children in a wide range of situations, all of the teachers utilized opportunities to draw children's attention to other children and their activities, interests or achievements. For example, Rhonda often suggested children display the products of their work with construction toys and casually raised children's interests as a topic for peer conversations.

Nan particularly emphasized her desire for children to enjoy being together, but through their interactions with children, all of these teachers enacted a similar goal. Another similarity was that in every setting teachers reminded children to act with care and show consideration for others.

All of these teachers modelled helping behaviour and often remarked on or praised children for assisting others. Beyond this, however, the teachers displayed different approaches to the promotion of helping interactions between children. Rodd in reporting on a study of preschoolers' helping behaviours suggests that: 'Potential helping roles for young children may be highlighted by early childhood professionals who stimulate children's awareness of the states and needs of others' (1989, p. 41). Brenda showed particular sensitivity in interpreting the 'states and needs' of children both for herself and for other would-be helpers. Her actions in first checking with the helpee before offering assistance, or suggesting another child help, reflected her concern with allowing children to retain ownership of their problem. Other teachers often verbally identified the need for help and specifically prompted children to help their peers.

It is interesting to note that during the tidy-up routine, the pattern of interaction between all of these teachers and children underwent something of a transformation. In most cases, the teacher was no longer a facilitator, but a supervisor, allocating tasks and trying to get the environment cleaned up in the minimum time, with as little fuss as possible. During tidy-up time, helping behaviour was expected of all children. Yet even here, the teachers displayed their preferences. Rhonda had a whole set of rules to deal with the pressures of tidy-up time. Nan began unobtrusively, by tidying up the messiest areas, leaving other children undisturbed as long as possible. Kathy postponed tidy-up time until late in the session, then became rather frustrated when children were uncooperative. Well into tidy-up time, Brenda continued to check with children before allocating joint tasks, but if the climate became chaotic, as it sometimes did, Brenda resorted to firm directives. If Marantz's conclusions from research are correct, such 'emotionally delivered verbal interventions from significant adults' (1988, p. 33) could reasonably be expected to have positive outcomes in terms of the development of children's prosocial behaviour.

As they spent these hours together each week, sharing the physical environment and the social world within, these young children and adults became a 'community' with some sense of common interests. It seemed that many members of the group did have a sense of pleasure in being together and were connected with bonds of affection and respect.

Influence of the Personal Factors of the Children

This study did not extend to an exploration of the inner lives of the children, but their influence on the social worlds that were constructed within these preschools was pervasive. It would appear appropriate that in the final section of this chapter, the children should have the last word.

It seemed that children's influences were both direct and indirect. Their actions made a direct contribution to the interactive life within the preschool as they operated within their own peer culture, attempting to control their lives and share this control with their peers (Corsaro, 1985). But beyond this, children had an indirect influence through the meanings they held for the teacher. As Gump writes: 'Logically, we could ask what the class does to the teacher as readily as we ask what the teacher does to the class' (1964, p. 181). More recent educational writers also have emphasized the importance of the students in shaping educational realities. For example, Riseborough writes: 'Sociologists, in their studies of how schooling happens, need to grant a far greater degree of cultural competency to children, especially when it comes to a consideration of the social construction of their teacher's identities and careers' (1985, p. 208).

In these settings, children were observed to be influential both as individuals and as a collective. For these teachers, 'The Group' seemed to have an identity of its own. Teachers compared it with other groups they had known and held an elaborate and persistent set of expectations for the group as a whole. For example, Kathy said that with her two-day group, she was 'sane', she thought 'Vacation time!' on Thursdays and Fridays. But on the first three days of the week, she 'braced [herself] to face the group'. The power of this group of children to affect Kathy's sense of well-being is reflected in Riseborough's words: 'children can present teachers with profound crises of self, can render teachers dramaturgically incompetent by not allowing them to play their official paradigmatic role' (1985, p. 227). Brenda, the most positive of teachers, also said this was the 'most demanding group ever'. When 'The Group' holds such meaning for the teacher, the teacher's self-image, interpretations of classroom events and subsequent actions must surely be affected.

Early childhood teachers, who routinely work with more than one group of children each week, provide a rare opportunity to explore the ways in which the children contribute to the teacher's image of self. Although it was not possible in this study to examine teacher beliefs and actions across groups, it would be interesting to try to tease out some of the differences between the teacher's 'situated' identity (Ball and Goodson 1985, p. 18) that is situation-specific, and the 'substantive' identity that remains a core belief across situations.

Quite apart from the meaning 'The Group' held for teachers, individual children also carried a wealth of meaning. Teachers had a multi-faceted knowledge of these individuals and this was shown to be a powerful factor in the ways in which teachers interpreted classroom events and made decisions about their own actions.

Although the teacher was the focus of this study, some of the most interesting data came from the children, as they interacted with peers and the teacher. Some of the children appeared very skilled in interpreting the teacher's actions and certainly were not powerless in the shaping of interactional sequences. They were not simply responding to the teacher's initiatives and, on occasion, seemed to be manipulating the situation for their own ends. This suggests skilled reading of subtle situational cues and sophisticated cognitions that are not consistent with much of our knowledge about young children's social or

The Human Encounter

cognitive skills. Much Piagetian research has led us to believe that young children are still basically egocentric and cognitively incapable of double-guessing the other player. Just as estimates of young children's cognitive competence have risen in the last decade, however, one suspects that we have not yet begun to appreciate the extent of social competence in some young children.

Chapter 8

Looking Forward; Looking Back

Teacher Development

As this study proceeded, it found more questions than it answered. It brought to the surface many of the taken-for-granted aspects of early childhood education and made me more aware of the powerful place the ideals of early childhood education hold in my own thinking. In examining the relationships between these ideals and the real life practices of early childhood teachers, it raised questions about the professional development of teachers, both during preservice programs and later in the career path, as experienced practitioners. When one appreciates the deep-rooted personal dimension of teaching, the importance of the teacher's personal practical knowledge in interpreting situations with children and making a never-ending series of teaching decisions, one must surely ask what this means for teacher development programs. How best can early childhood teachers be supported in their ongoing professional development?

In programs that have been concerned only with early childhood teacher behaviour (Holmberg *et al.*, 1972; Rubow and Fillerup, 1970), extensive resources have been devoted to attempts to change the pattern of interaction between teachers and children. But even in the case of narrowly focused strategies, teacher behaviour has been found to be extremely resistant to externally-driven change.

As Combs (1978) and others (Fenstermacher, 1978; Moustakas, 1968) suggest, teacher development involves far more than simply presenting to teachers a list of appropriate teaching strategies. There is no way to inject sterile knowledge into teachers' minds, because each teacher must make his/her own sense of new information and incorporate or discard it for action on the basis of his/her existing knowledge. As Grundy states: 'Even if regularities of action could be identified,

The Human Encounter

human action ... is never so predictable that principles can be applied without regard for the uniqueness of any individual event or interaction' (1987, pp. 66–7).

Although there can be no 'formula' for teaching, no foolproof recipe to follow, there may be some value in making teachers aware of the range of practical strategies used by other teachers. Such information would need to be presented as one colleague to another, so that teachers were empowered to accept or reject ideas, or like Talley, to 'try on new strategies' for a period, and then decide if they 'feel right' (McLean, 1986), if they are congruent with existing understandings. Comments from the teachers in this study (and in the preliminary study), however, suggested that even after a teacher decides to adopt a new strategy and add it to his/her repertoire, the process of behaviour change requires many months of devoted effort. Without the teacher's personal commitment to the new strategy and sheer determination, it would seem there is little hope of a change in teacher behaviour.

But teaching is not a simple selection and application of value-neutral strategies in value-neutral contexts. Whilst a degree of teacher comfort with new strategies is undoubtedly important, it is not a sufficient criterion for determining the worth of teacher actions. As a society we would hope our educators were aware of the broadest implications of their actions with children. Thus, what is at issue here is far more than a surface change in teacher behaviour (Meek, 1986). Interactions between teacher and child are rooted in the personhood of both, in the complexity of their cultural, social and (in the case of the teacher) professional understandings. Whilst the influence of young children in shaping these interactions cannot be denied, the teacher holds the major responsibility for the maintenance of quality in educational settings, and thus, changes in teacher-child interaction would seem to require deeper-level changes in the person's image-of-self-as-teacher.

Reflection

Self-scrutiny, an exploration of one's own beliefs (Combs, 1978; Greene, 1981; Griffin, 1986; Hosford, 1980) or contemplation (Fiske, 1980; Kelman, 1974), has long been seen as a path to personal and professional development, but reflection comes in many guises (Van Manen, 1977). The most recent advocates emphasize socially critical reflection (Smyth, 1987) and suggest that the path to a more just, humane society lies not in changing teacher behaviour alone, but in altering the ways in which teachers think about themselves, their work and their place in society. For example, Clandinin (1986, p. 173) writes of the need to inspect one's own images and seek out one's cultural resources. Giroux writes of teachers 'developing a critical appreciation of the situation in which they find themselves' (1981, p. 218). Smyth (1987) suggests practitioners probe the origins of their beliefs, through an examination of the history both of their professional ideas and their understandings about the broader social context in which they work. Similarly, in acknowledging that early childhood practitioners believe their field to be unique within education, Silin warns: 'as members of a collective enterprise, it is important for early childhood educators to recognize the degree to which such an identity is embedded in its own socializing institutions, sites of practice and tools of instruction' (1987, p. 28).

One wonders, however, if this expectation of a probing level of socially critical reflection might add to the burden of ideals already carried by teachers. As experienced early childhood practitioners live out their teaching lives in familiar contexts, dealing with the sometimes pressing demands of everyday teaching, what might cause them to engage in this level of critical reflection? In this study, Nan and Brenda had been motivated by quite different personal experiences, to reflect on their actions, their beliefs about children and learning, and their own place in children's lives. They believed their introspection had been a vital part of their personal and professional development. But in the terms of critical pedagogy, this hardly constituted socially critical reflection. In Habermas' (1972) theory of human interests, their concerns remained largely at the practical, rather than the emancipatory level.

Like so much of their teaching, the reflectiveness of these two teachers seemed to be a combination both of their personal predisposition towards reflection and their location in a teaching context that in some way challenged them to reconsider their beliefs. Reflectiveness may be encouraged in supportive contexts, but in the final analysis, reflection cannot be imposed (Gore and Bartlett, 1988). It must develop from within, as an integral part of professional life. Yet paradoxically, reflection is not a solitary process confined to the mind of an individual. A number of writers have suggested it is a highly interactive process. As Nias states: 'talk emerges as the critical element enabling the formation of individual values' (1985, p. 115). In this study, both Brenda and Nan saw 'talking things over' as a very important part of their development as teachers. Brenda's description of discussing with other teachers, her concern with the dilemma of providing appropriate

Aboriginal and Islander content in her curriculum, was similar to Clandinin's comment: 'The talking through of issues of concern was a way of coping with an uncertain society' (1986, p. 142). For Nan, the ongoing dialogue with her assistant had provided a means of clarifying her own philosophy of teaching.

But for those professionally concerned with the quality of educational provisions for young children and their families, the development of reflective practice cannot be left entirely to chance. Administrators and professional leaders in the early childhood networks will need to be reflective themselves and actively seek a greater level of understanding about the nature of the contexts in which they and the teachers work. They will need to ask what dimensions of these contexts support reflective practice and what actions they might take to increase the likelihood of teacher development through reflection.

One approach might be to make available to teachers wishing to engage in more reflective practice, a 'guide' (Smyth, 1987, p. 44) rather like Gould's 'friend of growth' (1980, p. 223) or Schon's 'coach' (1988, p. 22), a person without a specific end in mind, a facilitator who can help bring to the surface the taken-for-granted dimensions of practice. However, just as Buber's (1965) I-Thou relationship is unlikely between teacher and children, because it requires mutuality and a surrender of means to ends, within teacher inservice organizations this would be a difficult role to play. In such organizations, the 'end' of high quality teaching behaviour has been a powerful force in the relationships that exist between advisers and teachers and this could not easily be set aside, even in the interests of true mutuality and facilitation of reflection.

Another approach would encourage teachers to work collaboratively as peers, supporting each other through the reflective process (Smyth, 1987). In such a group of colleagues, teachers might reflect on the path of their career and professional development, writing and sharing their stories as teachers, as a way of making sense not only of their past, but also their present (Ayers, 1989; Diamond, 1988; Schon, 1988). Manley-Casimir and Wassermann (1989) describe yet another approach they have devised in a graduate-level course for experienced teachers. They use films about teaching to stimulate peer discussion about the complex, yet often taken-for-granted realities of teacher decision making.

Nias (1985) has found that even in schools, with colleagues close by, professional isolation is common. In early childhood education, where often there is only one teacher in each centre, the potential for isolation is even greater. Measor highlights the dangers of this isolation:

> for many teachers, the conditions of their employment promote an attitude of non-involvement with peers. Such conditions engender feelings of insecurity, status panic and self-protection though isolation and promote a form of alienation that social psychologists have called self-estrangement ... a loss of meaningful connection between worker and work. (1985, p. 85)

This description would appear to have some relevance to Kathy's position at the time of the study, after working in the same early childhood centre for more than a decade, with limited professional peer contacts. One of the greatest challenges facing early childhood networks is how to address this structural potential for professional isolation. In a study currently underway, Halliwell (1989) is investigating the ways in which early childhood teachers working at the primary level can support each other as they undergo the uncertainties of a period of curriculum change.

Whilst reflective practice in early childhood education cannot be mandated, a great deal of current research in education is investigating the nature and conditions of teacher (and student teacher) reflection. This body of research has much to offer those organizations which are concerned with the support of teacher development.

Preservice Teacher Education

Although preservice teacher education may be guided by similar principles and commitments to those described above, it occurs in quite a different context, with persons who are markedly dissimilar to experienced teachers. As adults, students in teacher education programs bring to their courses a wide-ranging cultural and social knowledge base and a wealth of experience as participants in education systems, but for the most part they do not have an extensive accumulation of practical knowledge of teaching.

Unlike practitioners in the field, they are not embedded in a context about which and in which they are extending their understandings of their work. With the exception of their practicums, they are located in university contexts that are most unlike early childhood working environments. Their studies about the education of young children are embedded in a very different set of educational and organizational constraints. This discontinuity between teacher education and teaching has been of major concern to early childhood teacher educators such as Jones who writes: 'I make the assumption that teachers are more likely to teach as they were taught than as they were taught to teach' (1986, p. 124).

Despite the lack of continuity between the educational principles of practice advocated for young children and those generally applied to adult college students, at least the content of early childhood teacher education has been guided by a similar set of ideological or philosophical commitments as has traditionally been used to define the nature of quality in early childhood services. Child-centred curricular approaches have been emphasized, and students have been exposed to a considerable amount of child development information in the hope that their practical teaching decisions will be based in sound knowledge of child development.

Perhaps because of the strength of commitment that has characterized early childhood education and the location of much of the teacher education program in settings that are dissimilar to real-life teaching contexts, early childhood teacher education traditionally has inculcated students with a strong set of ideals about the way teachers *should* act to enhance children's development and learning.

As Eisner (1984) and Greene (1981) suggest, beginning teachers certainly do need a 'vision of worthwhile-ness', a beacon that will help them identify and find a path towards high quality professional practice. Teaching *is* essentially a moral endeavour (Buchmann, 1984; Fenstermacher, 1986; Grundy, 1987), with every decision or interaction having a value dimension. Because the practical inevitably involves an element of moral judgment, practitioners must retain a concern with what 'ought' to be. But the question remains — is the inculcation of a set of ideals about how teachers *should* act, sufficient in a teacher education program? Will knowledge of the 'shoulds' enable novices to reach those ideals in their own practice?

Whilst not denying the importance of the range of research-generated disciplinary knowledge that informs teaching, this forms an incomplete basis for decisions about practical action (Buchmann, 1984; Silin, 1987). Particularly in the field of early childhood education, with its history of close connections with developmental psychology (Weber, 1984), there has been a widespread belief that: 'In the best of all possible worlds ... early childhood practice would be the embodiment of the latest findings and conceptions of developmental psychology' (Elkind, 1982, p. 4). In this little-examined relationship originate many of the present-day 'shoulds' that characterize early childhood teaching (Bredekamp, 1987).

In interpretive research projects such as this, an attempt is made to set aside those 'shoulds' and document the realities of life as they are experienced by practicing teachers. In 'thick' descriptions of interactions between teachers and children in classrooms, a different source of knowledge is made available to inform beginning teachers. In the minds of teacher educators, however, and in the minds of the already socialized students, the imperatives of how teachers *should* act are not easily set aside. There is a danger of harsh 'armchair criticism' of practising teachers, if they fail to act at all times, in all circumstances, in accordance with the model of a perfect early childhood education. As students become more aware of the academic status accorded knowledge generated through scientific research, they may well apply these standards to what they observe of others' practical actions, and find these wanting (Buchmann, 1984).

Should teacher educators acknowledge to their students that early childhood teaching is a complex, often ambiguous, and seldom perfect business? I believe so. All too often, it is left to the practicum to acquaint students with the realities of teaching and thus perpetuate the unfortunate, but commonly held belief that what you learn on campus is 'theory', whilst in the field, you learn about 'practice'.

Yinger (1987) emphasizes the importance of 'learning by doing', learning about teaching by teaching in real-life contexts, and few early childhood educators would disagree with him. Some understandings can only be developed through first-hand experience, through problem-finding and problem-solving in real-life contexts. Yet in Australian early childhood teacher education programs at least, the practicum is problematic. The articulation of the practicum with campus-based studies is made ever more difficult by increased pressures of a political, economic and administrative nature. At the most basic level, it is difficult simply placing large numbers of students in the field and allowing them to stay a sufficient time to develop practical competencies. Yet the problems are far more complex than the issue about what constitutes an adequate length of time in the field. They involve a qualitative as well as a quantitative dimension. In an ideal world of early childhood teacher education, committed, questioning, confident novices would be placed with exemplary reflective practitioners, who would share their own understandings of the complexities of professional decision making and act as facilitators to enhance the novice's reflective understandings of teaching. In this world, however, many contextual factors impinge on both the teacher and the student teacher, to make this an unlikely scenario. Thus, it would seem that the practicum alone cannot be relied upon to help students find their own path through the ideals and realities of teaching.

Yinger (1987) believes that what is needed is 'a language of practice' that goes beyond a vocabulary of the profession to provide a 'conceptual apparatus' (Eisner, 1984, p. 207) of 'the modes of thinking and acting employed by the practitioners to effectively accommodate the tasks at hand' (Yinger, 1987, p. 295). Such a language would have value not only in preservice teacher education, but also for the development of the profession as a whole. As Griffin (1986) suggests, teachers do need better ways to think (and talk) about teaching.

Although much remains to be understood about the nature of early childhood teaching, research studies such as this are beginning to contribute to such a 'language of practice'. The practical knowledge used by teachers as they make complex teaching decisions may be informed by disciplines such as developmental psychology, sociology, philosophy and the content area disciplines such as mathematics, science and the arts, yet it is more than the sum of these parts. To quote Yinger once again:

> A language of practice for teaching must be a language of ... practical action. It must be more than just a language of method, or a language of outcomes, or a language of content. It must weave these components together as integrated patterns that illustrate practice as an artful combination of ends and means. (1987, p. 313)

It would seem likely that conventional approaches to the transmission of information will not be appropriate for such an area of knowledge. This set of understandings will not easily be reduced to a collection of facts to be transmitted in a series of thirteen weekly lectures. In Yinger's (1987) conception, this knowledge was deeply embedded in real teaching-learning contexts and its acquisition required students to be actively teaching in the field for considerable periods of time. In many early childhood teacher education programs this is not an option, so other approaches need to be explored.

A central element to such a knowledge of practice is the personal dimension. Buchmann states: 'Practice is personal because action commits people and is ineluctably one's own' (1984, p. 435). Jones likens learning to teach to a young child's learning. She says it is 'the slow, untidy attempt to gain understanding of all the parts and pieces of a whole world. It can't be hurried, nor can it be detached from the person' (1986, p. 137).

This knowledge would not be 'out there', a vast collection of facts to be poured in, in the hope that if only the 'right' knowledge is added, practical action will in some way be better (Buchmann, 1984, p. 426). Rather, it would be 'in here', with students engaging with it, pondering and questioning it, playing with it, as it became part of them. Such a level of enagagement would suggest that students need to be highly motivated. But I believe they are highly motivated, when they can see a clear relationship between the ideas and practical action. They have chosen to be early childhood educators and are impatient to get on with it. Like a child who goes to school to learn to read and is disappointed if this is not accomplished by the end of the first day, beginning students are desperate to try on the shoes of the teacher. In a sense, this also returns us to Buber's (1967) notion of the I-Thou relationship, in which persons are able to take on another's perspective, to 'see things from the other side'. To work with students in this area of knowledge means to understand their desire to 'try on' being a teacher, to help them take on a little of the teacher's role, even for a brief period.

Several recent writers (Coles, 1989; Postman, 1989) have reawakened us to the power of stories as a means of helping others develop values, knowledge and dispositions. Although storytelling is rarely acknowledged as a strategy for professional education, I suspect that storytelling about real life practice has remained an important part of early childhood teacher education. A recent investigation of two preservice programs (McLean, Moyer and Gomez, 1990) found that these stories commonly are oral accounts based on the teller's personal experience as a teacher. Information from students suggests such stories have been a powerful means of communicating with novices, hungry for information about their future lives as early childhood educators. Some writers (Battersby, 1990) would see these simply as anecdotal material that has limited worth in developing critically reflective practice. But they can be far more than illustrative examples of technical points or paternalistic descriptions of 'how to do it'. Through the engagement such stories engender in the listener, they can be a means of helping students to try on the shoes of the teacher, of considering wider implications and appreciating complexities. They can be a way of integrating the theoretical with the practical, a way to communicate in 'the language of practice'.

A number of recent texts used by preservice students also include substantial blocks of material that is narrative in nature and provides

The Human Encounter

thick descriptions of practice or first-hand accounts using teachers' own words (Calkins, 1986; Conelly and Clandinin, 1988; Pollard, 1987).

Story-sharing also may be a useful strategy to encourage reflection as an integral part of practical action in preservice teacher education students, who, although lacking a vast body of practical experience, nevertheless have some experience of teaching through their practicums. Schon believes that 'story-telling is the mode of description best suited to transformation in new situations of action' (1988, p. 26). He asks, 'How may we be helped to learn from past experience in the mode of reflective transformation? We can encourage one another to tell stories about experiences that hold elements of surprise, positive or negative' (*ibid.*).

In a sense, interpretive investigations such as this, that provide thick descriptive accounts of teachers and children living together in classrooms, are stories to be told, to be shared amongst practitioners and novices, to encourage others to tell their stories. Such an approach relies on vicarious generalization, the hope that readers will find in the story something to resonate against their own experience and deepen their own understandings about their work. Neither teachers nor researchers can lay claim to perfection, but it is hoped that through this story, you may have found your own questions about life with children in early childhood contexts.

References

ABRAHAM, K. and CHRISTOPHERSON, V. (1982) 'Social structural influences on two indices of social competence in preschool children, *Early Child Development and Care*, **9**, pp. 33–43.

ALLPORT, G.W. (1981) 'The general and the unique in science', in REASON, P. and ROWAN, J. (Eds), *Human Inquiry*, Chichester, UK: John Wiley and Sons Ltd., pp. 63–76.

ANNING, A. (1988) 'Teachers' theories about children's learning', in CALDERHEAD, J. (Ed.) *Teachers' Professional Learning*, London: Falmer Press, pp. 128–145.

ANTONOVSKY, A. (1981) *Health, Stress and Coping*, San Francisco: Jossey Bass.

ARNOLD, M. (1979) 'Early child-child communication', *Theory Into Practice*, **18**, 4, pp. 213–19.

ASHER, S. (1983) 'Social competence and peer status: Recent advances and future directions', *Child Development*, **54**, 6, pp. 1427–34.

ASHER, S.R., ODEN, S.L. and GOTTMAN, J.M. (1977) 'Children's friendship in school settings', in KATZ, L.G. (Ed.) *Current Topics in Early Childhood Education*, Vol. 1, Norwood, New Jersey: Ablex.

ASHER, S., SINGLETON, L., TINSLEY, B. and HYMEL, S. (1978) 'A reliable sociometric measure of preschool children,' *Developmental Psychology*, **15**, pp. 443–4.

ASHTON-WARNER, S. (1963) *Teacher*, New York: Simon and Shuster.

AYERS, W. (1989) *The Good Preschool Teacher: Six Preschool Teachers Reflect on Their Lives*, New York, NY: Teachers College Press.

BACMEISTER, R.W. (1980) *Teachers of Young Children: The Person and the Skills*, paper presented to The Early Childhood Council of New York City (ERIC Document Reproduction Service No. ED 178 155).

BALL, S.J. and GOODSON, I.F. (1985) 'Understanding teachers: Concepts and contexts', in BALL, S.J. and GOODSON, I.F. (Eds) *Teachers' Lives and Careers*, London, UK: Falmer Press, pp. 1–26.
BANDURA, A. and WALTERS, R.H. (1963) *Social Learning and Personality Development*, New York: Holt, Rinehart and Winston.
BAR-TEL, D., RAVIV, A. and GOLDBERG, M. (1982) 'Helping behavior among preschool children: An observational study', *Child Development*, 53, pp. 396–402.
BATTERSBY, D. (1990) *How Does the Practicum Make a Difference?* paper presented at the first National Workshop on the Practicum in Early Childhood held at Frankston, VIC, June.
BAUMRIND, S. (1977) 'Some thoughts about childrearing', in COHEN, S. and COMINSKEY, T. (Eds) *Child Development: Contemporary Perspectives*, Itasca, IL: F.E. Peacock, pp. 248–58.
BEATY, J.J. (1984) *Skills for Preschool Teachers*, 2nd ed., Columbus, OH: Charles E. Merrill Pub. Co.
BERGER, P.L. and LUCKMAN, T. (1967) *The Social Construction of Reality*, Garden City, NY: Doubleday.
BERK, L.E. (1976) 'How well do classroom practices reflect teacher goals?', *Young Children*, 32, 1, pp. 64–81.
BERLAK, A. and BERLAK, H. (1981) *Dilemmas of Schooling: Teaching and Social Change*, London: Methuen.
BERLINER, D. and ROSENSHINE, B. (1978) 'The acquisition of knowledge in the classroom', in ANDERSON, R.C., SPIRO, R.J. and MONTAGUE, W.E. (Eds) *The Acquisition of Knowledge*, Hillsdale, NJ: Lawrence Erlbaum.
BERMAN, L.M. (1973) 'Not reacting but transacting: One approach to early childhood education', *Young Children*, 28, 5, pp. 275–82.
BEYNON, J. (1985) 'Career histories in a comprehensive school', in BALL, S.J. and GOODSON, I.F. (Eds) *Teachers' Lives and Careers*, London UK: Falmer Press, pp 158–79.
BLUMER, H. (1969) *Symbolic Interactionism: Perspective and Method*, Englewood Cliffs, NJ: Prentice Hall.
BOGDAN, R.C. and BIKLIN, S.K. (1982) *Qualitative Research for Education: An Introduction to Theory and Methods*, Boston: Allyn and Bacon.
BOLSTER, A.S. (1983) 'Toward a more effective model of research on teaching', *Harvard Educational Review*, 53, 3, pp. 294–308.
BREARLEY, M. (1970) *The Teaching of Young Children: Some Applications of Piaget's Learning Theory*, New York: Shoken Books.
BREDEKAMP, S. (Ed.) (1987) *Developmentally Appropriate Practice in*

Early Childhood Programs Serving Children from Birth Through Age Eight (expanded ed.) Washington DC: National Association for the Education of Young Children.

BRONFENBRENNER, U. (1979) *The Ecology of Human Development*, Cambridge, MA: Harvard University Press.

BRONSON, W.C. (1981) *Toddlers' Behaviors with Agemates: Issues of Interaction, Cognition and Affect*, Norwood, NJ: Ablex.

BROPHY, J.E. and EVERTSON, C.M. (1974) *Process-Product Correlations in the Texas Teacher Effectiveness Study: Final Report*, Austin TX: University of Texas, Research and Development Center for Teacher Education (ERIC Document Reproduction Service No. ED 091 394).

BRYAN, J.H. (1975) 'Children's cooperation and helping behaviors', *Review of Child Development Research*. 5, Mavis E. Heatherington (Ed.) Chicago: University of Chicago Press, pp. 127–181.

BUBER, M. (1965) *Between Man and Man*, New York: MacMillan.

BUBER, M. (1967) *A Believing Humanism*, New York: Simon and Schuster.

BUCHMANN, M. (1984) 'The use of research knowledge in teacher education and teaching', *American Journal of Education*, 92, 4, 421–39.

BURNINGHAM, J. (1970) *Mr. Gumpy's Outing*, Middlesex, UK: Puffin.

BUSSIS, A., CHITTENDEN, E. and AMAREL, M. (1976) *Beyond Surface Curriculum: An Interview Study of Teacher's Understandings*, Boulder, CO: Westview Press.

BUSSIS, A., CHITTENDEN, E., AMAREL, M. and KLAUSNER, E. (1982) *Inquiry Into Meaning*, Final Report, National Institute of Education Grant 79–0026.

BUZZELLI, C.A. and FILE, N. (1989) 'Building trust in friends', *Young Children*, 41, 3, pp. 70–5.

BYRNES, D.A. (1984) 'Forgotten children in the classroom: Development and characteristics', *Elementary School Journal*, 84, pp. 271–81.

CALDERHEAD, J. (Ed.) (1987) *Exploring Teachers' Thinking*, London, UK: Cassell Education.

CALDERHEAD, J. and ROBSON, M. (1988) *Images of Teaching and Learning: Student Teachers' Early Conceptions of Classroom Practice*, paper presented at the Annual Conference of the Australian Association for Research in Education, Armidale, NSW, December.

CALKINS, L.M. (1986) *The Art of Teaching Writing*, Portsmouth, New Hampshire: Heinemann.

CALDWELL, B.M. and HONIG, A.S. (1971) *Approach: A Procedure for Patterning Responses of Adults and Children*, Washington, DC: American Psychological Association.

CARINI, P.F. (1986) 'Building from children's strengths', *Journal of Education*, **168**, 3, pp. 13–24.

CARR, D. (1983) 'Personalites of a higher order', in MCBRIDE, W.L. and SCHRAG, C.O. (Eds) *Phenomenology in a Pluralistic Context*, Albany, NY: State University of New York Press, pp. 263–72.

CARTER, K. and DOYLE, W. (1987) 'Teachers' knowledge structures and comprehension processes', in CALDERHEAD, J. (Ed.) *Exploring Teachers' Thinking*, London, UK: Cassell Education, pp. 147–60.

CHAFEL, J.A. (1987) 'Social comparisons by young children in preschool: Naturalistic illustrations and teaching implications', *Journal of Research in Childhood Education*, **2**, 2, pp. 97–107.

CHARLESWORTH, R. and HARTUP, W.W. (1967) 'Positive social reinforcement in the nursery school peer group,' *Child Development*, **38**, pp. 993–1002.

CLANDININ, D.J. (1986) *Classroom Practice: Teacher Images in Action*, London, UK: Falmer Press.

CLARK, C.M. and PETERSON, P.L. (1986) 'Teachers' thought processes', in WITTROCK, M.C. (Ed.) *Handbook of Research on Teaching*, 3rd Ed. New York: American Educational Research Association, pp. 155–296.

CLARK, C.M. and YINGER, R.J. (1987) 'Teacher planning', in CALDERHEAD, J. (Ed.) *Exploring Teachers' Thinking*, London UK: Cassell Education Ltd., pp. 84–103.

COHEN, D.H. and STERN, V. (1978) *Observing and Recording the Behavior of Young Children*, rev. ed., New York, NY: Teachers College.

COLES, R. (1967) *Children of Crisis. Volume 1: A Study of Courage and Fear*, Boston, MA: Little, Brown and Company.

COLES, R. (1989) *The Call of Stories*, Boston, MA: Houghton Mifflin.

COMBS, A.W. (1978) 'Teacher education: The person in the process', *Educational Leadership*, **35**, 7, pp. 558–61.

COMBS, A.W., AVILA, D. and PURKEY, W. (1978) *Helping Relationships: Basic Concepts for the Helping Professions*, Boston, MA: Allyn and Bacon.

CONELLY, S.M. and CLANDININ, D.J. (1988) *Teachers as Curriculum Planners; Narratives of Experience*, New York, NY: Teachers College Press.

CORSARO, W. (1979) 'We're friends, right?: Children's use of access rituals in a nursery school', *Language in Society*, **8**, 3, pp. 315–36.

References

CORSARO, W. (1981) 'Entering the child's world: Researcher strategies for field entry and data collection', in GREEN, J. and WALLAT, C. (Eds) *Ethnography and Language in Educational Settings*, Norwood, NJ: Ablex, pp. 117–46.

CORSARO, W. (1985) *Friendship and Peer Culture in the Early Years*, Norwood NJ: Ablex.

CORTER, C., ABRAMOVITCH, R. and PEPLER, D. (1983) 'The role of the mother in sibling interaction', *Child Development*, 54, pp. 1599–1605.

DALLMAYR, F. (1973) 'Phenomenology and social science: An overview and appraisal', in CARR, D. and CASEY, E. (Eds) *Explorations in Phenomenology*, The Hague, The Netherlands: Martinus Nijhoff, pp. 133–66.

DALLMAYR, F. (1984) 'Introduction', in THEUNISSEN, M. *The Other: Studies in the Social Ontology of Husserl, Heidegger, Sartre and Buber*, Cambridge, MA: MIT Press, pp. i–xvii.

DAMON W. and KILLEN, M. (1982) 'Peer interaction and the process of change in children's moral reasoning', *Merrill-Palmer Quarterly*, 28, 3, pp. 347–67.

DAWSON, J.A. (1979) *Validity in Qualitative Inquiry*, paper presented at the annual meeting of the American Research Association, San Francisco, CA, April.

DAY, D.E. (1983) *Early Childhood Education: A Human Ecological Approach*, Glenview, IL: Scott Foresman.

DAY, D. and SHEEHAN, R. (1974) 'Elements of a better school', *Young Children*, 30, 1, pp. 15–23.

DEAN, J. and WHYTE, W. (1969) 'How do you know if the informant is telling the truth?', in MCCALL, G.J. and SIMMONS, J.L. (Eds) *Issues in Participative Observation: A Text and Reader*, Reading, MA: Addison-Wesley.

DIAMOND, C.T.P. (1988) 'Construing a career: A developmental view of teacher education and the teacher educator', *Journal of Curriculum Studies*, 20, 2, pp. 133–40.

DOYLE, W. (1977a) 'Paradigms for research on teacher effectiveness', *Review of Research in Education*, 5, pp. 163–98.

DOYLE, W. (1977b) 'Learning the classroom environment: An ecological analysis', *Journal of Teacher Education*, 28, 6, pp. 51–5.

DUBOS, R. (1981) *Celebrations of Life*, New York: McGraw-Hill.

DUNKIN, M. and BIDDLE, B. (1974) *The Study of Teaching*, New York: Holt, Rinehart and Winston.

EISNER, E. (1984) 'No easy answers: Joseph Schwab's contributions to curriculum', *Curriculum Inquiry*, 14, 2, pp. 201–10.

ELBAZ, F. (1983) *Teacher Thinking: A Study of Practical Knowledge*, London, UK: Croom Helm.

ELDEN, M. (1981) 'Sharing the research work: Participant research and its role demands', in REASON, P. and ROWAN, J. (Eds) *Human Inquiry*, Chichester, UK: John Wiley and Sons, pp. 253–66.

ELKIND, D. (1982) 'Child development and early childhood education: Where do we stand today?', in BROWN, J. (Ed.) *Curriculum Planning for Young Children*, Washington, DC: National Association for the Education of Young Children, pp. 4–11.

EMIG, J. (1983) 'Inquiry paradigms and writing', in GOSWANNI, D. and BUTLER, M. (Eds) *The Web of Meaning*, Upper Montclair, NJ: Boynton/Cook, pp. 157–70.

ENRIGHT, R. and SUTTERFIELD, S. (1979) *An Ecological Validation of Social Cognitive Development*, paper presented at the biennial meeting of the Society for Research in Child Development, San Francisco, CA.

ERIKSON, F. (1977) 'Some approaches to inquiry in school-community ethnography', *Anthropology in Education Quarterly*, **8**, 2, pp. 58–69.

ERIKSON, F. and SHULTZ, J. (1981) 'When is a context?: Some issues and methods in the analysis of social competence', in GREEN, J. and WALLAT, C. (Eds) *Ethnography and Language in Educational Settings*, Norwood, NJ: Aldex, pp. 147–60.

EVANS, R. (1981) 'Social integration of the young child: The management of change', *Early Child Development and Care*, **7**, pp. 57–82.

FARBER, B.A. (1984) 'Teacher burnout: Assumptions, myths and issues', *Teachers College Record*, **86**, 2, pp. 320–38.

FEENEY, S. and CHUN, R. (1985) 'Effective teachers of young children', *Young Children*, **41**, 1, pp. 47–52.

FEIN, G. and SWARTZ, P.M. (1982) 'Developmental theories in early education', in SPODEK, B. (Ed.) *Handbook of Research in Early Childhood Education*, New York: The Free Press, pp. 82–104.

FENSTERMACHER, G.D. (1978) 'A philosophical consideration of recent research on teacher effectiveness', *Review of Research in Education*, **6**, pp. 157–85.

FENSTERMACHER, G.D. (1986) 'Philosophy of research on teaching: Three aspects', in WITTROCK, M.C. (Ed.) *Handbook of Research on Teaching*, 3rd ed., New York: MacMillan, pp. 37–49.

FISKE, M. (1980) 'Changing hierarchies of commitment in adulthood', in SMELSER, N. and ERIKSON, E. (Eds) *Themes of Work and Love in Adulthood*, Cambridge, MA: Harvard University Press, pp. 238–64.

FLANDERS, N. (1964) 'Some relationships among teacher influence, pupil attitudes and achievement', in BIDDLE, B. and ELLENA, A. (Eds) *Contemporary Research on Teacher Effectiveness*, New York: Holt, Rinehart and Winston.

FROEBEL, F. (1901) *The Education of Man*, (W.N. Hailmann, trans.), New York: D. Appleton & Co. (original work published 1887).

FROMM, E. (1968) *The Revolution of Hope: Towards a Humanized Technology*, New York: Harper and Row.

FRYMIER, J., CORNBLETH, C. and DONMOYER, R. (1984) *One Hundred Good Schools*, West Lafayette, IN: Kappa Delta Pi.

FULLER, F. (1969) 'Concerns of teachers: A conceptualization', *American Educational Research Journal*, **6**, 2, pp. 207–25.

FULLER, F. and BROWN, O. (1975) 'Becoming a teacher' in RYAN, K. (Ed.) *Teacher Education: 74th Yearbook of the National Society for the Study of Education*, pp. 25–52.

FURLONG, J.J. and CARROLL, W.J. (1990) 'Teacher neutrality', *Education Forum*, **54**, 2, pp. 157–68.

GARVEY, C. and HOGAN, R. (1973) 'Social speech and social interaction: Egocentrism revisited', *Child Development*, **44**, pp. 562–8.

GEERTZ, C. (1973) *The Interpretation of Cultures*, New York: Basic Books.

GENDLIN, E.T. (1973) 'A phenomenology of emotions: Anger', in CARR, D. and CASEY, E. (Eds) *Explorations in Phenomenology*, The Hague, The Netherlands: Martinus Nijhoff, pp. 367–98.

GEORGE, C. and MAIN, M. (1979) 'Social interactions of young abused children: Approach, avoidance, and aggression', *Child Development*, **50**, pp. 306–18.

GESELL, A., ILG, F. and AMES, L. (1949) *Child Development*, New York: Harper.

GETZELS, J.W. and JACKSON, P. (1963) 'The teacher's personality and characteristics', in GAGE, N.L. (Ed.) *Handbook of Research on Teaching*, Chicago IL: Rand McNally, pp. 506–82.

GIROUX, H. (1981) 'Pedagody, pessimism and the politics of conformity: A reply to Linda McNeil', *Curriculum Inquiry*, **11**, 3, 211–22.

GLASER, B. and STRAUSS, A.L. (1967) *The Discovery of Grounded Theory: Strategies for Qualitative Research*, Chicago, IL: Aldine.

GOOD, T.L. and WEINSTEIN, R.S. (1986) 'Teacher expectations: A framework for exploring classrooms', in ZUMWALT, K.K. (Ed.) *Improving Teaching*, Alexandria, VA: Association for Supervision and Curriculum Development, pp. 63–86.

GOODSON, I.F. (1980) 'Life histories and the study of schooling', *Interchange*, 11, 4, pp. 62–76.
GORDON, A.M. and BROWNE, K.W. (1985) *Beginnings and Beyond: Foundations in Early Childhood Education*, New York: Delmar.
GORDON, R.L. (1975) *Interviewing: Strategies, Techniques and Tactics*, (rev. ed.) Homewood, IL: Dorsey Press.
GORE, J. and BARTLETT, L. (1988) 'Pathways and barriers to reflective teaching in an initial teacher education program', *Research Grants Series No. 4*, Board of Teacher Education, Brisbane, Qld., pp. 19–32.
GOULD, R. (1980) 'Transformations during early and middle adult years', in SMELSER, N. and ERIKSON, E. (Eds) *Themes of Work and Love in Adulthood*, Cambridge, MA: Harvard University Press, pp. 213–37.
GREENBERG, H.M. (1969) *Teaching with Feeling: Compassion and Self-awareness in the Classroom Today*, Indianapolis, IA: Pegasus.
GREENE, M. (1981) 'Contexts, connections, and consequences: The matter of philosophical and psychological foundations', *Journal of Teacher Education*, 32, 4, pp. 31–7.
GREENE, M. (1984) '"Excellence", meanings, and multiplicity', *Teachers College Record*, 86, 2, pp. 283–97.
GRIFFIN, G.A. (1986) 'Thinking about teaching', in ZUMWALT, K.K. (Ed.) *Improving Teaching*, Alexandria, VA: Association for Supervision and Curriculum Development, pp. 101–14.
GRIMMETT, P.P. and ERIKSON, G.L. (Eds) (1988) *Reflection in Teacher Education*, Vancouver, BC and New York: Pacific Education Press and Teachers College Press.
GROUNDWATER-SMITH, S. (1988) 'The interrogation of case records as a basis for constructing curriculum perspectives', in NIAS, J. and GROUNDWATER-SMITH, S. (Eds) *The Enquiring Teacher: Supporting and Sustaining Teacher Research*, London UK: Falmer Press, pp. 93–105.
GRUNDY, S. (1987) *Curriculum: Product or Praxis*, London UK: Falmer Press.
GRUSEC J.E. and ABRAMOVITCH, R. (1982) 'Imitation of peers and adults in a natural setting', *Child Development*, 53, pp. 636–42.
GRUSEC, J.E. and LYTTON, H. (1988) *Social Development: History, Theory and Research*, New York: Springer-Verlag.
GUMP, P.V. (1964) 'Environmental guidance', in BIDDLE, B. and ELLENA, A. (Eds) *Contemporary Research on Teacher Effectiveness*, New York: Holt, Rinehart and Winston.
HAAS, J. and SHAFFIR, W. (1980) 'Fieldworkers' mistakes at work:

Problems in maintaining research and researchers' bargains', in SHAFFIR, W., STEBBINS, R. and TUROWETZ, A. (Eds) *Fieldwork Experience*, New York: St Martin's Press, pp. 244–55.

HABERMAS, J. (1972) *Knowledge and Human Interests*, 2nd ed., London: Heinemann.

HALL, E.T. (1976) *Beyond Culture*, Garden City, NY: Anchor Books.

HALLIWELL, G. (1989) *Teachers Initiating Change Towards More Flexible Curriculum Practices*, paper presented at Childhood in the 21st Century, an international conference on early childhood development and education, Hong Kong, July-August.

HALPERIN, M. (1976) 'First-grade teachers' and children's developing perceptions of school', *Journal of Educational Psychology*, **68**, pp. 638–48.

HALPERN, E.S. (1983) *Auditing Naturalistic Inquiries: The Development and Application of a Model*, unpublished doctoral dissertation, Indiana University, Indiana.

HAMILTON, M.L. and STEWART, D.M. (1977) 'Peer models and language acquisition', *Merril Palmer Quarterly*, **23**, 1, pp. 45–55.

HARTUP, W. (1983) 'Peer relations', in MUSSEN, P. (Ed.) *Handbook of Child Psychology*, Vol. 4, New York: John Wiley, pp. 103–96.

HARTUP, W.W., GLAZER, J.A. and CHARLESWORTH, R. (1967) 'Peer reinforcement and sociometric status', *Child Development*, **38**, pp. 1017–24.

HARVEY, O., WHITE, B.J., PRATHER, M. and ALTER, R. (1966) 'Teacher's belief systems and preschool atmospheres', *Journal of Educational Psychology*, **57**, 6, pp. 373–81.

HAZDEN, N., BLACK, B. and FLEMING-JOHNSON, F. (1984) 'Social acceptance: Strategies children use and how teachers can help children learn them', *Young Children*, **39**, 6, pp. 26–36.

HENRY, J. (1971) *Pathways to Madness*, New York: Random House.

HERON, J. (1981) 'Experiential research methodology', in REASON, P. and ROWAN, J. (Eds) *Human Inquiry*, Chichester, UK: John Wiley and Sons, pp. 153–66.

HILDEBRAND, V. (1981) *Introduction to Early Childhood Education*, 3rd ed., New York: MacMillan.

HILDEBRAND, V. (1985) *Guiding Young Children*, 3rd ed., New York: MacMillan.

HILL, T.C. (1982) *Promoting Empathy in the Preschool: An Important Part of the Curriculum*, paper presented at the annual meeting of the National Association for the Education of Young Children Washington DC.

HOLMBERG, M.C. (1980) 'The development of social interchange patterns from 12 to 42 months', *Child Development*, **51**, pp. 448–56.

HOLMBERG, M.C., THOMSON, C.L., BAER, D.M., GOERTZ, E.M. and HOLT, W.J. (1972) *The Experimental Analysis of Preschool Teachers' Behaviors. Final Report*, Lawrence, Kansas: Kansas Center for Early Childhood Education (ERIC Document Reproduction Service No. ED 129 405).

HONIG, A.S. (1982) 'Research in review: Prosocial development in children', *Young Children*, **37**, 5, pp. 51–62.

HOSFORD, P. (1980) 'Improving the silent curriculum', *Theory Into Practice*, **19**, 1, pp. 45–50.

HOWES, C. and RUBENSTEIN, J.L. (1979) *Influences on Toddler Peer Behavior in Two Types of Daycare*, unpublished manuscript, Harvard University.

HUGHES, M.M. (1958) 'Teaching is interaction', *Elementary School Journal*, **5**, pp. 457–64.

HUSTON-STEIN, A., FRIEDRICH-COFER, L. and SUSMAN, E. (1977) 'The relation of classroom structures to social behavior, imaginative play and self-regulation of economically-disadvantaged children', *Child Development*, **48**, pp. 908–16.

HYMES, J.L. (1981) *Teaching the Child Under Six*, 3rd ed., Columbus, OH: Charles E. Merrill.

JACKSON, P.W. (1968) *Life in Classrooms*, New York: Holt, Rinehart and Winston.

JACKSON, P.W. (1970) 'The consequences of schooling', in OVERLY, N.V. (Ed.) *The Unstudied Curriculum: Its Impact on Children*, Washington, DC: Association for Supervision and Curriculum Development, pp. 1–15.

KALKER, P. (1984) 'Teacher stress and burnout: Causes and coping strategies', *Contemporary Education*, **56**, 1, pp. 16–19.

KATZ, L.G. (1972) 'Developmental stages of preschool teachers', *The Elementary School Journal*, **72**, 1, pp. 50–4.

KATZ, L.G. (1984) 'The professional early childhood teacher', *Young Children*, **39**, 5, pp. 3–10.

JONES, E. (1986) 'Perspectives on teacher education: Some relations between theory and practice', in Katz L. (Ed.) *Current Topics in Early Childhood Education*, Vol. VI, Norwood, NJ: Ablex, pp. 123–41.

KELMAN, H.C. (1968) *A Time to Speak: On Human Values and Social Research*, San Francisco, CA: Jossey-Bass.

KELMAN, H. (1974) 'Attitudes are alive and well and gainfully employed in the sphere of action', *American Psychologist*, **19**, 5, pp. 310–24.

KISIEL, T. (1973) 'Scientific discovery: Logical, psychological or hermenetical', in CARR, D. and CASEY, S. (Eds) *Explorations in Phenomenology*, The Hague, The Netherlands: Martinus Nijhoff, pp. 263–84.

KOHLBERG, L. (1970) 'The moral atmosphere of the school', in OVERLY, N.V. (Ed.) *The Unstudied Curriculum: Its Impact on Children*, Washington, DC: Association for Supervision and Curriculum Development, pp. 104–27.

KRASNOR, L.R. (1982) 'An observational study of social problem solving in young children', in RUBIN, K. and ROSS, H. (Eds) *Peer Relationships and Social Skills in Childhood*, New York: Springer-Verlag.

KRASNOR, L.R. and RUBIN, K. (1983) 'Preschool social problem solving: Attempts and outcomes in naturalistic interaction', *Child Development*, **54**, pp. 1545–58.

KROGH, S.L. (1984) 'Preschool democracy — ideas from Montessori', *The Social Studies*, **75**, 4, pp. 178–81.

KROGH, S.L. and LANNE, L.L. (1985) 'But what about sharing?: Children's literature and moral development', *Young Children*, **40**, 4, pp. 48–51.

LAING, R.D. (1969) *Self and Others*, New York: Pantheon Books.

LAMPERT, M. (1985) 'How do teachers manage to teach?: Perspectives on problems in practice', *Harvard Educational Review*, **55**, 2, pp. 178–94.

LANGUIS, M. and WILCOX, J. (1981) 'A life-span human development model of learning for early education', *Theory into Practice*, **20**, 2, pp. 79–85.

LAZARUS, R.S. and COHEN, J.B. (1977) 'Environmental stress', in ALTMAN, I. and WOHLWILL, J. (Eds) *Human Behavior and Environment*, New York: Plenum Press, pp. 90–127.

LE COMPTE, M.D. and GOETZ, J.P. (1984) 'Ethnographic data collection in evaluation research', in FETTERMAN, D.M. (Ed.) *Ethnography in Educational Evaluation*, Beverly Hills, CA: Sage, pp. 37–59.

LEIBERMAN, A. and MILLER, L. (1978) 'The social realities of teaching', *Teachers College Record*, **80**, 1, pp. 54–68.

LEINHARDT, G. (1986) 'Expertise in mathematics teaching', *Educational Leadership*, **43**, 7, pp. 28–33.

LEINHARDT, G. (1988) 'Situated knowledge and expertise in teaching', in CALDERHEAD, J. (Ed.) *Teachers' Professional Learning*, London, UK: Falmer Press, pp. 146–68.

LINDBERG, L. and SWEDLOW, R. (1985) *Young Children: Exploring and Learning*, Boston, MA: Allyn and Bacon.

LEVINSON, D.A. (1980) 'Toward a conception of the adult life course', in SMELSER, N. and ERIKSON, E. (Eds) *Themes of Love and Work in Adulthood*, Cambridge MA: Harvard University Press, pp. 265–85.

LINCOLN, Y.S. and GUBA, E.G. (1985) *Naturalistic Inquiry*, Beverly Hills, CA: Sage.

McLEAN, S.V. (1986) 'Facilitating social interaction: Ideal or reality?' *Early Childhood: Ideals/Realities*, Vol. 2, proceedings of the 17th National Conference of the Australian Early Childhood Association, Brisbane, September, 1985.

McLEAN, S.V. (1990) 'Teachers in multicultural settings', *Educational Forum*, **54**, 2, pp. 197–204.

McLEAN, S.V., MOYER, J. and GOMEZ, R. (1990) *Stories About Teaching: Student and Faculty Perceptions in Two Preservice Teacher Education Programs*, paper presented at the 36th World Congress of the International Council on Education for teaching, Singapore, July.

McPHERSON, G. (1972) *Small Town Teacher*, Cambridge MA: Harvard University Press.

MAGOON, A.J. (1977) 'Constructivist approaches in educational research', *Review of Educational Research*, **47**, 4, pp. 651–93.

MANLEY-CASIMIR, M. and WASSERMANN, S. (1989) 'Connecting self with the practice of teaching: The teacher as decision-maker', *Childhood Education*, **65**, pp. 288–93.

MARANTZ, M. (1988) 'Fostering prosocial behaviour in the early childhood classroom: Review of the research', *Journal of Moral Education*, **17**, 1, pp. 27–39.

MARGOLIN, E. (1982) *Teaching Young Children at School and Home*, New York: MacMillan.

MARLAND, P.W. (1977) *A Study of Teacher's Interactive Thoughts*, unpublished doctoral dissertation, University of Alberta.

MASSARIK, F. (1981) 'The interviewing process re-examined', in REASON, P. and ROWAN, J. (Eds) *Human Inquiry*, Chichester, UK: John Wiley and Sons, pp. 201–6.

MEASOR, L. (1985) 'Critical incidents in the classroom: Identities, choices and careers', in BALL, S.J. and GOODSON, I.F. (Eds) *Teachers' Lives and Careers*, London, Falmer Press, pp. 61–77.

MEEK, A. (1986) 'Whatever happened to good vibrations?', *Educational Leadership*, **43**, 7, pp. 80–1.
MEHAN, H. and WOOD, H. (1975) *The Reality of Ethnomethodology*, New York: John Wiley and Sons.
MINCEY, E. (1982) 'The preschool as an ecological approach to early education', *Early Child Development and Care*, **9**, pp. 45–63.
MINUCHIN, P.P. and SHAPIRO, E.K. (1983) 'The school as a context for social development', in MUSSEN, P.H. (Ed.) *Handbook of Child Psychology*, Vol. 4, New York: John Wiley, pp. 197–254.
MISCHEL, T. (1977) 'Conceptual issues in the psychology of the self: An introduction', in MISCHEL, T. (Ed.) *The Self: Psychological and Philosophical Issues*, Totowa NJ: Rowman and Littlefield, pp. 3–28.
MISCHLER, E. (1979) 'Meaning in context: Is there any other kind?', *Harvard Educational Review*, **49**, 1, pp. 1–19.
MITMAN, A.L., MERGENDOLLER, J.R., WARD, B.A. and TIKUNOFF, W.J. (1981) *Verification Inquiry, Vol. 6: Ecological Case Studies of Classroom Instruction in a Successful School*, (Report No. EPSSP-81-15), San Francisco, CA: Far West Laboratory for Educational Research and Development.
MONTESSORI, M. (1963) *The Secret of Childhood*, Calcutta, India: Orient Longmans Ltd.
MONTESSORI, M. (1964) *The Absorbent Mind*, Wheaton, IL: Theosophical Press.
MONTESSORI, M. (1974) *Childhood Education*, Chicago, IL: Henry Regnery Company.
MOORE, S. (1981) 'The unique contribution of peers to socialization in early childhood', *Theory Into Practice*, **20**, 2, pp. 105–88.
MOORE, T. (1975) 'Exclusive early mothering and its alternatives: The outcomes in adolescence', *Scandinavian Journal of Psychology*, **16**, pp. 255–72.
MOOS, R.M. and MOOS, B.S. (1978) 'Classroom social climate and student absences and grades', *Journal of Educational Psychology*, **10**, 2, pp. 263–9.
MORTON, A. (1980) *Frames of Mind*, Oxford, UK: Clarendon Press.
MOUSTAKAS, C. (1966) *The Authentic Teacher*, Cambridge MA: Howard A. Doyle.
MOUSTAKAS, C. (1968) *Individuality and Encounter*, Cambridge, MA: Howard A. Doyle.
MOYER, J. and KUNZ, J. (1985) 'The symbolization of teaching', *Dimensions*, **13**, 4, pp. 20–3.

MUELLER, E. and BRENNER, J. (1977) 'The origins of social skills and interaction among playgroup toddlers', *Child Development*, **48**, pp. 854–61.

NATIONAL COMMISSION ON EXCELLENCE IN EDUCATION (1983) *A Nation at Risk*, Washington, DC: US Government Printing Office.

NESPOR, J. (1987) 'The role of beliefs in the practice of teaching', *Journal of Curriculum Studies*, **19**, July–August, pp. 317–28.

NIAS, J. (1985) 'Reference groups in primary teaching: Talking, listening and identity', in BALL, S.J. and GOODSON, I.F. (Eds) *Teachers' Lives and Careers*, London, UK: Falmer Press, pp. 105–19.

OVERLY, N. (Ed.) (1970) *The Unstudied Curriculum: Its Impact on Children*, Washington, DC: Association for Supervision and Curriculum Development.

OWENS, R.G. (1982) 'Methodological perspective', *Educational Administration Quarterly*, **18**, 2, pp. 1–21.

PALEY, V.G. (1986) 'On listening to what children say', *Harvard Educational Review*, **56**, 2, pp. 122–31.

PATTON, M.Q. (1980) *Qualitative Evaluation Methods*, Beverly Hills: Sage.

PEERY, D., JENSEN, L. and ADAMS, G. (1984) *Relationships Between Parent's Attitudes Regarding Child Rearing and the Sociometric Status of Their Preschool Children*, unpublished manuscript, Brigham Young University, Salt Lake City.

PEERY, J.C. (1979) 'Popular, amiable, isolated, rejected: A reconceptualization of sociometric status in preschool children', *Child Development*, **50**, pp. 1231–4.

PENDLETON, V.M. (1980) *Emotional Development and Delay: The Child in the Context of the School Environment*, paper presented at a topical conference of The Council for Exceptional Children, Minneapolis, MN, August.

PERRY, R. (1986) *An Examination of Two Contrasting Approaches to Teaching Preschool Children and Their Effects on Linguistic and Social Behaviour*, unpublished doctoral thesis, University of Queensland, Australia.

PETERS, D. and KLEIN, E. (1981) 'The education of young children: Perspectives on possible futures', *Theory Into Practice*, **20**, 2, pp. 141–7.

PETERS, R.S. (1967) *Ethics and Education*, London, UK: Scott Foresman and Company.

PETKAU, H. and WHEELER, A. (1981) *Inviting Teacher Professional Growth*, paper presented to the annual meeting of the American

Educational Research Association, Los Angeles (ERIC Document Reproduction Service No. ED 200 598).

PHYFE-PERKINS, E. (1982) *Effects of Teacher Behavior on Preschool Children: A Review of Research*, Urbana, IL: ERIC Clearinghouse on Elementary and Early Childhood Education.

PINES, M. (1984) 'Children's winning ways', *Psychology Today*, 18, 12, pp. 58–65.

POLANYI, M. (1967) *The Tacit Dimension*, Garden City, NY: Doubleday.

POLLARD, A. (Ed.) (1987) *Children and Their Primary Schools: A New Perspective*. London, UK: Falmer Press.

POPKEWITZ, T. and WEHLAGE, G. (1977) 'Schooling as work: An approach to research and evaluation', *Teachers College Record*, 79, 1, pp. 70–84.

PORTER, C. and POTENZA, A. (1983) 'Alternative methodologies for early childhood research', in KILMER, S. (Ed.) *Advances in Early Education and Day Care*, Vol. 3, Greenich, CT: JAI Press, pp. 157–86.

POSTMAN, N. (1989) 'Learning by story', *The Atlantic*, 264, 6, pp. 119–24.

PRAWAT, R.S. and NICKERSON, J.R. (1985) 'The relationship between teacher thought and action and student affective outcomes', *The Elementary School Journal*, 85, 4, pp. 529–40.

READ, K. and PATTERSON, J. (1980) *The Nursery School and Kindergarten: Human Relationships and Learning*, 7th ed., New York: Holt, Rinehart and Winston.

REASON, P. and ROWAN, J. (1981) 'Issues of validity in new paradigm research', in REASON, P. and ROWAN, J. (Eds) *Human Inquiry*, Chichester, UK: John Wiley and Sons, pp. 239–50.

REIK, T. (1948) *Listening with the Third Ear: The Inner Experiences of a Psychoanalyst*, New York: Farrar, Straus and Giroux.

RICHARDSON, E. (1967) *The Environment of Learning Conflict and Understanding in the Secondary School*, New York: Weybright and Talley.

RISEBOROUGH, G.F. (1985) 'Pupils, teachers' careers and schooling: An empirical study', in BALL, S.J. and GOODSON, I.F. (Eds) *Teachers' Lives and Careers*, London UK: Falmer Press, pp. 202–65.

ROBERTS, M. (1985) 'A celebration of the centenary of the birth of Susan Issacs', *International Journal of Early Childhood*, 17, 2, pp. 53–5.

ROBISON, H. (1983) *Exploring Teaching in Early Childhood Education*, Boston, MA: Allyn and Bacon.

RODD, J. (1989) 'Is preschoolers' helping behaviour egocentric or altruistic?: The effects of cost and need', *Australian Journal of Early Childhood*, **14**, 4, pp. 37–42.
ROGERS, C. (1969) *Freedom to Learn*, Columbus, OH: Charles E. Merrill.
ROGERS, D.L. and ROSS, D.D. (1986) 'Encouraging positive social interaction among young children', *Young Children*, **44**, 3, pp. 12–17.
ROGERS, R. (1967) *Coming Into Existence: The Struggle to Become an Individual*, Cleveland, OH: World Publishing Company.
ROOPNARINE, J. and ADAMS, G. (1985) *The Interactional Teaching Patterns Between Mothers and Fathers and Their Popular, Moderately Popular, or Unpopular Preschool Children*, unpublished manuscript, Syracuse University, New York.
ROOPNARINE, J.L. and HONIG, A. (1985) 'The unpopular child', *Young Children*, **40**, 6, pp. 59–64.
ROSENSHINE, B. (1971) 'Teaching behaviors related to pupil achievement: A review of research', in WESTBURY, I. and BELLACK, A.A. (Eds) *Research Into Classroom Practice*, New York: Teachers College Press, pp. 51–98.
ROWAN, J. and REASON, P. (1981) 'On making sense', in REASON, P. and ROWAN, J. (Eds) *Human Inquiry*, Chichester, UK: John Wiley and Sons, pp. 113–37.
RUBIN, K.H. (1977) 'The social and cognitive value of preschool toys and activities', *Canadian Journal of Behavioral Science Review of Canadian Science*, **9**, pp. 382–5.
RUBIN, K. (1983) 'Recent perspectives on social competence and peer status: Some introductory remarks', *Child Development*, **54**, pp. 1383–5.
RUBOW, C.L. and FILLERUP, J.M. (1970) *The Professional Response*, unpublished manuscript, University of Arizona (ERIC Document Reproduction Service, No. ED 048 922).
RUSSELL, T. (1988) 'From pre-service teacher education to the first year of teaching: A study of theory and practice', in CALDERHEAD, J. (Ed.) *Teachers' Professional Learning*, London UK: Falmer Press, pp. 13–34.
SAPON-SHEVIN, M. (1980) 'Teaching cooperation in early childhood settings', in CARTLEDGE, G. and MILBURN, J. (Eds) *Teaching Social Skills to Children: Innovative Approaches*, New York: Pergamon Press, pp. 229–48.
SCHON, D.A. (1983) *The Reflective Practitioner: How Professionals Think in Action*, New York: Basic Books.

SCHON, D.A. (1987) *Educating the Reflective Practitioner: Towards a New Design for Teaching and Learning in the Professions*, San Francisco, CA: Jossey-Bass.

SCHON, D.A. (1988) 'Coaching reflective teaching', in GRIMMETT, P.P. and ERICKSON, G.L. (Eds) *Reflection in Teacher Education*, Vancouver and New York: Pacific Educational Press and Teachers College Press, pp. 19–30.

SEEFELDT, C. and BARBOUR, N. (1986) *Early Childhood Education: An Introduction*, Columbus, OH: Charles E. Merrill.

SHATZ, M. and GELMAN, R. (1973) 'The development of communication skills: Modification in the speech of young children as a function of listener', *Monographs of the Society for Research in Child Development*, 33, 152, whole issue.

SHULMAN, L.S. (1984) 'The practical and the eclectic: A deliberation on teaching and research', *Curriculum Inquiry*, 14, 2, pp. 183–200.

SHULMAN, L.S. (1987) 'Knowledge and teaching: Foundations of the new reform', *Harvard Educational Review*, 57, 1, pp. 1–23.

SHULMAN, L.S. and LANIER, J.E. (1977) 'The institute for research on teaching: An overview', *Journal of Teacher Education*, 28, 4, pp. 44–9.

SHURE, M. and SPIVAK, G. (1979) 'Interpersonal cognitive problem solving and primary prevention programming for preschool and kindergarten children', *Journal of Clinical Child Psychology*, 28, 2, pp. 89–94.

SIKES, P. (1985) 'The life cycle of the teacher', in BALL, S.J. and GOODSON, I.F. (Eds) *Teachers' Lives and Careers*, London, UK: Falmer Press, pp. 27–60.

SILIN, J.G. (1987) 'The early childhood educator's knowledge base: A reconsideration', in KATZ, L. (Ed.) *Current Topics in Early Childhood Education*, Vol. 7, Nowood, NJ: Ablex, pp. 17–31.

SMITH, C.A. (1982) *Promoting the Social Development of Young Children: Strategies and Activities*, Palo Alto CA: Mayfield.

SMITH, J.K. and HESHUSIUS, L. (1986) 'Closing down the conversation: The end of the qualitative-quantitative debate among educational inquirers', *Educational Researcher*, 15, 1, pp. 4–12.

SMITH, L.M., KLEINE, P.F., DWYER, D.C. and PRUNTZ, J.J. (1985) 'Educational innovators: A decade and a half later', in BALL, S.J. and GOODSON, I.F. (Eds) *Teachers' Lives and Careers*, London, UK: Falmer Press, pp. 180–201.

SMITH, P.K. and CONNOLLY, K.J. (1977) 'Social and agressive behavior in preschool children as a function of crowding', *Social Science Information*, 16, pp. 601–20.

SMYTH, W.J. (1986) *Reflection in Action*, Victoria: Deakin University Press.
SMYTH, W.J. (1987) *A Rationale for Teachers' Critical Pedagogy: A Handbook*, Victoria: Deakin University Press.
SOAR, R.S. and SOAR, R.M. (1972) 'An empirical analysis of selected Follow-Through programs: An example of a process approach to evaluation', in GORDON, I. (Ed.) *Early Childhood Education, 71st Yearbook of the Society for the Study of Education, Part 2*, Chicago, IL: University of Chicago Press, pp. 229–59.
SPILTON, D. and LEE, L.C. (1977) 'Some determinants of effective communication in four-year-olds', *Child Development*, **48**, pp. 968–77.
SPIVAK, G. and SHURE, M. (1974) *The Social Adjustment of Young Children*, San Francisco, CA: Jossey-Bass.
SPODEK, B. (1985) *Teaching in the Early Years*, 3rd ed., Englewood Cliffs, NJ: Prentice Hall.
SPODEK, B. (1987) 'Thought processes underlying preschool teachers' classroom decisions', *Early Child Development and Care*, **29**, pp. 197–208.
SPRADLEY, J. (1979) *The Ethnographic Interview*, New York: Holt, Rinehart and Winston.
SROUFE, L.A., FOX, N. and PANCAKE, V. (1983) 'Attachment and dependency in developmental perspective', *Child Development*, **54**, pp. 1615–27.
STALLINGS, J. (1975) 'Implementation and child effects of teaching practices in Follow-Through classrooms', *Monographs of the Society for Research in Child Development*, **40**, pp. 7–8.
TAYLOR, C. (1973) 'Interpretation and the sciences of man', in CARR, D. and CASEY, E. (Eds) *Explorations in Phenomenology*, The Hague, The Netherlands: Martinus Nijhoff, pp. 47–101.
TEILHARD DE CHARDIN, P. (1959) *The Phenomenon of Man*, New York: Harper and Row.
THEUNISSEN, M. (1984) *The Other: Studies in the Social Ontology of Husserl, Heidegger, Sartre and Buber*, Cambridge, MA: MIT Press.
TORBERT, W.R. (1981) 'Why educational research has been so uneducational: The case for a new model of social science based on collaborative inquiry', in REASON, P. and ROWAN, J. (Eds) *Human Inquiry*, Chichester, UK: John Wiley and Sons, pp. 141–52.
TOULMIN, S.E. (1977) 'Self-knowledge and knowledge of the "self",' in MISCHEL, T. (Ed.) *The Self: Psychological and Philosophical Issues*, Totowa, NJ: Rowman and Littlefield, pp. 292–317.

TYLER, L. and GOODLAD, J. (1979) 'The personal domain: Curriculum meaning', in GOODLAD, J. (Ed.) *Curriculum Inquiry: The Study of Curricular Practice*, New York: McGraw-Hill, pp. 191–207.

VANDELL, D.L. and MUELLER, E.C. (1977) *The Effects of Group Size on Toddler's Social Interactions with Peers*, paper presented at the meeting of the Society for Research in Child Development, New Orleans, March.

VANDELL, D.L., WILSON, K.S. and BUCHANAN, N.R. (1980) 'Peer interaction in the first year of life: An examination of its structure, content, and sensitivity to toys', *Child Development*, **51**, pp. 481–8.

VAN MANEN, M. (1977) 'Linking ways of knowing with ways of being practical', *Curriculum Inquiry*, **6**, pp. 205–28.

VERMA, S. and PETERS, D. (1975) 'Day care teacher practices and beliefs', *The Alberta Journal of Educational Research*, **21**, pp. 46–55.

WAGNER, A.C. (1987) '"Knots" in teacher thinking', in CALDERHEAD, J. (Ed.) *Exploring Teachers' Thinking*, London, UK: Cassell Educational Ltd., pp. 161–78.

WALLAT, C. and GREEN, J. (1979) 'Social rules and communicative contexts in kindergarten', *Theory Into Practice*, **18**, 4, pp. 275–84.

WEBER, E. (1984) *Ideas Influencing Early Childhood Education: A Theoretical Analysis*, New York: Teachers College Press.

WILLIAMS, C., NEFF, A. and FINKELSTEIN, J. (1981) 'Theory into practice: Reconsidering the preposition', *Theory Into Practice*, **20**, 2, pp. 93–6.

WILSON, S.M., SHULMAN, L.S. and RICHERT, A.E. (1987) '150 different ways of knowing: Representations of knowledge in teaching', in CALDERHEAD, J. (Ed.) *Exploring Teachers' Thinking*, London, Cassell Educational Ltd., pp. 104–24.

YAMAMOTO, K. (1972) *The Child and his Image*, Boston: Houghton Mifflin.

YAMAMOTO, K. (1984) 'My problems in understanding human beings', *Journal of Humanist Psychology*, **24**, 4, pp. 65–74.

YARDLEY, A. (1971) *The Teacher of Young Children*, London, UK: Evans Brothers.

YARROW, M. and WAXLER, C. (1977) 'The emergence and functions of prosocial behaviors in young children', in SMART, R. and SMART, M. (Eds) *Readings in Child Development and Relationships*, 2nd ed., New York: Macmillan, pp. 77–81.

YARROW, M. and WAXLER, C. (1979) 'Observing interaction: A confrontation with methodology, in CAIRNS, B. (Ed.) *The Analysis of*

Social Interaction: Methods, Issues and Illustrations, Hillsdale, NJ: Erlbaum, pp. 37–65.

YINGER, R.J. (1987) 'Learning the language of practice', Curriculum Inquiry, 17, 3, pp. 299–318.

YONEMURA, M.V. (1986) A Teacher at Work: Professional Development and the Early Childhood Educator, New York, NY: Teachers College Press.

ZEICHNER, K.M., TABACHNICK, R. and DENSMORE, K. (1987) 'Individual, institutional and cultural influences on the development of teachers' craft knowledge', in CALDERHEAD, J. (Ed.) Exploring Teachers' Thinking, London, UK: Cassell Educational Ltd., pp. 21–59.

Appendix

Examples of Coding Systems

Coding System Used for Brenda's Interviews

The Child
Individual differences
Characteristics
Motivation
Trust/expectation
Development
Respect for children
Importance of the broadest context

The Interface
Rules
Peer groups
Performing
General program comments
Social development program
Own family in program
Evaluation (what is good and not good)
Physical environment

Other
Details of centre
Staff relations
Parents
Professional networks
Reflections on the study

The Human Encounter

The Teacher

Personal
- Self-child connections
- What's me — not me
- Personal factors:
  - confidence
  - fears/anxieties
  - anger
- Acceptance of complexity
- Personal development
- Self-teacher connections
- Present/future orientation
- Awareness of specific actions (their development)
- If not a teacher, then what?
- Why have you stayed?

- *Interrelatedness
- *Talking things over
- *It all takes time
- *Being positive
- *Particularistic
- *Paradoxes

History
- Mentors and others
- College
- Work history
- Personal history

Teaching activity not directly involving children
- Changes as children arrive
- Mental activities:
  - Mental preparation
  - on-the-spot
  - post-hoc
  - *staying calm

Networking
- Staff relations
- Parents
- Professional networks

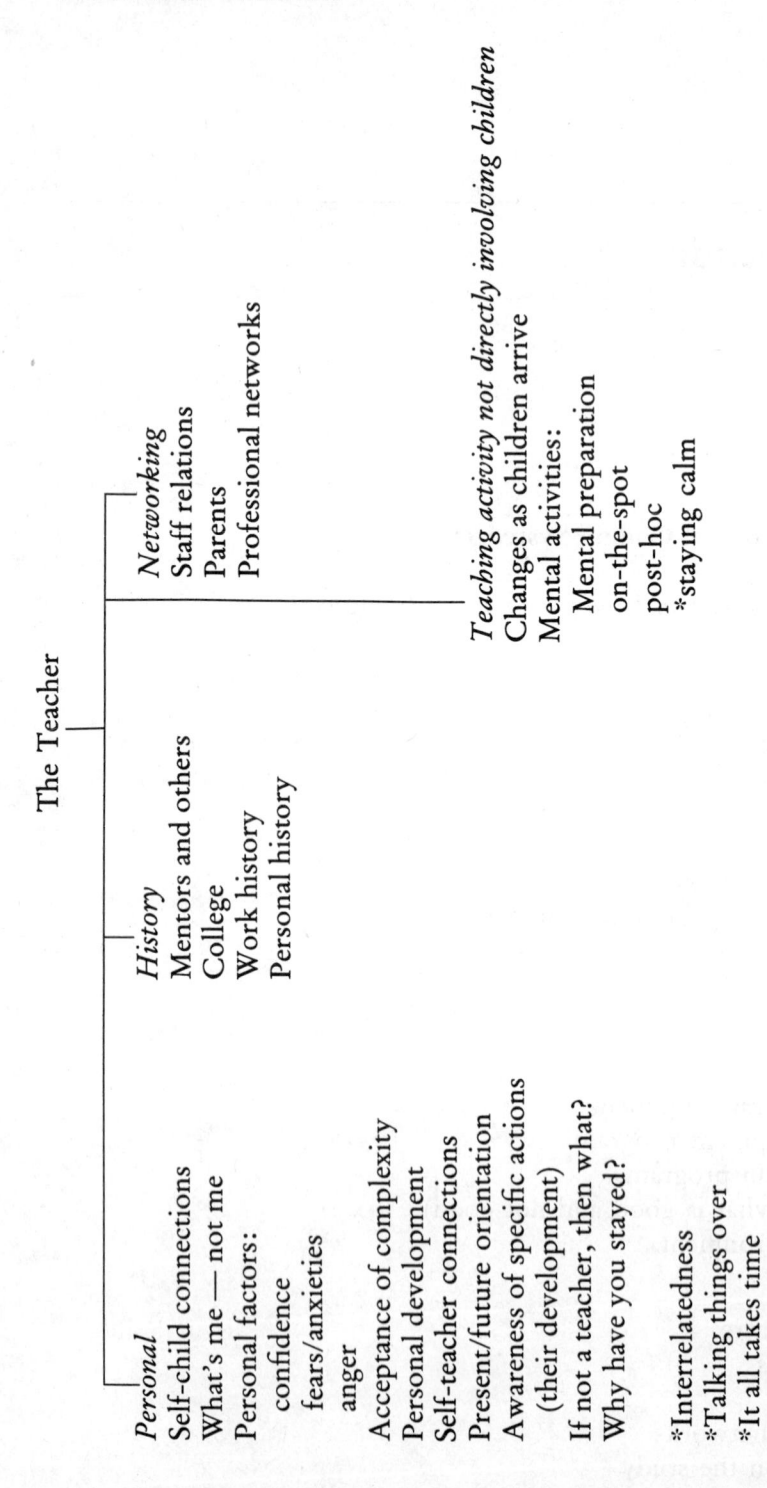

*Categories added specifically for Brenda

Appendix: Examples of Coding Systems

Coding System Used for Observation in Kathy's Setting

Teacher Qualities
Movement
Speech
Physical contacts
Responsiveness
Praise
Respect for children
Trust and expectation

Program Details
General atmosphere
Content notes
Timetable
Independence/dependence
Performance
Warnings of departure
Rituals

Developing a Sense of Community
Drawing children's attention to the social aspect of life
Drawing children's attention to other's achievements/actions
Indicating consideration for others
Developing social skills
Personal aspects of the teacher verbalized
Protecting
Sharing

Environment
Adjustments to the environment

Access
Helping children gain access to peer groups
Splitting peer groups

Involvement in Play
Involvement in play
Offering extending ideas
Using content as a tool

Peer Conflicts
Conflicts
Conditionals/threats
Interprets peer situation

Questions peer situation
Tale-telling
Observes
Suggests alternatives
Offers content solution
Putting in perspective
Asks child to relay message to peer
Accompanies/speaks for child
Pronouncements/rulings/nominations

Rules
Rules
Directives
Non-directives
Chastisements
'Being sensible'

Other
Reflection on the study
Parents
Staff

Index

Aboriginal: education, 106, 107
  discontinuities in, 105
  people, 101
access: coding system, 245
  to peer play groups, 65–6, 83–4, 86–90, 124–5, 154–5, 202–4
achievements: appreciation of, 113, 123–4, 199
  pressure for, 134
actions: children's negative, 168–9
  interpreting children's, 111
  teacher's, ambiguities of, 162, 178
    consistency of, 167
    future-directed orientation, 166
    and social development, 200
    student perspectives of, 164
activities: physical, 101
adults: effects on children's peer interactions, 11
age-definition: and children's development, 141–2
  and teaching behaviour, 46
ambiguity: of teacher's actions, 161–5, 178
analysis: of data, 32–6
  of human phenomena, 162
  teacher, time for, 163
assistants, at preschool, 43, 71, 101–2, 131
  Kathy's relationship with, 133
  criticism of, 137
  and supervision of children, 195
attitude: social, 13
  teacher, 4
audiotape recordings, 25
  interviews, 27
  transcription, 26
authenticity, 188
  value to Nan, 77–8, 97–8, 188
awareness of others, 114

behaviour, 2, 162
  helping, 209
  and interpretation, 164
  meanings for, 6
  problem, 115
  'professional' teacher –, 197
  prosocial, 10
  of teachers, 3
    goal-directed, 5
belief: about self, 176–7
  and action, 7
  Brenda's, 103
  Kathy's, 134
  Rhonda's, 48, 56
    and behaviour, 46
  teacher, 4, 162
    and resistance to change, 213–14
  underlying order in, 183
Brenda, 20, 180, 186, 193, 197, 198, 200, 201, 204, 209, 211, 215
  biography, 102, 105–8
  calmness of, 102–3, 104, 108–9, 111, 116, 168, 196
  career path, 107–8
  case study, 14, 99–128
    participation in, 126
  flexibility of, 127
  interview coding scheme, 33, 34, 243–4

257

Index

and observations, 23
own development, 103–4, 108
self-awareness, 126, 178
burned-out: Kathy's feeling of, 132, 138, 143, 159, 182

calmness: importance of, 168
see also Brenda's
card sort, 29–30, 140
case studies, 14–15
coding systems, 243–6
dissimilarities in, 194
format, 35–6
program details, 243, 245
children: extent of social competence, 212
as Group, 210–11
identity of, 34, 168
impact of observers, 24–5
individual, 211
influences of, 210–12
invisible, 190
number of, in case studies, 42, 70, 101, 130
pressures on, 133–4
problem, 133
see also teachers: respect for children
classroom: actions in, 36
and concept of 'living', 165–6
environment, 167
holistic perspective, 19
life of, 18–19
coding schemes: interview, 32–3, 243–4
micro-level, 34
observational, 33–5, 245–6
communications: transactional nature of, 162, 163
community: coding system, 245
sense of, 54, 58–61, 95–6, 114–15, 122–4, 153–4, 208–10
confidence: Rhonda's, 45
of teachers, 165
conflict resolution: non-violent strategies for, 13
see also peer conflict
contact: lack of direct, with Kathy, 151

see also physical contact
context: social, 173–4
stripping, 17
contextual: influences on human interactions, 173
information, 35
continuities: between teacher and children, 104–5
control strategies, 146–7
conversations (stimulated recall), 27, 28–9
critical: incidents, 179
pedagogy, and social context, 173–4, 215
reflection, 181
curriculum: 'hidden', 11
planned, 11
tensions, and Aborigines, 105

data collection, 22–32, 37
decision making, 191–4
objectivity, 163
on-the-spot, 51–2, 80, 111, 167, 190–1, 192, 194
and questions, 85
see also differentiation
decontextualization, 17
development: adult, transformation, 178
teacher's, 213–22
developmental continuum, 104, 166
developmentally appropriate practice, 172
dialogue: written 'skeleton' of, 25
differentiation: in decision making, 192–3
directive strategies, 85, 111, 119–21, 141, 150
gradations of, 117
phrasing of, 152
discussions: with other teachers, 215–16
dramatic play: involvement in, 61–2, 92–4, 126, 155–6, 204–6

education: beliefs about, 165
effective teaching, 3–4, 5
empathy, 187
enculturation: of children, 2

Index

enticement: use of, 170, 171
environment: classroom, 167
  coding system, 245
  coherent, 198
  effects of physical, 11, 189–1
  physical, and peer conflicts, 90, 147, 207
    and peer interaction, 96, 125–6, 156–8, 207–8
  teachers, adjustments by, 66, 69–70
  as providers, 12, 26–7
equally-valued relationships: with children, 169, 184–5
event sampling, 25
  in tidy-up routine, 26
eye contact: as social skill, 96

facial expressions, children's, 170
facilitative strategies, 170–2 *passim*, 188, 198
  and peer conflicts, 111, 119–20, 150
families: of preschool children, 42, 70, 101, 130
films: use, in teacher peer discussions, 210
flexibility: as essential skill, 190
foreknowledge: need for, 21
Forebel, Friedrich (1782–1852), 8
frustration: Kathy's, 137

games, 203
  group, 13
Group, The, 211–12
group membership rules, 89

'here and now': management of, 194–9
hermaneutic: approach, 27
  circle, of knowledge, 18
  and interpreter's understanding, 161, 192
human: becoming, 2
  encounter, 183–9
    and 'being there', 187
  essence of, 162
  inquiry, interpreter's understanding, 161

  as knowing being, 17
  phenomena, analysis, of, 162
  understanding, 17
humanist psychology movement, 12, 173
humour, sense of, 44

'ideal of citizenship', 13
ideals: model, 164
  for student teachers, 167, 218
  of teaching, 164–5, 167–8, 180, 215
  and realities, 167, 213, 219
image: concept of, 35
  -of-self-as-teacher, 35–6, 162, 176–83
    Brenda's, 103–15
    Kathy's, 132–44, 180
    Nan's, 72–84
    Rhonda's, 45–56
independence: development of, 147–8
  importance of children's, 49–50, 56
inflexibility, 44
Intentionalist Account of Teacher Effectiveness, 5
interactions: children's peer, 10–12
  confirmation in, 185–7
  consummatory, 185
  social, 10
  between teachers and young children, 1, 2, 9–10, 15
  see also under peer interaction
interdependence, 176
interpretive: research, 2–3
  statements, 91, 124, 150–1, 163
  neutral, 151
interruptions: response to, 60–1
intervention: adult, and children's interactions, 12
  see also peer conflict; peer interaction
interview coding schemes, 32–3
interview data: dependability, 30–2
interviews, 27–32, 37
  'clinical judgment' in, 31
  depth, 27–8

259

Index

Kathy's response, 132
Rhonda's response, 67
introspection: Kathy's lack of, 182
   value of, 180–3, 215
Isaacs, Susan (1885–1948), 8
isolation, professional, 136, 144, 216–17

judgment; children's, in designated activities, 147–8

Kathy, 20, 187, 196, 200, 201, 204, 205, 209, 211
   biography, 131, 135–6
   and card sort, 30, 140
   case study, 14, 129–59
      observation coding system, 245–6
      participation, 158
   confusion of, 133
   interviews with, 27, 32, 132
   and introspection, 182–3
   isolation, 217
   own development, 136, 159
   principles, 133
   and teaching stress, 20–1, 132–3, 138, 143, 159
   and trust, 21–2
   self-protective, 158
   speech, 131
knowledge: -in-action, 5, 37
   in hermaneutic circle, 18, 192
   and personal interpretation, 17–18
   situated, 192
   see also foreknowledge
knowledge base: of teachers, 172–6

learning environment, 4

manipulation: by children, 211–12
   use of, 171
manners: importance of, 55, 60, 209
maturationist view, 12, 173
meanings: search for, 18, 19
mental preparation, for teaching, 80, 108, 111
   importance of, 168
   lack of, 140

methodological techniques: of research, 17–39
models, 175
   intentionalist, 174
   in social development, 172
   constructivist, 174
molecular behavioural analysis, 10
Montessori, Maria (1870–1952), 7, 8
   and sharing, 208
moral: stories with, and social attitudes, 13,
mothering style: and children's peer interactions, 11
   and teching, 46
motivation: of children, 47
   of teachers, 221
multiculturation, 13
multidimensionality: in physical environment, 89

Nan, 20, 168, 171, 180, 186, 187, 193, 197, 198, 200, 202, 204, 205, 207–8, 209, 215
   biography, 71, 74–7
   and card sort, 30
   case study, 14, 69–98
      and observations, 23–4
      views on, 97
   connection, as parent, 74
   identity crisis, 76–7
   own development, 97, 178
   philosophy, 76
neutrality: of teachers, 162–3
non-authoritarian stance: Brenda's, 117–18
non-directive: remarks, use of, 72
   teaching strategies, 85, 86, 170–1, 206
non-verbal teaching behaviour, 43

observational: coding schemes, 33–5
   strategies, 25
observations, 22–7
   coding system, 245–6
   consecutive schedule, 24, 37
   corroboration, 37–8
   discomfort of, 23
   in free playtimes, 25–6
   nature of, 25–7

overt, 21
timing for, 22–4
observer: distance, 24
  role of, 24–5
  second, 38
orderliness, 56
organization: by Rhonda, 45

parents: contact with, 136–8 *passim*
peace education, 13
peer conflict: coding system, 245–6
  resolving, 62–5, 84, 90–2, 111, 114, 118–21, 145, 148–52, 162, 197, 200–2
peer interaction, 10–11, 93, 143, 200
  coding system, 245
  helping, 59
  and physical environment, 96, 125–6
  and teachers, 11, 19
    intervention, 94
    involvement, 55, 144
peer play groups: disbandment, 89
  involvement in creation of, 83–4, 86–90, 124–5, 154–5, 202–4
peer success: strategies for, 83
personal dimension: and sense of community, 124
personal identification: with children, 180
personality: of teachers, 3
personally memorable events, 179
perspectives: inside-out, 31, 37
  outside-in, 31, 37, 48, 56, 144
persuasion: use of, 170, 171
physical contact: by teachers, 43, 71, 102, 131, 168
planning: teaching program, 51
play: versus work, 145–6, 154
popularity; degree of, 203
positive statements: Brenda's, 103, 118
post-hoc thinking, 111, 140
power: differential of children and teacher, 184
  Kathy's lack of, 137
  Rhonda's, 57
praise: role of, 57
preschool centres: Brenda's, 99–100
  Kathy's, 129
  Nan's, 69–70
  Rhonda's, 41–2
preservice teacher education, 217–22
problem solving, 116, 147
  and peer interactions, 13
  questions for, 85
process behaviours, 33
product behaviours, 33
professional distance: in relationships, 135
punctuality: enforcement by Rhonda, 45
punishment: role of, 57
purpose, 56

questioning, 181
  as means of control, 146–7
  open-ended, 81
questions: in decision making, 193
  in dramatic play, 92, 205
  focusing, 124
  and peer conflict, 90–1, 119
  use of, 85

realities: of teaching, 167, 213, 219
records: keeping, 38
  running, 25
reevaluation: of teacher's actions, 126
referential adequacy, 38
reflection, 214–17
  by Brenda, 112
rejection: of children, 203
relationships: difficult, 169–70
  'I-Thou', 184–5, 221
  with parents, 135
  between teachers and young children, 1, 7
relaxation: Nan's ability for, 73
research: interpretive, 2–3
researcher: as interpretor, 3
resources: use of, 70
repsect: for children, 8, 53–4, 81–2, 112–13, 186
responses: measuring children's, 115
responsibility: children's sense of, 84
  Rhonda's sense of, 49
Rhonda, 20, 43, 180, 186, 195, 196, 200, 201, 204–6 *passim*, 209

Index

behaviour, 43
biography of, 47–8
case study, 14, 41–67
consistency, 67
interviews, 67
rituals: importance of, 60, 130
role: of teachers, 73
room to grow: need for, 9
rules, 49, 58, 94–5, 206–7
  coding system, 246
  formal, 152
  group, 121
  infringements, 58
  procedural, 95, 152
  safety, 94–5, 152, 195
  structure, 50, 56, 206
'ruling' statements, 91, 150

safety: physical, of children, 195
  psychological, 196
  see also under rules
sampling: event, 25
self: acceptance of, 79
self-concept, 7, 176–7
  Kathy's, 136–9
  see also image-of-self-as-teacher
self confidence: children's, 82
  of teachers, 165
self-control, 116, 169
self-observation, 181
  see also introspection
self-questioning, 20, 181
sensitivity: use of, 113
settled, being: importance of, 50–1
shaming, 150
  trilogy, 124
sharing: learning to, 96, 208
simultaneity: in physical environment, 189–90
situations: factors of, 198
  interpretation, in context, 197
social development: of children, 10–11, 36, 54–6, 114–15, 142–4
  promoting, 199–210
social interactions: and physical environment, 26–7
  and self confidence, 82–3

social: language, 10
  Learning Theory, 12
  rejection, 73
  skills, 96
socialization: of children, 2
solitude: need for, 202–3
speech patterns: Nan's, 72
statements, 162
  interpretive, 91, 124, 150–1, 163
  teacher, inconsistencies in, 31
stimulated recall, 10
story-telling: as strategy in professional education, 221–2
'stream-of-behaviour' chronicle, 25
study, overall plan, 18–22
  participants in, 19–21
supervision: burden of, 148, 195
survival: in classroom, 194–5
symbolic-interactionist approach: in development, 173

task completion: importance of, 145–6
teachers: anonymity of, 37
  as authority figure, 12
  behaviour, 4
  belief, 4, 176–7
  collaboration with peers, 216
  development, 213–22
  as facilitator, 3
  'ideal', 9
  identity, 177
  interview coding system, 244
  as model, 12, 60, 209
  out of school life, 7
  as plerson, 7, 18, 28, 106
  personality, 3
  personal qualities of, 8–9
  and physical environment, 26–7
  respect, for children, 8, 53–4, 81–2, 112–13, 140–2, 186
  selection, for study, 19–20
  therapeutic role, 12–13
  uniqueness of, 34
  well-being, 196
teaching: cognitive aspects of, 79–81
  definition, 165
  early childhood, 3
  effectiveness, 3–4, 5, 9

Index

idealized view of, 164, 167–8
instructional approach, 170
moods, 168
myths of, 166
as performance, 28, 77, 187–8
practice, 219–22
  language of, 220
realities of, 167
strategies, economical, 43
view of, 6
team-teaching, 48
team: working as, 60
thick description: in case studies, 35, 219, 222
tidy-up routines, 42, 209–10
  and rules, 121–2
time: Brenda's attitudes to, 109–10
timetable, 42, 70, 100, 129–30
  flexibility, 70, 100
tolerance: of children, 13

trust: in children, 82
  foundations for, 21–2, 37
  in Nan's personal feelings, 78

unpredictability: in physical environment, 189, 190–1
usefulness: value of, 73

verbal behaviour: chastisement, 57
  in teaching, 43–4
verbal contact, direct: between children, 114
visitor; role of, in dramatic play, 92–3, 205
vulnerability: of teacher, 172

watershed experiences, 179
wordiness: Nan's, 79
work: activities, 145
  versus play, 145–6, 154